http://www.easybib.com

Fifth Edition

SURVIVAL

A Sequential Program for College Writing

Robert M. Frew
Richard C. Guches
Robert E. Mehaffy

American River College
Sacramento, California

T. H. Peek Publisher
P. O. Box 50123, Palo Alto, California 94303

ISBN 0-917962-32-X

02   01   00
30   29   28

Manufactured in the United States of America

Preface to the Fifth Edition

Welcome to the fifth revised edition of *Survival*. Within these chapters are the tools for successful writing, enhanced by sample papers written by students and professional writers. As always, it is our hope that *Survival's* carefully structured exercises will serve as your stepping-stones to thoughtful, creative papers.

We have retained the strengths that have always made *Survival* an effective composition text. The step-by-step, sequential approach is still here: each chapter focuses on a particular writing assignment, and each exercise takes you a step toward mastery of that assignment.

In this edition the step-by-step approach is integrated into a three-phase writing process: planning, writing and editing. We believe that this is a major improvement that will help you to approach your writing projects with skill and confidence. For example, within the planning phase, techniques such as brainstorming and clustering are powerful tools for generating ideas and narrowing topics. In *Survival* the writing process emphasizes collaborative feedback and revision, but the process always leads to a polished product, possible because you have mastered the details of the final manuscript format.

As requested by instructors, we have changed the chapter sequence slightly in this edition. Chapter One: "Sentence Structure and Mechanics," now allows you to review the fundamental principles of sentence construction and punctuation before beginning Chapter Two: "Essay Structure," which introduces you to the writing process and the basics of organizing a paper. Also new to this edition is an exciting "Critical Review" chapter that instructors using the book have suggested. This chapter provides the opportunity to review books, movies, performances, or events with a subjective emphasis. We believe that the rhetorical strategies presented here, and throughout the book, will develop valuable critical thinking and communication skills—skills needed in other courses and in understanding the significant issues of our times.

The fifth revised edition of *Survival* steps fully into the era of the computer. With its emphasis on revision, the writing process presented in the book is ideally suited for students using computers. The library research chapter has been greatly enhanced by explaining computer use in the library, including suggestions for using electronic card catalogs and online databases. In addition, all aspects of documentation for sources, both print and electronic, are thoroughly discussed with the 1995 Modern Language Association (MLA) guidelines.

This text is still about survival. We are confident that our book will equip you to survive and thrive in all classes requiring writing, and beyond, The goal of *Survival* is to illuminate the writing process in all its phases and to help all students realize their writing potential.

Contents

CHAPTER ONE

Sentence Structure and Mechanics

Objectives

When you have completed this chapter, you will

1. avoid errors in agreement, tense, and person.

2. revise sentences to achieve variety and effective coordination, subordination, and transitions.

3. punctuate simple, compound, and complex sentences correctly.

4. properly use semicolons and colons.

5. avoid run-on, comma-splice, and fragment errors.

1

Writing is one of the gauges that scholars employ to judge the level of intellectual development achieved by a civilization. Ancient peoples who had not perfected a written language had to rely wholly upon oral communication. The oral tradition of our ancestors is, of course, rich in story and myth. However, speaking to contemporary people across the centuries without writing means that much of what these people's lives were like, what frightened them, what brought them joy, what they thought about, is left to our speculation from hints derived from their technology, their art, and the stories that survive from their oral tradition.

In the contemporary world, writing has become of paramount importance to our lives. Moreover, the need for absolute clarity in communication, especially in areas such as science, government, business, and diplomacy, has obligated us to agree upon certain principles in the selection of vocabulary, the construction of sentences and their punctuation, the development of paragraphs, and the creation of compositions. These principles (or rules) are sometimes referred to as grammar, usage, mechanics, or conventions. Although you may often find them to be a nuisance, if not an irritation, these conventions do, if fact, ensure a clarity of communication that might not otherwise be achieved.

This first chapter of *Survival* reviews the fundamental conventions of writing at the sentence level. While most students already know and employ these rules, some may benefit from a refresher. Others may profit from reaffirming what they are already doing. Still others need to learn the rules of writing for the first time. What you learn or review in this chapter will assist you throughout all the chapters of the book as well as throughout your future courses. Chapter One, then, will familiarize you with many of the commonly observed conventions and rules of formal writing by reviewing the fundamentals of effective sentence structure and punctuation.

LESSON ONE: *Agreement, Pronoun Reference, Tense,*
and Person

This lesson is designed to help you with several of the conventions of standard English that may give you trouble. Most of these conventions have been around for generations and are now so rigidly adhered to in writing that they are called rules. Once mastered, they are not usually difficult, and they will seem quite logical after they have been in your written "vocabulary" for a while. If you already know them, scan over the lesson quickly; if you do not know these rules, be certain that you learn them before you take the Chapter One Test.

Subject-Verb Agreement

The subject of a sentence must agree with the verb in number. A great many nouns and pronouns in English have one form to refer to a single item (the singular form) and another form to refer to more than one item (the plural form). Frequently, verbs also have two forms: one for singular subject nouns and another for plural subject nouns.

Singular		**Plural**
is	. . . .	are
was	. . . .	were
has	. . . .	have
asks	. . . .	ask

Examples

> The average **American child** *watches* too much television.
> Many **men** *watch* organized sports all year around.
> The **dandelion** *is* a prolific plant.
> **Dandelions** *were used* for herbal medicines by our ancestors.
> **She** *owns* a small red sports car.
> **They** *have* three hunting dogs.

Difficulty arises when you encounter expressions not obviously singular or plural. Words such as **each, either, neither, someone, one,** and especially **everyone** and **everybody** often seem to designate more than one person or item, but they all require singular verbs. These are called **singular indefinite pronouns.**

Examples

> **Everybody** at the new Warehouse Video *is planning* to attend the store's huge grand opening celebration.
> **Neither** of the sisters *has applied* herself with the enthusiasm necessary to win a spot on the soccer team.
> **Each** of the Australian shepherds *is losing* all ability to hear anything but the sharpest sounds.

In the last of the preceding examples, the subject of the sentence is each, which requires a singular verb, not Australian shepherds, which would require a plural verb.

On the other hand, compound subjects require the plural form even when each subject is singular.

Examples

> **Walking and bicycling** *are* both good exercise and invigorating.
>
> **Ariel and Alisa** *are working* to register new voters before the next election.

Even more troublesome for many students is the agreement of quantities. Even though they normally look as if they are plural, they must be treated as singular.

Examples

> **One thousand megabytes** *is* a gigabyte.
>
> When Cheryl was treasurer, **$500** *was* too expensive for printing the newsletter.
>
> **Sixty pounds** of camping equipment and food carefully packed in a backpack *is* sufficient to make most anyone wish to have taken up a less strenuous activity.

Collective nouns, words that designate groups, are singular when you are thinking of the group as a whole, but they are plural when you are thinking of individual members of the group. Most contemporary writers, however, consider collective nouns to be singular.

Some Collective Nouns

audience
committee
family
group
jury
police
team

Singular—

> The entire Heller family is planning to spend the summer at their grandparents' beach cottage.

Plural—

> The Brown family are divided about whether to spend their vacation camping in the mountains, sunbathing at the beach, or resting at home.

Note—There are many other confusing and irregular singular and plural forms. If you are ever in doubt about the agreement of a sentence that you have written, consult a good dictionary to be certain whether the verb you have used is singular or plural. Computer word-processing programs often feature a grammar check function that may be useful when checking for agreement problems.

By permission of John Hart and Field Enterprises Inc.

EXERCISE 1.1

In each of the following sentences, circle the correct form of the verb. (Answers on page 48)

1. Neither of the failing students (do / does) any homework.
2. Violence on television (has / have) become a troublesome political issue.
3. America (is / are) moving rapidly into the high-tech communications age.
4. The difference between last year's model and this year's new design (was / were) easy to recognize.
5. Five one-dollar bills (fill / fills) a wallet but buy little.
6. The jury (come / comes) in to deliver the verdict only after the audience stands.
7. Everyone in the class (is / are) expected to have his or her rough draft finished on Friday.
8. Twelve miles (is / are) too far for me to walk to work every day.
9. Each of the cars (require / requires) expensive repairs.
10. Odelia and Gladys (was / were) planning a trip for Sunday.

Pronoun Reference

A pronoun must refer clearly to its *antecedent:* the person, place, or thing substituted for by the pronoun. Do not, for example, let a pronoun seem to point to more than one antecedent, or the resulting sentence will create unintended double meanings.

Ambiguous—

> The **painter** agreed to give the **writer** an interview because *she* knew *she* needed more media exposure.

Here the reader cannot tell who knew what, the painter or the writer. Sometimes the easiest way to solve this problem is to repeat the noun.

Revised—

> The *painter* agreed to give the **writer** an interview because the **writer** knew the *painter* needed more media exposure.

Although this sentence is no longer ambiguous, it appears awkward. The apparent awkwardness may be overcome by reordering the sentence so that the pronoun comes before only one antecedent.

Revised—

> Because the *painter* knew the writer understood the need for media exposure, **she** granted the writer an interview.

Just as the subject and verb must agree in number, so must a pronoun agree in number with its antecedent. Difficulty with pronoun agreement occurs typically when a pronoun is used to refer to an indefinite pronoun. Such agreement problems come about because informal, conversational English frequently includes these agreement errors. In conversations they are not considered serious errors, but in written work you do for class, agreement errors will be considered incorrect.

> Informal—**Everyone** in the stands stood and clapped **their** hands.
> Formal— **Everyone** in the stands stood and clapped **his** or **her** hands. (See gender fairness below.)
> Formal— **All** of the spectators stood and clapped **their** hands.
>
> Informal—**Everybody** in the class did **their** personal best.
> Formal— **Everybody** in the class did **his** or **her** personal best. (See gender fairness below.)
> Formal— **All** of the students in the class did **their** personal best.

Gender Fairness (Sexist Language)

Gender fairness in writing is desirable because sexist language offends many readers. Simply stated, the use of one gender, usually masculine, to refer to everyone, sounds sexist.

Example

> Before selecting a doctor, check *his* qualifications carefully.

Those who are aware of sexist language would correctly assert that the speaker or writer does not know the gender of the doctor. Using the pronoun *his* completely ignores over half of the population. You should make it your goal to remove gender-specific references where they are unnecessary.

Examples

> Sexist— A *citizen* in a free society should be able to read, view, or listen to just about whatever **he** wishes, without fear of censorship.
>
> Improved— *Citizens* in a free society should be able to read, view, or listen to just about whatever **they** wish, without fear of censorship.

> Sexist—An *American* can be harshly punished if **he** violates the law in some foreign countries.
>
> Improved—*Americans* can be harshly punished if **they** violate the law in some foreign countries.

Notice that in each of the improved sentences above, the subject and pronoun were changed to plural. This is the preferred method of removing sexist language from your writing. However, you should be aware that you have other options.

Examples

> Sexist—*Nobody* should try to avoid **his** civic duty to serve on a jury.
>
> Improved—*Nobody* should try to avoid **his** or **her** civic duty to serve on a jury.
>
> Better—*People* should not try to avoid **their** civic duty to serve on juries.

While the "his or her" solution to the sexist language problem (the second example above) is technically correct, it is not favored because it too often produces wordy sentences.

Three Additional Pronoun Reminders

1. Always make pronouns refer to a basic element of a sentence; never let the pronoun refer to a modifier.

Unclear:	He reached for the **car** door handle, but **it** rolled away.
Clear:	The car rolled away as he reached for the door handle.

2. Eliminate indirect or indefinite pronoun reference.

Unclear:	Riding across the mountains on horseback, **you** had to worry about rattlesnakes.
Clear:	Riding across the mountains on horseback, **pioneers** had to worry about rattlesnakes.
Clear:	**Pioneers** had to worry about rattlesnakes while they rode across the mountains on horseback.
Unclear:	In a surprise *attack* on June 25, rebel forces surrounded the capital. **This** caught the president and his military advisors off guard.
Clear:	In a surprise *attack* on June 25, rebel forces surrounded the capital. **This attack** caught the president and his military advisors off guard.

3. Avoid ambiguous use of **it** and **they**.

Unclear:	In last month's edition of *Oceans*, **it** presents a good explanation of whale migration.
Clear:	**An article** in last month's edition of *Oceans* gives a good explanation of whale migration.
Unclear:	**They** do not allow Olympic athletes to use steroids.
Clear:	Olympic **officials** do not allow Olympic athletes to use steroids.

EXERCISE 1.2

Rewrite each of the following sentences, correcting the pronoun reference and gender-specific errors. (Answers on page 48)

1. A senior military officer is responsible for the decisions of the subordinate members of his unit.

_____

_____

_____

2. My brother-in-law is an accident liability lawyer, and he never misses an opportunity to practice it.

_____

_____

3. The leader of the group asked each person to bring their own camping equipment.

_____

_____

4. Whenever Katie meets Joyce, she starts criticizing her decision to move out.

_____

_____

5. On the evening news last night, it said to plan for a bus strike starting tomorrow.

_____

_____

_____

6. After the engine stopped working, the ship's captain asked each crew member to decide if they wanted to continue the voyage.

_____

_____

_____

7. She reinstalled the new program on the hard drive, but it was still slow.

_____

_____

_____

8. A good public official should always try to fulfill his promises to the voters.

_____

_____

9. Everybody in the auditorium saw the police come in but could not believe their eyes when they arrested the lead singer on stage.

_____

_____

_____

10. The road repair crew scraped through the insulation on the cable television feed buried under the roadway. This resulted in a television blackout for the whole Westwood district.

_____

_____

_____

Tense

When you write a paper, every verb and verb phrase helps create a sense of time. You may write as if events are happening simultaneously with your writing, as if they have already happened, or as if they will be happening in the future.

Present—
A good education **gives** one a sense of self-worth.

Past—
A good education **gave** one a sense of self-worth.
Future—
A good education **will give** one a sense of self-worth.

Time perspective in a sentence—tense—is determined by the verb form or combination of verb forms you use.

Examples

They **work** for Ken Burns, the documentary filmmaker.
They **worked** on the Civil War documentary.
They **had worked** for a small studio right after college.
They **have worked** in film production for eleven years.
They **are working** on a new documentary.
They **will work** together on the next project.
They **will be working** in Mexico later this year.
They **will have worked** for Ken Burns for six years this July.
They **may work** on a sequel to their baseball documentary.
They **could have worked** for a larger studio.
They **should have worked** for the production company longer.
Work!
Will you **work** for a documentary filmmaker again?
Have you **worked** at any job outside the film business?

Although six tenses are considered basic, it is possible to identify *thirty* tenses, plus other word combinations within which these tenses work. However, you need not label all thirty tenses. What is important is that you use the verb-form combinations that will most accurately communicate the time of an action or state of being and most accurately show the time relationship of different actions and events within a sentence, a paragraph, and the various paragraphs in a paper.

The Six Basic Tenses

1. Present tense—designates an action or event taking place when the statement is made.

   Example

   They **see** the signals.

2. Past tense—designates an action or event that happened before the statement is made.

   Example

   They **saw** the signals.

3. Future tense—designates an action or event that will happen but that has not happened yet when the statement is made.

Example

> They **will see** the signals.

4. Present perfect tense—designates an action or event begun in the past and continuing to or into the present. To form the present perfect tense, add **has** or **have** to the past participle form of the verb. (Often the past participle will end -ed.)

Examples

> He **has seen** the signals.
> They **have seen** the signals.
> They **have worked** hard on the project.

5. Past perfect tense—designates an action or event begun and finished in the past before another action or event in the past. To form the past perfect tense, add **had** to the past participle form of the verb.

Examples

> They **had seen** the signals.
> They **had worked** hard on the project.

6. Future perfect tense—designates an action or event that will be completed in the future prior to some future time. To form the future perfect tense, add **will have** or **shall have** to the past participle.

Example

> They **will have seen** the signals.

Do not restrict yourself to the six basic tenses described above—use whatever verb form combination you need to communicate accurately and to follow the conventions of proper usage.

Once you begin writing in one tense you must continue using it, avoiding **unnecessary** shifts in time perspective.

> Wrong—
> Although she **had** a stack of work on her desk she wanted to do, she **is** simply too sick to work.
> (Shift from past tense to present tense.)

> Right—
> Although she **had** a stack of work on her desk she wanted to do, she **was** simply too sick to work.
> (Past tense used consistently.)

> Right—
> Although she **has** a stack of work on her desk she wants to do, she **is** simply too sick to work.
> (Present tense used consistently.)

Shifts in tense sometimes are necessary to communicate a sense of time exactly, but you must carefully construct your sentences to avoid any confusion in time perspective when you write of two or more events that happen at different times or different places.

Necessary tense shifts—
Tonight Ronald Hammersmith **will discuss** (future) the actions Franklin Delano Roosevelt **took** (past) during his first one hundred days in office as he **attempted** (past) **to implement** (present—infinitive used as direct object) emergency measures against the depression that **had taken** (past perfect) America to the brink of disaster.

Be alert to the necessity of choosing tenses carefully, and do not shift tense without good reason. Careless use of the verb forms may result in confusing statements.

Example

Confusing—
Last summer Edith Smith **explained** to visiting Rotarians what **is** happening in Northern Ireland.
Clear—
Last summer Edith Smith **explained** to visiting Rotarians what **was** happening in Northern Ireland.

The first sentence suggests that Ms. Smith knew last summer what would be happening now. The second sentence is better because it obviously refers only to what was happening in Northern Ireland last summer.

EXERCISE 1.3

Circle the correct verb form. If both choices seem correct, choose the more accurate tense. (Answers on page 49)

The sugar sensor (1. looks / looked), at this time, to be the most promising device (2. to help / to helping) diabetics lead a life with fewer complications. This device, the Dextrometer, (3. is / was) a home test that (4. let / lets) the diabetic (5. to know / know) immediately how much insulin (6. was taken / should be taken) or if any should be taken at all. To perform the test, the diabetic (7. need / needs) one small drop of blood from a finger. This drop (8. is placed / will be placed) on a specially treated strip; after waiting for sixty seconds and washing the strip off with water, the diabetic (9. should place / places) the strip into the meter, and within two seconds the blood sugar level (10. registered / registers). This testing of the blood (11. allows / allowed) a more accurate dose of insulin to be given. By allowing better control over the times and amounts of insulin injected, the

Dextrometer (12. increased / increases) safety and (13. will reduce / reduces) the chance of infection. Thus, the diabetic (14. will have felt / feels) better. The light weight of this device (15. would make / makes) it attractive to diabetics. Earlier devices (16. were / would have been) big, heavy, and (17. would have had to be / had to be) plugged into an electrical outlet. By contrast, the Dextrometer (18. is / will be) about the size of a cassette player and light enough to be carried around in its own case. Although the Dextrometer (19. has been / is) too complicated and not reliable enough to be a commercial success, it (20. does / would) offer hope for diabetics in the future.

Person—First, Second, and Third

Everything is written in first, second, or third person, depending upon the writer's purpose and audience. "Person" is the perspective used to distinguish between the writer and those to whom or about whom the writer writes. *First person* is used when the writer or the character in the writing is speaking. *Second person* is used when someone is addressed. *Third person* is used when someone or something is written about. The writer must choose one of these three perspectives—first, second, or third person—and then use it consistently to avoid **shifts in person**, which can be awkward or confusing.

First Person

First-person writing is characterized by the use of the pronouns **I, my, me, we, our,** and **us.** Either the author or a character in the writing is speaking firsthand. First person is commonly used in narratives, descriptions, anecdotes, fiction, and autobiographical essays. Traditionally, first person was avoided in explanatory and argumentative essays. Contemporary writers, however, are using first person references in their writing. Some instructors even go so far as to encourage their students to use the first-person *we* and *our* on the theory that first person promotes a feeling of involvement among the readers, thus making the writing more persuasive. Since this practice is not fully accepted, you should be careful to determine your instructor's preferences before using first person in your own writing.

Example

Unacceptable—

I think *I* am right in saying that no woman can be denied the right to use her original name after she is married.

Better—

Under *our* legal system, no woman can be denied her right to use her original name after she is married.

Best—

No woman can be denied the right to use her original name after she is married.

Exceptions to this general rule occur when you are writing about activities or events in which you actually participated or at least observed firsthand, for example, when writing an anecdote or when writing an autobiographical essay. In these instances it is acceptable to refer to yourself.

Example (anecdote)

A child's mind does not clearly comprehend death. When a traumatic event occurs that a child has never experienced before, however, it is not atypical for the child to decide death is near. I can still recall my first truly frightening experience. As the calf's head hit the side of my mouth, I felt the blow but no pain. However, when I had finally calmed the calf, and it had resumed eating, I began to feel a dull ache in my jaw. I felt my face in the darkness and suddenly realized that the sticky mess on my face and shirt was blood, my blood. As my fingers explored my face, my brain came to the realization that my face now had two mouths rather than one. As my brain attempted to comprehend this discovery, my fingers explored the hole to the left of my mouth. Suddenly, my composure dissolved; the pain, the blood, the hole, all overwhelmed my six-year-old mind. What started as a whimper ended as a yell of anguish that trailed along behind me while I ran into the barn to tell my mother I was dying.

While some instructors will not accept first-person *we* or *our* in persuasive writing, many will now accept this practice if used only occasionally and very carefully. Also, to be acceptable, the first person must refer to all people, not to first-person I.

Example

Unacceptable—

We should complete the Jackson County's light rail system in order to reduce the number of cars on the freeway. (Only the people of a special audience are the "we" in this sentence.)

Acceptable—

We must work to reduce the pollution of water and air if the planet is to remain habitable by the human species. (Presumably, the writer of this sentence is referring to all of the people in the world.)

Second Person

Second-person writing is characterized by the use of the pronouns *you* and *your*. The writer's intention is to direct his or her words directly to the reader as an individual. Commands (imperative sentences) are always written using second person because the subject of a command is always "you" understood. Generally, second person is acceptable only in directions and textbooks; consequently, second-person usage should be carefully avoided in school and job-related writing.

Example

Unacceptable—

> When *you* are competing for a management job in a large company, *you* have to be better qualified than everyone else who applies.

Acceptable—

> After *you* have formed the mold in the sand, melt the paraffin. *You* can use one of *your* old coffee cans to heat the paraffin in until the wax is liquefied. As it is melting, mix pieces of crayon in with the wax until the color is right. *You* can also add a few drops of scented oil at this stage.

Third Person

In third-person writing, people, places, and events are referred to objectively by name or description. Third-person writing is characterized by use of the following pronouns: *he, his, him, it, its, she, hers, her, one, they, their,* and *them.* The writer is writing about someone or something. Most academic writing—essays, reports, and tests—are written in third person. The same holds true for reports, proposals, and other writing on the job.

Example

> Three hundred years ago during the plague, London was not a very sanitary place to live. *Londoners,* both rich and poor, bathed infrequently. Most *families* bought a limited amount of water daily from *waterbearers,* and there were no private baths. *Samuel Pepys* wrote in *his* secret diary that *his wife* actually dared to wash *herself* all over at a public "hothouse" and that a few days later *he* bathed also, an unusual event. The city had no underground sewer system. Instead of sewers, kennels (open gutters) were used for waste liquids from chamber pots and wash-up water.

Continue to use third person throughout the entire paper unless you are including an anecdote to illustrate a particular point. Unnecessary shifts in person appear awkward and are often confusing to your reader.

Example

Awkward shift—

> Vincent did not want to run for student body office. *He* would rather work from behind the scenes without *you* always knowing what they were doing.

Revised—

> Vincent did not want to run for student office. *He* would rather work from behind the scenes without people knowing what *he* was doing.

EXERCISE 1.4

Revise the following paragraph. Begin by removing the gender-specific language. Then correct all agreement, reference, tense, and person errors. (Sample revision on page 49)

The hospice program is committed to helping both patients and families adjust to terminal illness and impending death. Often the acceptance of death is easier for the patient than his family. A dying person needs time to work things out emotionally with himself and his family. Prior to the mid-1970s few classes dealing with death and dying could be found in the United States. Today, however, there is many choices of classes, group sessions, or lectures. According to Clare Curran, R.N., the Patient Care Coordinator for the Mercy San Juan Hospice program, hospitals in most metropolitan areas offer a series of informative programs for the cancer patient and their family. In addition, many chapters of the American Cancer Society hold weekly meetings for family members undergoing the stress of cancer in a loved one. Counseling was also offered by trained volunteers who visit patients at home and in the hospital on a regular basis. Often the patient and his family members will be more receptive to a volunteer than a health care professional. In hospice, I believe, the grieving process is understood by all who care for the patient, and special attention is given to those emotionally involved with the dying person.

LESSON TWO: *Sentence Structure and Punctuation; Transitions*

To be a good writer, you must be a skillful sentence editor—aware of the types of sentences you are using and how to punctuate them. Good writing is characterized by a variety of simple, compound, and complex sentences. Appearing at the beginning, in the middle, and at the end of sentences, phrases and dependent clauses create sentence variety and a fuller expression. Some sentences are long and complicated, but others are short, producing interesting contrast. Punctuation is used effectively to prevent confusion and to make reading easier. Smooth transitions are made between sentences and paragraphs. Always, whether by instinct or design, sentence structure enhances what is being said. The overall effect is sentences that flow with pleasing balance and rhythm. As you write, you will naturally be concerned with the task of saying what you want to say clearly. But you should try to write with style, rewriting, experimenting with options, correcting, trying different word combinations, until you are thoroughly satisfied with the results.

THE SIMPLE SENTENCE

By definition, a **simple sentence** is one that contains only one independent clause and no dependent clauses. Simple refers to one of anything: simple sentence means one independent clause in the sentence, simple subject means one subject, and simple predicate means one verb in the predicate.

By contrast, compound refers to two or more of any one thing: compound sentence means two or more independent clauses, compound subject means two or more subjects, and compound predicate means two or more verbs.

Examples

A massive oil slick drifted closer to the coast. (simple subject and predicate)

A massive oil slick and debris from the sinking tanker drifted closer to the coast. (compound subject and simple predicate)

A massive oil slick and debris from the sinking tanker drifted closer to the coast and threatened its delicate marine life environment. (compound subject and compound predicate)

A simple sentence can actually be quite complicated. But as long as it contains only one independent clause and no dependent clauses, it is still a simple sentence.

Example

To the dismay of the clean-up crews, the massive oil slick and debris from the sinking tanker drifted closer to the coast, threatening its delicate marine environment with irreparable damage from the sticky goo.

Phrases

A **phrase** is a meaningful group of words that does not contain a subject and a predicate. A phrase functions as a single part of speech, often as an adjective or adverb. Although a simple sentence contains no dependent clauses, it usually contains one or more phrases. These phrases are indispensable if you are to express yourself effectively. In order to punctuate a sentence correctly, you must be aware that you are using a phrase.

Examples

The scientist *has created* a perfect artificial emerald. (verb phrase)

She read *for an hour before lunch.* (prepositional phrases)

Falling asleep at the wheel, the truck driver drove off the highway, *demolishing a roadside fruit stand.* (participial phrases)

Eating more fruit and vegetables and less red meat is gaining acceptance from those who wish to maintain good health. (gerund phrases)

Her term paper finished, she let out a huge sigh. (absolute phrase)

Carol went to *find a newspaper.* (infinitive phrase)

His brother, *a track star at Borg High School,* suffered a pulled hamstring muscle. (appositive phrase)

The most financially successful movie of all time, *for example,* is *Jurassic Park.* (transitional phrase)

Dirty and bedraggled, the puppy was obviously lost. (adjective phrase)

Two weeks earlier, he lost his watch. (adverb phrase)

EXERCISE 1.5

Underline the phrases in the following simple sentences. (Answers on page 49)

1. After the conference the committee members will visit the Faulkner home in Oxford, Mississippi.

2. Following an ancient instinctual urge, the salmon, a huge Oregon Chinook, hurled itself up the fish ladder.

3. Fearful of the high surf, the crew paddled the little sportboat away from the rocks.

4. A whiz with computers, Barbara Jean installed additional RAM and a sound card in her Pentium multimedia system.

5. Having a job is the most important consideration for Michelle.

6. His purpose accomplished, the new premier returned to Pretoria.

7. Starving and desperate, the stragglers crossed the border into the refugee camp in search of safety.

8. In 1965 at age 16, Robin Lee Graham sailed alone around the world.

9. Twenty years later, Tania Aebi, only 18 years old at the time, set out from New York in a 26-foot sailboat to sail around the world alone.

10. As a matter of fact, Graham and Aebi completed their respective circumnavigations at age 21.

Punctuating Simple Sentences

INTRODUCTORY PARTS

Commas may be needed in simple sentences to set off introductory parts.

1. Transitional Words and Phrases

Transitional words and phrases are used to build bridges between sentences. Use a comma to set off an introductory transitional word or phrase.

Examples

They wanted to hike to the summit. *However,* the storm grew worse.

Nils had been acting differently for about a month. *For instance,* he would suddenly begin singing during class.

2. To Prevent Confusion

A comma after an introductory word or phrase may be necessary to keep the reader from mistakenly connecting the word or phrase to what follows, forcing the reader to reread the sentence.

Examples

Surprised, Fred barely had time to push his dirty clothes under his bed.

Three inches below, the heat shield tile had developed a crack.

3. To Create a Pause

You can direct a reader to pause after an introductory word or phrase by setting it off with a comma.

Examples

On the road to the enchanted castle, the miller's son met a wizard.

Somehow, the miller's son misunderstood the directions to the castle.

Two miles later, the fog began to form.

Warm and peaceful, the moss-covered tree looked inviting.

Sleeping peacefully under the branches of the tree, he did not notice the evil sorceress.

"*Miller's son,* you are trespassing on sacred ground."

Alas, he was turned into a frog!

INTERNAL PUNCTUATION

Words and phrases in the middle of a simple sentence may need to be separated from one another or set off from the rest of the sentence with commas.

1. Transitional Words and Phrases

    Examples

> The next day, *however*, the storm became worse.
> He would, *for instance*, suddenly start singing in class.

2. To Prevent Confusion

    Examples

> Bill, *John's brother*, will visit us in December.
> The ranger, *seeing the climber's plight*, radioed for a rescue helicopter.

3. To Separate Words and Phrases

    Examples

> It was a *hot, sultry* day in July.
> They rented *sleeping bags, backpacks*, and *cooking equipment* for their camping trip.
> The jeep *crossed the ravine, forded the stream*, and *began to climb* the steep slope below the cabin.

4. To Set Off a Word or Phrase

    Examples

> You see, *Dr. Jones*, you will never escape.
> The miller's son, *alas*, was turned into a frog!
> Leonard Greene, *my next-door neighbor*, has decided to sell his house.
> The problem, *corrosion*, was discovered by a plumber.

In some cases the presence or absence of a pair of commas will tell the reader how to interpret the meaning of a sentence.

Examples

> The car *stalled in the intersection* blocked traffic for miles.
> The car, *stalled in the intersection*, blocked traffic for miles.

In the first version above, the one without commas, the -ed verb phrase tells which car is being talked about—perhaps there are many cars at the intersection. The phrase is essential to the identification of the car. In that sense it is a *restrictive modifier* and should not be set off with commas. In the second version, the pair of commas acts like parentheses, showing that the reader already knows which car is being talked about. The phrase—*a nonrestrictive modifier*—is information that is not vital to the meaning of the sentence.

END PARTS

A word or phrase at the end of a simple sentence may need to be set off with a comma. In general, however, end parts are less likely to need separation than are introductory parts.

1. Transitional Words and Phrases

   Examples

   > The bird feeder remained standing after the windstorm, however.
   > Even while visiting England, most Americans want to start their day with a cup of coffee, of course.

2. To Prevent Confusion

   Examples

   > The band performed in several states, in Michigan, Florida, New York, and Ohio.
   > The crack in the bridge upper deck grew more pronounced, causing the Highway Department to close the crossing altogether.
   > Eric darted up the street, the county truant officer close behind.

3. To Separate or Create a Pause

   Examples

   > Lynne's report was late, as usual.
   > "Thank you for an outstanding presentation, Ms. VanderSchaaf."
   > Joshua's large dictionary lay under his desk all during the test, unconsulted and forgotten.
   > Trenton received three dozen orders for the new printer during the first week it was available, the direct result of his presale promotional mailings.
   > She served his favorite dessert, Jello with Cool Whip.
   > The miller's son was turned into a frog, alas!

EXERCISE 1.6

Correctly punctuate each of the following simple sentences. If a sentence needs no punctuation, write **C** in the left margin next to the sentence. (Answers on page 50)

1. Athletes from all over the world gathered in the little mountain town and competed in winter games.

2. The town a replica of an Alpine village was small and picturesque.

3. Close to the narrow winding brick and cobblestone streets stood tall colorful Swiss-style chalets.

4. Near the center of town a town hall complete with a tower and clock was surrounded by small shops.

5. Three miles from town an elaborate winter sports complex had been built for the games.

6. It contained two stadiums for ice skating and hockey a bobsled run and of course various ski runs and jumps.

7. Everyone except some of the townspeople overwhelmed by the crowds and the lack of parking eagerly anticipated the forthcoming events.

8. The unpredictable mountain weather however refused to cooperate.

9. A fierce blizzard the worst in thirty years struck the area covering everything with three to five feet of snow.

10. To everyone's chagrin the blizzard continued for five days making roads impassable.

11. Many spectators' cars trapped in the snow drifts were abandoned.

12. As a result snowplow crews had difficulty clearing the roads.

13. "Mr. Smith your automobile has been found" announced the manager over the hotel intercom.

14. Nevertheless athletes game officials spectators and townspeople carried on conducting most of the events on schedule a remarkable feat.

15. However in some instances ski and sled run times were slow due to the heavy snow.

16. Late in the afternoon of the second day ski jump competitors midway through their jumps disappeared into the falling snow magically reappearing near the bottom of the slope.

17. The outdoor ice rink the largest in the country had to be cleared every fifteen minutes.

18. Spectators and athletes enjoyed the sports events during the day and participated in the endless parties during the night.

19. Parvo Jones the owner of a popular ski lodge had once been a world champion downhill racer.

20. Now twenty years later he was famous for his Midnight Supper party.

21. Through the huge windows facing the mountain guests watched a column of tuxedoed skiers snaking single-file down the slope each holding a lighted lantern.

22. A German band played by the crowded pool of course.

23. According to rumor some guests never left the lodge to attend a single sports event.

24. On Thursday an old pine tree broke from the weight of the snow crashing down on a restaurant in the town square.

25. Naturally the snow stopped on Saturday the last day of the games.

THE COMPOUND SENTENCE

When two or more simple sentences (independent clauses) are joined correctly, the resulting sentence is called a compound sentence. Study the following sentences.

Examples

The brakes failed, *and* the car crashed into the tree. (comma and conjunction)
The class was canceled; the teacher had chicken pox. (semicolon)

The road was covered with snow; *therefore*, the trucker drove very slowly. (conjunctive adverb)

You can write compound sentences using any of the three methods illustrated above. However, the most common connector is the comma and conjunction shown in the first example. You must not omit any part of the punctuation, or you will create a sentence error.

Examples

INCORRECT	The brakes failed and the car crashed.
INCORRECT	The brakes failed, the car crashed.
CORRECT	The brakes failed, and the car crashed.

The two independent clauses in a compound sentence are equal in importance and subject matter. The word used to describe any two things that are equal in rank or importance is called a coordinate. Logically the term *coordinating conjunction* describes any word used to join simple sentences to create a compound sentence. Other than using a semicolon, the only way to correctly join two simple sentences is to use a coordinating conjunction.

COORDINATING CONJUNCTIONS

and	yet
but	nor
or	so
for	

Whenever you use a coordinating conjunction to join two simple sentences, you must place a comma before the conjunction. Some authorities hold that when two short, closely related independent clauses are joined, a comma before the conjunction is not necessary. However, while working with this book you should use a comma. The comma and the conjunction work together; neither may be omitted.

Example

The storm-spawned waves rocked the boat, and the sailors became seasick.

Coordinating conjunctions confuse some writers because the same conjunctions that are used to join two sentences into a compound sentence are also used to join two subjects or predicates in a simple sentence. The difference is that no comma is used in the simple sentence while a comma must be used in the compound sentence.

Examples

SIMPLE	The storm hit the city just before dark and made the roads impassable by dawn.
COMPOUND	The storm hit the city just before dark, and the roads became impassable by dawn.

Each of the previous example sentences has the same number of words, but one is simple and the other compound. In order to correctly punctuate each, you must first be able to distinguish one from the other.

Easy Test for Commas

When you see two sentence parts connected with the conjunction **and, but, or, for, yet, nor,** or **so,** conduct this simple test to determine whether or not a comma is needed in front of the conjunction.

1. Using your pen, cover the conjunction and the portion of the sentence after the conjunction.

   Example

   The storm hit the city just before dark *and the roads were impassable at dawn*.

2. Ask yourself, could the exposed portion before the conjunction stand alone as a sentence?

   Example

   Yes. "The storm hit the city just before dark" is a sentence.

3. Next, cover the portion of the sentence in front of the conjunction and the conjunction itself.

   Example

   The storm hit the city just before dark and the roads were impassable at dawn.

4. Ask yourself, could the exposed portion stand alone as a sentence?

   Example

   "The roads were impassable at dawn." Yes, is the answer.

5. Since your answer would be yes to both questions, you know you must use a comma before the conjunction to join these two independent clauses.

   Example

   The storm hit the city just before dark, *and* the roads were impassable at dawn.

6. If your answer is no to either question, you would not precede the conjunction with a comma.

   Example

   The storm hit the city just before dark and made the roads impassable by dawn.

Since the part of the sentence after the conjunction is not a complete sentence, you would not place a comma before the conjunction in the example.

USING A SEMICOLON IN COMPOUND SENTENCES

The semicolon can be used instead of the comma and conjunction in some compound sentences. In other words, the semicolon can sometimes be used to join two closely related simple sentences. Three possible reasons that you might want to use this technique are as follows:

1. Joining two closely related simple sentences is one way to achieve sentence variety, thus making your writing more interesting for your readers.

2. Joining two closely related simple sentences may help you develop smoother-flowing sentences.

3. Joining two closely related simple sentences emphasizes the close relationship of the ideas in the two independent clauses being connected.

The reader comes to a semi-stop upon encountering the semicolon instead of a full stop signaled by a period. The semicolon creates a tighter connection than the comma-conjunction combination. Study the examples below.

Examples

Ben and Jerry are active environmentalists; their business practices promote those causes.

Ruth spoke to the city council about bus service for the elderly last week; this week she is writing to seven state legislators.

Maria was so late to class that she had time to finish only half the test; her grade suffered because of her tardiness.

In each of the sentences above, the semicolon is preferable to a comma and the conjunction *and* or to two sentences, which would sound choppy. Notice that in each case the connection is brisk, and the sentences connect smoothly. Occasional use of semicolons will improve your writing style, but be careful not to overuse them.

Perhaps one of the most effective uses of the semicolon is in the *semicolon + conjunctive adverb + comma* connection between two simple sentences.

Examples

The funding for the new computer classroom has again been delayed; *however,* several businesses have agreed to lend the school some new computers for next year.

She wants to enroll in advanced science and math courses as soon as she starts college; *therefore,* she studies several hours each evening.

The fuel economy of American-made automobiles has improved dramatically the past few years; *moreover,* their overall quality now rivals that of most imports.

Some Conjunctive Adverbs

; accordingly,	; clearly, then,	; for one thing,	; heretofore,
; afterward,	; consequently,	; fourth,	; however,
; afterwards,	; finally,	; furthermore,	; in addition,
; all in all,	; first,	; granted,	; in fact,
; also,	; for example,	; hence,	; in general,
; as a matter of fact,	; for instance,	; hereafter,	; in other words,

; in particular,	; nevertheless,	; second,	; thereupon,
; in short,	; notwithstanding,	; similarly,	; third,
; in summary,	; obviously,	; still,	; thus (,)
; indeed,	; of course,	; then(,)	; to be sure,
; likewise,	; on the whole,	; thereafter,	; to make matters worse,
; moreover,	; otherwise,	; therefore,	; unfortunately,

The conjunctive adverb builds a smooth transition between the two simple sentences being connected. But be aware that it is the semicolon that connects the two sentences, not the conjunctive adverb. Notice in the following examples that the conjunctive adverb *however* could be omitted but that the semicolon could not be omitted without creating a punctuation error. Remember, too, that a comma is usually placed after the conjunctive adverb to complete the connection.

Examples

INCORRECT   The swan was the Queen's favorite bird however, the poacher killed it.

INCORRECT   The swan was the Queen's favorite bird, however, the poacher killed it.

CORRECT   The swan was the Queen's favorite bird; however, the poacher killed it.

CORRECT   The swan was the Queen's favorite bird; the poacher killed it. (conjunctive adverb removed)

Note: Since many of the same kinds of words and phrases used in simple sentences are used in compound sentences, the same punctuation rules apply for both kinds of sentences. The following compound sentence, for example, contains an introductory participial phrase and a transitional word in the middle of the second independent clause. Such transitions must be set off with commas.

Example

Believing strongly in her principles, his grandmother tried to convince Nicholas to be a lawyer for the elderly and poor; he, *however*, was determined to be a corporate lawyer in the electronics industry.

EXERCISE 1.7

Label the sentence **SS** if it is a simple sentence and **CD** if it is a compound sentence. Then punctuate the sentence correctly; some will need no punctuation. (Answers on page 51)

_____ 1. Three passersby broke the windows of the burning car to rescue the elderly lady but one of the rescuers was badly burned.

_____ 2. The rain continued to fall and the river rose almost to the top of the levee.

_____ 3. However the members of both teams looked unbelievably dirty at the end of the game.

_____ 4. The city plans to hire crews to clean the downtown sidewalks regularly however merchants in the area may be assessed for the costs.

_____ 5. He had dated the girl three times yet he still did not know her last name.

_____ 6. The terrier never tired of digging holes he would even dig in the flower beds at night.

_____ 7. The student worked all night in a film lab and she usually fell asleep in her morning classes.

_____ 8. Dave will not be there Sunday but he will stop by sometime next week.

_____ 9. The recently hired paramedics were enthusiastic about their work but very inexperienced.

_____ 10. The downtown J.C. Penney's store will be closed and converted into an office building.

_____ 11. Without her testimony about the bribery attempts there will not be enough evidence and convictions in the case will be impossible.

_____ 12. They will fly to Dublin next summer and drive from there to Northern Ireland to take photographs.

_____ 13. He had to take his cousin to the Senior Prom the whole idea was his mother's.

_____ 14. The older model was actually better than the new one for the newer model was built with inferior parts.

_____ 15. Alexander Hamilton the leader of the Federalists argued for a strong national government but Thomas Jefferson leader of the Democratic-Republicans favored state's rights.

_____ 16. The gaunt old gunfighter laughed and then slumped over dead his face crashing into his plate of steak and pumpkin pie.

_____ 17. The cafeteria should be one of the cleanest places on campus but it is one of the dirtiest.

_____ 18. Food is left on the trays and silverware and detergent is caked inside the glasses.

_____ 19. Landing the Concorde jetliner is not much noisier than the Boeing 747 but taking off it is much louder.

_____ 20. Brian read the directions three times yet he still did not know how to solve the algebra problems.

_____ 21. Serious problems hampered efforts to distribute food to the refugees for instance there were not enough trucks to transport the food to distribution points.

_____ 22. She slammed on the brakes and swerved onto the shoulder.

_____ 23. Will you drive back to Springfield on Sunday or will you wait until Monday morning?

_____ 24. The sleet beat on the bay windows the wind howled down the chimney.

_____ 25. Definitely a Type-A person she was irritated by red lights and became impatient in supermarket lines .

EXERCISE 1.8

Write each sentence as requested. Make sure each is punctuated correctly.

1. Simple sentence with simple subject and compound predicate

_____

_____

_____

2. Compound sentence using comma and conjunction

_____

_____

_____

3. Simple sentence with compound subject and compound predicate

_____

_____

_____

4. Compound sentence using conjunctive adverb

_____

_____

_____

5. Compound sentence using semicolon without conjunctive adverb

_____

_____

_____

Have your sentences checked.

THE COMPLEX SENTENCE

In order to understand the complex sentence, you must first know the difference between independent and dependent clauses. An **independent clause** is any group of words that contains a subject and a predicate and can stand alone as a complete sentence.

Examples

> Wolves howl.
> Julie showed Bill the shawl.

By contrast, a **dependent clause** is any group of words that begins with a subordinating conjunction or relative pronoun and contains a subject and a predicate. The dependent clause cannot stand alone as a sentence.

Examples

> *when* wolves howl (subordinating conjunction)
> *that* she bought in Mexico (relative pronoun)

Every grammatically complete sentence must contain at least one independent clause. When a dependent clause is added to an independent clause, the idea contained in the dependent clause is of less importance. The dependent clause, therefore, is subordinated to the independent clause through the use of a **subordinating conjunction** (sometimes referred to as a subordinating connective). These conjunctions indicate the subordinate status of dependent clauses.

Some Subordinating Conjunctions

after	before	though	where
although	even though	unless	whereas
as	if	until	while
as long as	provided	when	
because	since	whenever	

In addition to subordinating conjunctions, **relative pronouns** are used to create subordinate dependent clauses.

Relative Pronouns
that
what
which
who
whom

Relative pronouns and subordinating conjunctions are known collectively as **signal words.** These subordinating conjunctions and relative pronouns are used to join two clauses, making one dependent upon the other. That is, the clause to which one of these words is attached becomes a dependent clause and can no longer stand alone. Therefore, whenever one of these dependent clauses is created, it must be attached to an independent clause; the resulting sentence is a **complex sentence.** Complex sentences will give your writing variety and life when interspersed among simple and compound sentences. While editing, you can convert some simple and compound sentences to complex sentences.

Examples

1. He did not like his new job. However, the salary was high. (two simple sentences)
    He did not like his new job, but the salary was high. (compound sentence)
    He did not like his new job *even though* the salary was high. (complex sentence with a subordinating conjunction)

2. She saw a police car. She stopped. (two simple sentences)
    After she saw the police car, she stopped. (complex sentence with a subordinating conjunction)

3. She wanted a Chinese basket. It would have to be large enough for her jade plant. (two simple sentences)
    She wanted a Chinese basket *that* would be large enough for her jade plant. (complex sentence with a relative pronoun)

Punctuating Complex Sentences

INTRODUCTORY DEPENDENT CLAUSES

Ordinarily, a dependent clause must be followed by a comma when the dependent clause is placed at the beginning of the sentence, preceding the independent clause. The effect of the comma is to create a pause.

Examples

Although an oil surplus developed, gasoline prices remained high.
When she saw Juan's picture, she screamed, "He's so cute!"

DEPENDENT CLAUSES IN THE MIDDLE

If a dependent clause in the middle of a sentence is essential to the meaning of the sentence (restrictive) no commas are used to separate it from the rest of the sentence.

Examples

The woman *who is wearing the bright red blouse* will show you the exhibit.
An automobile *that has a long wheelbase* often rides more comfortably on the highway.

But if a dependent clause that interrupts a sentence can be removed from the complex sentence without altering the intended meaning of the sentence, a pair of commas should be used to set the interrupting dependent clause apart from the rest of the sentence. In cases where you cannot decide whether or not a dependent clause is restrictive or nonrestrictive, ask yourself if the reader should pause at the beginning and end of the dependent clause in question. If pauses are necessary for proper reading, place a comma at the beginning and end.

Examples

> Theresa, who is wearing the bright red blouse, will show you the exhibit.
> Teri's pickup truck, which she bought just last year, leaves her stranded at least twice a month.

DEPENDENT CLAUSES AT THE END

Whenever possible, refrain from using a comma to separate an independent clause and a dependent clause that follows it at the end of a sentence. You must have a very good reason for using a comma to set off an end clause.

Examples

> The magazine editor wore a smile *although she was obviously annoyed.*
> They worked for a new car dealer *until they started their own auto parts business.*

However, a comma placed between an independent clause and the dependent clause that follows may be needed to create a pause or to prevent confusion. A pause may be needed so that the dependent clause will be read with more emphasis than if the comma were not used. Or the pause may be used to show that the dependent clause is not needed, an extra or a nonrestrictive clause.

Examples

> The theater manager plans to begin evening productions one hour earlier, *whether the audience likes it or not.* (emphasis)
> Devon and Sandra plan to buy a new refrigerator, *although their son Charles would rather have them buy a computer.* (signaling readers that the dependent clause is not essential)

A comma may be necessary to prevent confusion.

Examples

> Jody has announced that she will return to college, *after she just told everyone she was going to quit school to find work.* (prevents confusion by separating main and subordinate ideas)
> Carlton wants part of his mother's estate, *which he is entitled to according to the will.* (prevents confusion by separating thoughts)

EXERCISE 1.9

Write complex sentences according to the following directions. (Have your sentences checked.)

1. Write a complex sentence *beginning* with a dependent clause. Punctuate the sentence correctly.

_____

_____

_____

2. Write a complex sentence with the dependent clause *in the middle*. In this sentence make the interrupting dependent clause essential and punctuate the sentence correctly.

_____

_____

_____

3. Write another complex sentence with a dependent clause *in the middle*. In this sentence make the interrupting dependent clause nonessential and punctuate it accordingly.

_____

_____

_____

4. Write a complex sentence in which the independent clause *is followed* by a dependent clause. Punctuate it correctly.

_____

_____

_____

By permission of John Hart and Field Enterprises Inc.

EXERCISE 1.10

Revise the following sentences by inserting appropriate coordinating conjunctions or signal words. Note that the punctuation often suggests the correct answer. (Answers on page 52)

1. The rain today was unexpected, _____ it was welcome.

2. _____ the computer breaks down, no one knows how to make the company function any longer.

3. Everyone attempted to look busy _____ the supervisor entered the room.

4. The order arrived on schedule, _____ the parts we wanted most had been back ordered.

5. Every educated person in the audience claimed to understand the situation, _____ _____ no one actually did.

6. The players on the opposing team were secretly elated _____ they heard about the quarterback's injuries.

7. _____ they installed a word-processing program, they spent many hours retyping manuscripts.

8. Clear-cutting is a logger's dream _____ it is an environmentalist's nightmare.

9. _____ the rest of us were spending our money on luxury items, Mark was putting his in the bank.

10. _____ the airplane had come to a stop, we saw the armed guards take up positions all around the aircraft.

11. The dog _____ Nola purchased for her daughter is an Australian shepherd.

12. _____ millions of dollars have been spent on highway improvement, there are still roads throughout the United States _____ are considered "death traps."

EXERCISE 1.11

Write two compound and two complex sentences in which you use coordinating conjunctions and signal words respectively to join the clauses. Punctuate the sentences properly. (Have your sentences checked.)

1. Compound _____

_____

_____

_____

2. Compound _____

_____

_____

_____

3. Complex _____

_____

_____

_____

4. Complex _____

_____

_____

_____

EXERCISE 1.12

In the blanks, write **SS** if the sentence is simple, **CD** if the sentence is compound, and **CX** if the sentence is complex. Then insert any punctuation needed; some sentences will not need punctuation. (Answers on page 52)

_____In ten days a billion could be reproduced. _____Diatoms a class of microscopic plants belonging to the group algae multiply by division and often cloud the water brown. _____More than 25,000 kinds of these single-celled plants exist and no shell is the same. Each one is a living jewel. _____Many of them have such delicate symmetry and perfection that if they were larger they would be used by jewelry designers. _____It is necessary to use a microscope to study and admire their structure because they are too small to be seen by the unaided eye. _____Diatoms are found everywhere there is water and in incredible numbers. _____Just one liter of sea water may contain as many as 10 million. _____But not all are aquatic under moist conditions some live in topsoil tree trunks attached to moss and even on brick walls. _____Diatoms living and dead are important because of the large role they play in nature their help in science and their multiple uses in industry.

_____Billions of prehistoric diatoms make up deposits called diatomaceous earth which when mined have many uses in industry. _____Composed of silica a transparent substance harder than glass many diatoms are found fossilized. _____Eventually they deplete themselves of nutrients and great numbers sink and die carpeting the ocean floor with a layer of diatomaceous ooze. _____Through the passing of time as oceans rise and continents drift this ooze fossilizes into rich deposits of diatomaceous earth. _____Diatomaceous earth is mined throughout the United States. _____The Western states have cubic miles of it in varying purity. As many as 75,000 individual diatoms are contained in one cubic inch of diatomaceous earth.

_____Once it is mined it is very useful to industry and it is used in many products. _____Because it is not combustible it is used as an insulator. _____Its light weight and multitude of pores make it an ideal filter of raw sugar solutions petroleum products some alcohols and other chemicals. _____Diatomaceous earth helps save lives by providing the sparkle in roadway reflectors. _____It is the grit in toothpaste and cleansing powders. _____Many insecticides contain diatomaceous earth. _____Some people even line their cupboards with it to keep weevils out. _____Death comes in twelve hours after an insect ventures into it. _____Its skin is cut and the insect is drained of its vital juices. _____Thus diatomaceous earth is a very useful resource.

TRANSITIONS

After you have made certain your writing contains a variety of sentence patterns, you may have to make another kind of revision. You may have to add transitional words and phrases that make your paper more coherent by more clearly showing the connection between different ideas.

Examples

Before revision—
A college education is very expensive. Typical college graduates earn much more during their lifetime than do typical high school graduates.

After revision—
Of course, a college education is very expensive. But typical college graduates earn much more during their lifetimes than do typical high school graduates.

Common Transitions

When you want to show that one idea is an **addition** to another, use — too, also, furthermore, similarly, moreover, and, or, nor, indeed, in fact, first, second . . .

When you want to **illustrate**, use — for example, for instance, for one thing, similarly, likewise

When you want to **summarize**, use — that is, in short, in other words

When you want to **concede** a point, use   no doubt, to be sure, granted that . . . , it is true that . . . , of course, doubtless, certainly, admittedly

When you want to show a **contrast** between one idea and another, or when you want to **refute** a previously stated concession, use   but, nevertheless, conversely, on the other hand, yet, however, on the contrary, not at all, surely, no

When you want to **conclude**, use   hence, accordingly, so, therefore, consequently, as a result, in conclusion, thus, finally, on the whole, all in all, in other words, in short

Here are some additional points you should remember about the use of transitions:

1. Use transitions to make your sentences and paragraphs flow together smoothly. Study the way the italicized words and phrases have been used to smoothly connect ideas in the following student-written paragraph.

    Example

    > *Finally*, on the topic of personal integrity opponents of amnesty raise three points. *First*, they argue that to grant amnesty for acts done willfully would be a disservice to the individuals who performed them. *After all*, if the act of dissent is to have meaning, then it must not be forgotten. *Second*, opponents contend that most dissenters did not stand up for their beliefs in spite of the law and bear the penalty. Daniel Oliver speaks to this point in the *National Review*: "It is not the willingness of the man of conscience to break the law that impresses, but rather his willingness to pay the penalty for breaking the law." *In this way*, their protest does not show conviction and consequently does not have merit. *Third*, they argue that such a relaxation of the law will compound the problem in the future. Despite the fact that the Selective Service Act is no longer being used, there is still a principle of personal integrity with respect to the law which must not be violated.

2. Use the logical connections that will help your reader follow your argument. In other words, when you want to show contrast, use a transition from the contrast group, and so forth.

3. Avoid repeating the same transitional words or phrases in a short paper. They can become repetitious and cause the paper to seem awkward or mechanical.

4. Smooth transition can be achieved by repeating key words from a previous sentence.

    Example

    > The District Attorney and the defendant's lawyer arranged *a deal*. *This deal* was contingent upon *several conditions*. The *first condition* was that . . . .

5. In longer papers a whole sentence (and in very long papers, even a complete paragraph) may be needed to establish the transition from one major point to another. These papers often develop two or more important concepts, and their

relationship must be shown to the reader to justify their appearance in the same paper.

6. Parallel construction in sentences, especially in introductory phrases or clauses, can be used to effect transition. This device is very useful in showing the continuity of several topic sentences (see Appendix B).

Example—

> *Winston's first act of rebellion* is to purchase a diary.
> *Winston's second act of rebellion* is to enter into a relationship with Julia. (Parallel topic sentences)

EXERCISE 1.13

Circle the conjunctive adverb or transition that would work best in each of the following sentences. (Answers on page 53)

1. The accident occurred at the peak of rush-hour traffic; (consequently / in addition), a major traffic jam developed.
2. The optimistic person sees a half-full glass on the counter; (for instance / however), the pessimistic person sees a half-empty glass.
3. Some students, (indeed / unfortunately), refuse to become actively involved in their own education.
4. (Of course / In other words), other students push relentlessly to derive the most benefits from their educational experience.
5. (For instance / Nevertheless), some dedicated students go home immediately after lectures to type the lecture notes they took that day, recalling the instructor's every word.
6. The election will be held next month; (consequently / however), polls show many voters are apathetic about the candidates and issues.

LESSON THREE: *Semicolons, Colons, Run-ons, Comma Splices, and Fragments*

The Semicolon

Lesson Two reviewed the use of the semicolon to join two simple sentences to form a compound sentence. That is its most common use. You should be aware, however, that the semicolon can also be used to prevent confusion in long sentences that contain several commas. Perhaps the most common of these is the compound sentence in which a semicolon is used before a conjunction (and, or, but, for, yet, nor, so) to prevent confusion.

Example

> War was inevitable, or so it appeared at the time; *but* Americans, as if denying reality would prevent it, continued to demand that President Roosevelt remain neutral.

The semicolon is used here before the conjunction because numerous commas are used elsewhere in the sentence. By using the semicolon to break the sentence into its two major parts, the sentence is made easier to read.

Some writers also use a semicolon in compound sentences with *yet* or *so*.

Example

> Gina was sure she understood how to drive in America two weeks after she moved here from England; *yet* she caused an accident almost immediately when she drove the wrong way on a freeway.

A semicolon may also be used in a sentence to separate the major items in the series from the lesser items.

Example

> Three people were killed in the boating mishap: Jerry, the skipper; Pamela, his fourteen-year-old daughter; and Adele, the skipper's sixty-four-year-old mother-in-law.

The Colon

Although the colon is not used as frequently as the semicolon, you must know when it is used to avoid misusing it. You will most commonly use the colon to introduce a list. Note that the lead-in should be a complete sentence—do not place a colon after a preposition or a verb.

Examples

> Long after the devastating hurricane, people remembered the three heroes: the 10-year-old girl who pulled the toddler from the pond, the 67-year old grandmother who pushed the car off the tracks, and the anonymous man who helped the children safely out of the wrecked school bus.

> "To be really successful, you will have to be trilingual: fluent in English, Spanish, and computer."—John Naisbitt, *Megatrends*

Colons and semicolons may not be used interchangeably. A colon is used to separate a sentence from a series or a phrase. A semicolon is used to join two complete sentences (unless it is used for clarification, which is rather rare.)

Colons are also used to introduce quotations in a formal manner.

Example

Addressing the risks of voyaging in *Destination Mexico*, the authors remind would-be adventurers of an important point: "Whether in one's own backyard or on a remote island off the Mexican coast, the unexpected can occur. A sudden storm may appear. Accidents happen. But wherever we are, we all try to minimize the consequences of the unexpected by our preparations."

Finally, colons can be used to emphasize an appositive.

Examples

Automobile accidents most often result from two dissimilar causes: alcohol and speed.
Human beings are faced with many problems, but almost all of them can be attributed directly or indirectly to one single cause: overpopulation.

EXERCISE 1.14

Punctuate the following sentences correctly. If the sentence is already correctly punctuated, write **C** on the first line. (Answers on page 53)

1. Many scholars suggest that most of the world's problems can be traced to a single cause; overpopulation.

_____

_____

_____

2. Pamela and Randy met for the first time in the fall of their senior year at the university; they married after graduation at the end of the spring semester.

_____

_____

_____

3. Procrastination is his greatest failing, he rarely completes any task in a timely manner.

_____

_____

_____

4. The best-known quotation from Shakespeare is the following "To be, or not to be—that is the question."

_____

_____

_____

5. Rachel neither misses nor is late to her classes: consequently, her grades reflect her effort and her abilities.

_____

_____

_____

6. During times of crisis and danger, most people realize that there is but one truly important concern; family.

_____

_____

_____

7. Some people use seasonings to enhance the flavor of their food others use it to hide the flavor.

_____

_____

_____

8. The desire to make friends and be accepted is a priority of most children; they seem to realize early that happy people need social interaction.

_____

_____

_____

9. After decades of only three television networks, ABC, CBS, and NBC, suddenly three new networks are competing for audience share Fox, WB, and UPN.

_____

_____

_____

10. They longed to travel to some tropical country with a palm tree-lined, white sand beach and warm water to swim in and sunbathe, unfortunately, they knew they must remain at their work in the blustery cold north.

_____

_____

_____

_____

_____

Run-ons and Comma Splice Errors

Many instructors assume that a student who does not correct run-on sentences in a paper is a poor writer. A run-on sentence consists of two or more independent clauses joined without any punctuation, thus giving the impression that two sentences have been fused, or run together.

Examples

Run-on error—
He never seems to answer questions he always counters with questions of his own.

Revised—
He never seems to answer questions; he always counters with questions of his own.
OR
He never seems to answer questions, *and* he always counters with questions of his own.

In the run-on sentence above, some indication of the relationship of the two clauses is necessary. Their relationship may be shown only through the use of appropriate punctuation or through the use of linking words and correct punctuation. The linking word you choose depends upon the emphasis and meaning that you want to give each of the clauses.

Independent clauses (IC) may be joined in the following ways:
1. semicolon IC ; IC
2. semicolon+ conjunctive adverb+comma
   IC ; however, IC
   ; moreover,
   ; nevertheless,
3. comma+conjunction
   IC , and IC
   , but
   , or
   , for
   , nor
   , so
   , yet

Remember: Independent clauses cannot be joined with commas alone; the comma must be followed by a conjunction to avoid a *comma splice error*.

Examples

Comma splice error—
Fossil fuel is not an unlimited energy source, it is being swiftly depleted.

Revised—
Fossil fuel is not an unlimited energy source; it is being swiftly depleted.

OR

Fossil fuel is not an unlimited energy source; *moreover*, it is being swiftly depleted.

OR

Fossil fuel is not an unlimited energy source, *and* it is being swiftly depleted.

Exception: If a sentence contains a series of three or more short independent clauses, and the last two are separated by *and*, *or*, or *but*, commas may be used between the other independent clauses.

Example

She wanted equality, she demanded it, and she received it.

EXERCISE 1.15

Revise the sentence if it contains a run-on or comma splice error. If the sentence is correct, write **C** on the first line. (Answers on page 53)

1. The old dirt road became a soggy mess during the storm, by the end of the week it was a sea of mud.

_____

_____

_____

2. In most colleges and universities today, the computer is not a luxury it is a necessity.

_____

_____

_____

3. Jeffery desperately wanted to earn an "A" for the semester; nevertheless, he could not seem to bring himself to arrive at class on time.

_____

_____

_____

4. In spite of her strong will, Dr. Williamson was unable to overcome her illness, however, she never gave up the fight as long as she lived.

_____

_____

_____

5. All students should carry a dictionary it is a bother to have to borrow one.

_____

_____

6. She had missed many classes during the semester consequently, she was unable to correctly answer enough test questions to pass.

_____

_____

_____

7. The insects went into hibernation early this year some say that means winter will be abnormally cold.

_____

_____

8. Team sports are losing popularity among college-aged men they are, however, maintaining popularity among college coaches, alumni, and television audiences.

_____

_____

_____

_____

9. The river flooded every two or three years, consequently, regulations now prohibit building in the flood plain.

_____

_____

_____

10. Some television programs have been criticized for containing too much violence nevertheless, these shows seem to be among some of the most popular.

_____

_____

_____

_____

Fragments

As your papers are graded, your instructors may find stylistic, spelling, punctuation, typing, and format errors, all of which you could have corrected by thorough proofreading; however, the most serious error in the eyes of many instructors is the *fragment*, an incomplete sentence, one that does not contain a complete thought.

Example

While some former big-name musical artists still produce good material.

It is difficult to tell just what the writer of this sentence wishes the reader to know. What the writer has written is a dependent clause without an independent clause to complete the thought. Perhaps the removal of the signal word will make the meaning clear:

Some former big-name musical artists still produce good material.

On the other hand, the writer may have wished to write this clause as an introductory part of a complex sentence (a sentence that contains an *independent* and a *dependent* clause).

Example

While some former big-name musical artists still produce good material, they are not creating the musical excitement produced in the 1940s by Frank Sinatra, in the 1950s by Elvis Presley, and in the 1960s by the Beatles.

Although most fragments are dependent clauses that their writers thought were complete sentences, phrases (groups of words without subjects and verbs) sometimes are written as though they could stand alone as complete sentences. Often these phrases are appositives.

Example

> *Terminator 2, Jurassic Park,* and *Star Trek: Generations.*

While this phrase makes even less sense standing alone as a sentence than did the dependent clause in the first example, it is easy to understand how the writer happened to write it. Obviously, the phrase is intended as an appositive to illustrate the sentence preceding it, or possibly as an introductory phrase for the sentence that follows.

Example

> Highly technical special effects have often become a prerequisite to success for movies as demonstrated in *Terminator 2, Jurassic Park,* and *Star Trek: Generations.*

> OR

> As demonstrated in *Terminator 2, Jurassic Park,* and *Star Trek: Generations,* highly technical special effects have often become a prerequisite to success for movies.

EXERCISE 1.16

Convert all fragments into complete sentences. Write **C** after each correct sentence. (Answers on page 54)

1. The most endangered animals in the zoological garden along with fourteen of their keepers.

2. Writing her last term paper in three hours and printing it the next morning before class.

3. Moreover, the substitute teacher assigned the class an extra test because of the widespread cheating during the first examination.

4. The proliferation of CD ROM options with their many entertainment and educational references.

_____

_____

_____

5. Although public education has been accused of stagnation and critics continue to attack the system at nearly every opportunity.

_____

_____

_____

As with a great many rules and guidelines in the use of English, this prohibition against fragments may be broken for stylistic reasons. An occasional stylistic fragment can add emphasis if the technique is not overused. Fragments are sometimes used in novels and newspaper and magazine articles. Academic writing, however, is generally considered too formal to allow them. If you want to use them, be certain to obtain your instructor's permission.

Stylistic fragment—

"Man is the only animal that blushes. *Or needs to.*"
—Mark Twain

Answers to Chapter One

Many of the answers and revisions given for Chapter One exercises are only suggestions. Your answers and revisions may be correct even though they are not exactly the same as those listed. Ask about any of your answers or revisions that are different than those suggested.

Exercise 1.1

1. does	6. comes
2. has	7. is
3. is	8. is
4. was	9. requires
5. fill	10. were

Exercise 1.2

1. Senior military officers are responsible for the decisions of the subordinate members of their units.
   or
   A senior military officer is responsible for the decisions of subordinate members of his or her unit.

2. My brother-in-law is an accident liability lawyer, and he never misses an opportunity to practice his profession.

3. The leader of the group asked each person to bring his or her own camping equipment.
   or
   The leader of the group asked the campers to bring their own camping equipment.

4. Whenever Katie meets Joyce, she starts criticizing Joyce's decision to move out.
   or
   Whenever Katie meets Joyce, Joyce starts criticizing Katie's decision to move out.

5. On the evening news last night, the commentator said to plan for a bus strike starting tomorrow.

6. After the engine stopped working, the ship's captain asked each crew member to decide if he or she wanted to continue the voyage.
   or
   After the engine stopped working, the ship's captain asked the crew members to decide if they wanted to continue the voyage.

7. She reinstalled the new program on the hard drive, but the program was still slow.

8. A good public official should always try to fulfill his or her promises to the voters.
   or
   Good public officials should always try to fulfill their promises to the voters.

9. All who were in the auditorium saw the police come in but could not believe their eyes when the police arrested the lead singer on stage.

10. The road repair crew scraped through the insulation on the cable television feed buried under the roadway. This damage resulted in a television blackout for the whole Westwood district.

Exercise 1.3

1. looks	11. allows
2. to help	12. increases
3. is	13. reduces
4. lets	14. feels
5. know	15. makes
6. should be taken	16. were
7. needs	17. had to be
8. is placed	18. is
9. places	19. is
10. registers	20. does

Exercise 1.4

The hospice program is committed to helping both patients and families adjust to terminal illness and impending death. Often the acceptance of death is easier for the patients than their families. Dying patients need time to work things out emotionally with themselves and their families. Prior to the mid-1970s few classes dealing with death and dying could be found in the United States. Today, however, there are many choices of classes, group sessions, or lectures. According to Clare Curran, R.N., the Patient Care Coordinator for the Mercy San Juan Hospice program, hospitals in most metropolitan areas offer a series of informative programs for cancer patients and their families. In addition, many chapters of the American Cancer Society hold weekly meetings for family members undergoing the stress of cancer in a loved one. Counseling is also offered by trained volunteers who visit patients at home and in the hospital on a regular basis. Often the patients and their family members will be more receptive to a volunteer than a health care professional. In hospice, the grieving process is understood by all who care for the patient, and special attention is given to those emotionally involved with the dying person.

Exercise 1.5

1. <u>After the conference</u> the committee members will visit the Faulkner home <u>in Oxford, Mississippi</u>.

2. <u>Following an instinctual urge,</u> the salmon, <u>a huge Oregon Chinook,</u> hurled itself <u>up the fish ladder</u>.

3. <u>Fearful of the high surf</u> the crew paddled the little sportboat <u>away from the rocks</u>.

4. <u>A whiz with computers,</u> Barbara Jean installed additional RAM and a sound card <u>in her Pentium multimedia system</u>.

5. <u>Having a job</u> is the most important consideration <u>for Michelle</u>.

6. <u>His purpose accomplished,</u> the new premier returned <u>to Pretoria</u>.

7. <u>Starving and desperate,</u> the stragglers crossed the border <u>into the refugee camp</u> <u>in search of safety</u>.

8. <u>In 1965</u> <u>at age 16</u>, Robin Lee Graham sailed alone <u>around the world</u>.

9. <u>Twenty years later,</u> Tania Aebi, <u>only 18 years old at the time,</u> set out <u>from New York</u> <u>in a 26 foot sailboat</u> <u>to sail around the world alone</u>.

10. <u>As a matter of fact,</u> Graham and Aebi completed their respective circumnavigations <u>at age 21</u>.

Exercise 1.6

1. C
2. The town, a replica of an Alpine village, was small and picturesque.
3. Close to the narrow, winding brick and cobblestone streets, stood tall, colorful Swiss-style chalets.
4. Near the center of town, a town hall, complete with a tower and clock, was surrounded by small shops.
5. Three miles from town, an elaborate winter sports complex had been built for the games.
6. It contained two stadiums for ice skating and hockey, a bobsled run, and, of course, various ski runs and jumps.
   or
   It contained two stadiums, for ice skating and hockey, a bobsled run, and, of course, various ski runs and jumps.
7. Everyone, except some of the townspeople overwhelmed by the crowds and the lack of parking, eagerly anticipated the forthcoming events.
   or
   C
8. The unpredictable mountain weather, however, refused to cooperate.
9. A fierce blizzard, the worst in thirty years, struck the area, covering everything with three to five feet of snow.
10. To everyone's chagrin, the blizzard continued for five days, making roads impassable.
11. Many spectators' cars, trapped in the snow drifts, were abandoned.
12. As a result, snowplow crews had difficulty clearing the roads.
13. "Mr. Smith, your automobile has been found," announced the manager over the hotel intercom.
14. Nevertheless, athletes, game officials, spectators, and townspeople carried on, conducting most of the events on schedule, a remarkable feat.
15. However, in some instances ski and sled run times were slow due to the heavy snow.
    or
    However, in some instances, ski and sled run times were slow due to the heavy snow.
16. Late in the afternoon of the second day, ski jump competitors midway through their jumps disappeared into the falling snow, magically reappearing near the bottom of the slope.
17. The outdoor ice rink, the largest in the country, had to be cleared every fifteen minutes.
18. C
19. Parvo Jones, the owner of a popular ski lodge, had once been a world champion downhill racer.
20. Now twenty years later, he was famous for his Midnight Supper party.
    or
    Now, twenty years later, he was famous for his Midnight Supper party.
21. Through the huge windows facing the mountain, guests watched a column of tuxedoed skiers snaking single-file down the slope, each holding a lighted lantern.
22. A German band played by the crowded pool, of course.
23. According to rumor, some guests never left the lodge to attend a single sports event.
24. On Thursday an old pine tree broke from the weight of the snow, crashing down on a restaurant in the town square.
    or
    On Thursday, an old pine tree broke from the weight of the snow, crashing down on a restaurant in the town square.
25. Naturally, the snow stopped on Saturday, the last day of the games.

Exercise 1.7

CD 1. Three passersby broke the windows of the burning car to rescue the elderly lady, but one of the rescuers was badly burned.

CD 2. The rain continued to fall, and the river rose almost to the top of the levee.

SS 3. However, the members of both teams looked unbelievably dirty at the end of the game.

CD 4. The city plans to hire crews to clean the downtown sidewalks regularly; however, merchants in the area may be assessed for the costs.

CD 5. He had dated the girl three times, yet he still did not know her last name.

CD 6. The terrier never tired of digging holes; he would even dig in the flower beds at night.

CD 7. The student worked all night in a film lab, and she usually fell asleep in her morning classes.

CD 8. Dave will not be there Sunday, but he will stop by sometime next week.

SS 9. The recently hired paramedics were enthusiastic about their work but very inexperienced.

SS 10. The downtown J.C. Penney's store will be closed and converted into an office building.

CD 11. Without her testimony about the bribery attempts, there will not be enough evidence, and convictions in the case will be impossible.

SS 12. They will fly to Dublin next summer and drive from there to Northern Ireland to take photographs.

CD 13. He had to take his cousin to the Senior Prom; the whole idea was his mother's.

CD 14. The older model was actually better than the new one, for the newer model was built with inferior parts.

CD 15. Alexander Hamilton, the leader of the Federalists, argued for a strong national government, but Thomas Jefferson, leader of the Democratic-Republicans , favored state's rights.

SS 16. The gaunt old gunfighter laughed and then slumped over dead, his face crashing into his plate of steak and pumpkin pie.

CD 17. The cafeteria should be one of the cleanest places on campus, but it is one of the dirtiest.

CD 18. Food is left on the trays and silverware, and detergent is caked inside the glasses.

CD 19. Landing, the Concorde jetliner is not much noisier than the Boeing 747, but taking off, it is much louder.

CD 20. Brian read the directions three times, yet he still did not know how to solve the algebra problems.

CD 21. Serious problems hampered efforts to distribute food to the refugees; for instance, there were not enough trucks to transport the food to distribution points.

SS 22. She slammed on the brakes and swerved onto the shoulder.

CD 23. Will you drive back to Springfield on Sunday, or will you wait until Monday morning?

CD 24. The sleet beat on the bay windows; the wind howled down the chimney.

SS 25. Definitely a Type-A person, she was irritated by red lights and became impatient in supermarket lines.

Exercise 1.8

Answers will vary; have your work checked.

Exercise 1.9

Answers will vary; have your work checked.

Exercise 1.10

1. but, yet,
2. If, When, After
3. when, as, after
4. but, yet
5. but, yet
6. when, after
7. Before, Until
8. although, though
9. While, Although, Though
10. When, After
11. that, which
12. Although, Though that, which

Exercise 1.11

Answers will vary; have your work checked.

Exercise 1.12

SS In ten days a billion could be reproduced. SS Diatoms, a class of microscopic plants belonging to the group algae, multiply by division and often cloud the water brown. CD More than 25,000 kinds of these single-celled plants exist, and no shell is the same. SS Each one is a living jewel. CX Many of them have such delicate symmetry and perfection that if they were larger they would be used by jewelry designers. CX It is necessary to use a microscope to study and admire their structure because they are too small to be seen by the unaided eye. SS Diatoms are found everywhere there is water and in incredible numbers. SS Just one liter of sea water may contain as many as 10 million. CD But not all are aquatic; under moist conditions some live in topsoil, tree trunks, attached to moss, and even on brick walls. CX Diatoms, living and dead, are important because of the large role they play in nature, their help in science, and their multiple uses in industry.

CX Billions of prehistoric diatoms make up deposits called diatomaceous earth, which when mined have many uses in industry. SS Composed of silica, a transparent substance harder than glass, many diatoms are found fossilized. CD Eventually they deplete themselves of nutrients, and great numbers sink and die, carpeting the ocean floor with a layer of diatomaceous ooze. CX Through the passing of time as oceans rise and continents drift, this ooze fossilizes into rich deposits of diatomaceous earth. SS Diatomaceous earth is mined throughout the United States. SS The Western states have cubic miles of it in varying purity. SS As many as 75,000 individual diatoms are contained in one cubic inch of diatomaceous earth.

CX or CD-CX Once it is mined, it is very useful to industry, and it is used in many products. CX Because it is not combustible, it is used as an insulator. SS Its light weight and multitude of pores make it an ideal filter for raw sugar solutions, petroleum products, some alcohols, and other chemicals. SS Diatomaceous earth helps save lives by providing the sparkle in roadway reflectors. SS It is the grit in toothpaste and cleansing powders. SS Many insecticides contain diatomaceous earth. SS Some people even line their cupboards with it to keep weevils out. CX Death comes in twelve hours after an insect ventures into it. CD Its skin is cut, and the insect is drained of its vital juices. SS Thus, diatomaceous earth is a very useful resource.

Exercise 1.13

1. consequently
2. however
3. unfortunately
4. Of course
5. For instance
6. however

Exercise 1.14

1. Many scholars suggest that most of the world's problems can be traced to a single cause: overpopulation.
2. C
3. Procrastination is his greatest failing; he rarely completes any task in a timely manner.

   or

   Procrastination is his greatest failing. He rarely completes any task in a timely manner.
4. The best-known quotation from Shakespeare is the following: "To be, or not to be—that is the question."
5. Rachel either misses or is late to most of her classes; consequently, her grades do not reflect her true abilities.
6. During times of crisis and danger, most people realize that there is but one truly important concern: family.
7. Some people use seasonings to enhance the flavor of their food; others use it to hide the flavor.
8. C
9. After decades of only three commercial television networks, ABC, CBS, and NBC, suddenly three new networks are competing for audience share: Fox, WB, and UPN.
10. They longed to travel to some tropical country with a palm-tree-lined, white sand beach and warm water to swim in and sunbathe; unfortunately, they knew they must remain at their work in the blustery, cold north.

Exercise 1.15

1. The old dirt road became a soggy mess during the storm; by the end of the week, it was a sea of mud.
2. In most colleges and universities today, the computer is not a luxury; it is a necessity.
3. C
4. In spite of her strong will, Dr. Williamson was unable to overcome her illness; however, she never gave up the fight as long as she lived.
5. All students should carry a dictionary; it is a bother to have to borrow one.
6. She had missed many classes during the semester; consequently, she was unable to correctly answer enough test questions to pass.
7. The insects went into hibernation early this year; some say that means winter will be abnormally cold.
8. Team sports are losing popularity among college-aged men; they are, however, maintaining popularity among college coaches, alumni, and television audiences.
9. The river flooded every two or three years; consequently, regulations now prohibit building in the flood plain.
10. Some television programs have been criticized for containing too much violence; nevertheless, these shows seem to be among some of the most popular.

Exercise 1.16

1. The most endangered animals in the zoological garden, along with fourteen of their keepers, were transferred to the new wildlife park.
2. Writing her term paper in three hours and printing it the next morning before class resulted in a poor grade.
3. C
4. The proliferation of CD ROM options with their many entertainment and educational references has dramatically increased the desirability of computers.
5. Although public education has been accused of stagnation and critics continue to attack the system at nearly every opportunity, students are more successful than ever.

CHAPTER TWO

Essay Structure

Objectives

When you have completed this chapter, you will have:

1. practiced the three-phase writing process.
2. demonstrated an understanding of basic essay structures.
3. created thesis statements.
4. written topic sentences.
5. written primary and secondary support sentences.
6. composed introductory, body, and concluding paragraphs.
7. written and revised a 500-750 word paper about a social problem.

2

Survival is a textbook that will help you learn the form of writing most widely assigned in the academic world: the **essay**, or **paper**, as it is commonly called. The fact is that your instructors in a variety of subject areas will assign papers and expect you to deliver high-quality written work. As you work your way through *Survival*, you will master a writing process that will enable you to manage almost any writing project with skill and confidence.

Writing skill is absolutely necessary for your success. This skill goes hand in hand with reading, oral communication, mathematics, and critical thinking, making up the five basic skills crucial to your **survival** in this complex, competitive world of continuous change. Furthermore, you must learn to adapt your writing for different audiences and situations encountered in school and at work. For example, in school you are often assigned to write term papers, book reports, lab reports, and written exams. Your reader is usually your instructor, but occasionally other students in your class will read your papers, offering their responses and editing suggestions.

At work you may need to write letters, memos, different types of reports, feasibility studies, grant proposals, competitive proposals, instruction manuals, promotional literature, and other types of writing, each with a different purpose and audience. Frequently you will be asked to work collaboratively on writing projects, for example, peer editing or co-writing with other employees. In these situations the success of your group with its project depends on your ability to handle your part of the writing assignment competently.

LESSON ONE: *The Writing Process—Planning, Writing, Editing*

A process is a series of steps to achieve a desired outcome or produce a finished product. Whether writing for school or work, you need to know a process you can rely on for each writing project. *Survival* recommends a **writing process** that moves back and forth between three phases:

PLANNING
WRITING
EDITING

Your ability to produce successful writing projects will increase dramatically if you adopt this process.

A linear process is one that proceeds generally along a straight line from start to finish. The writing process you will practice in *Survival* is a linear, step-by-step process—step one, step two, step three, and so on. The rhetorical path is clear: choose a subject to write about, propose an idea about the subject, then explain and defend that idea. However, along the way the process becomes nonlinear. You will find yourself planning and replanning, writing and rewriting, thinking your paper is perfect and then discovering it isn't. Each of the three phases includes different stages. You will find yourself interrupting one of the phases to loop back or ahead to a different phase or stage. The overlapping characteristic of the process can be represented by the illustration below:

Three-Phase Writing Process

The Planning Phase

The **planning phase** of the writing process is often called the "prewriting" phase because it includes all of the activities completed before you actually begin composing the introductory paragraph of a paper. Essentially, you are organizing to begin writing. You are clarifying the assignment, finding something to write about, gathering information, and formulating your main idea for the paper along with an outline to follow in developing that idea. Within the planning phase you complete several steps:

DISCOVERING A SUBJECT
NARROWING THE SUBJECT TO A TOPIC
RESEARCHING THE TOPIC
WRITING A THESIS
DEVELOPING AN OUTLINE

The Writing Phase

The first or preliminary version of a piece of writing that will be revised, corrected, and retyped in a desired format is called "a draft," often "the rough draft." Any succeeding version of the original draft is also called a draft—second draft, revised draft, and on to the final draft. During the **writing phase** of the process you write a series of drafts, proceeding step-by-step:

DRAFTING
REVISING
RECEIVING FEEDBACK
REWRITING

Of course, the computer has blurred the distinction between first, second, and successive drafts somewhat. If you use a computer, you know how easy it is to rewrite. The glowing monitor beckons you again and again to tinker with the text just one more time before you print a final copy. For the sake of definition, therefore, you can say that a draft is produced each time you actually print a new version of your paper or retype it or write it over with pen or pencil.

The procedure for writing the first draft is simple: Find a quiet place or sit at your computer and write steadily and rapidly, without stopping, if possible, until the first draft is complete. As you write, do not worry about punctuation, spelling, or proper grammar; you will go back over your paper to remove the errors later. Whenever you stop to look up a word in the dictionary or check a punctuation rule, you run the risk of losing your momentum and forgetting what you were saying. Concentrate on what you want to say in your paper.

The Editing Phase

During the **editing phase** of the writing process, you prepare your final draft. Your main concern will be the final appearance of your manuscript. You will present the finished document to be read by others, perhaps seeking the response of your classmates, and, most important, evaluation by your instructor. Therefore, your goal should be to turn in a paper that is carefully edited, free of errors, and attractively presented in an appropriate format. Three steps must be completed in the editing phase:

EDITING
PROOFREADING
MANUSCRIPT PREPARATION

EXERCISE 2.1

1. Describe the process that you typically employ when you are given a writing assignment.

_____

_____

_____

_____

2. What are the three phases of the writing process advocated in *Survival*?

(1) _____

(2) _____

(3) _____

3. Explain why the writing process is not entirely a step-by-step linear process.

_____

_____

_____

_____

_____

Have your answers checked.

LESSON TWO: *Managing Your Writing Projects*

Assignment Analysis

As soon as possible after you are given a writing assignment, **analyze the assignment** by asking a set of questions and then writing down the answers:

1. What is the assignment? Required length?
2. What type of paper is it, and what is its purpose?
3. When is the paper due? Are there other deadlines? What are the consequences of missing any of these deadlines?
4. Is there a recommended organization and format?
5. Are library research and documentation required? Interviews? Focus Groups? Surveys?
6. Who will be reading your paper, and how do you want to affect them?
7. Are any oral reports required in connection with the project?
8. Will collaborative work such as peer editing be required? If you will be working with co-authors or on a writing team, what are your responsibilities?
9. Do you have the skills you need, or will you need help?
10. How will your performance be evaluated? Will revisions be allowed?

Work Schedule

In order to finish your paper on time, you will need to organize a **work schedule** that includes completion dates for each task in the project. If you are working by yourself, the schedule is essential to help you determine whether you are working fast enough to complete the paper on time. This schedule becomes even more important if you are working with a co-author or on a writing team because each person needs to know when his or her part of the assignment is due so that everyone's work can be integrated and reviewed. Sometimes your instructor will break down the assignment for you, assigning a due date for each part. Often, however, the scheduling will be your responsibility. Because no schedule ever works perfectly, you must learn how to adjust your schedule to cope with unanticipated difficulties and temporary setbacks. Every day you should study your work schedule for the writing project, noting in writing the parts of the project you have completed and any changes you find it necessary to make.

Audience Analysis

Who are you writing for—who is your **audience**? What is the technical expertise of your readers? Are they likely to be biased by a particular point of view? How do you want to affect them? Should you adopt a particular writing strategy to affect your readers the way you want to? These are questions you must consider whenever you embark upon a writing project, usually as part of the planning phase.

How you want to affect your readers will mainly depend on your purpose. Is your purpose to explain, compare, analyze, evaluate, propose, or argue? If your purpose is to explain, your basic assumption is that your readers do not completely understand something. If, on the other hand, your purpose is to argue in favor of your opinion on a controversial subject, your assumption is that you can persuade your readers that your view is worth considering. Your purpose may be to go even further, persuading your readers that they should take a particular course of action. Whenever you write, you should create the impression that you are knowledgeable, objective, organized and articulate, sometimes humorous, but always honest and sincere.

Writing with Computers

Computers can make your writing projects more manageable. Increasingly, to be a successful writer in school or on the job, you need to master word processing on a computer. If you are not now using a computer for one reason or another, you will be before long. It's inevitable! You can compose, revise, and format written documents on a computer with relative ease. You can also use computer technology to search electronically for information in the library and on other databases accessible by computer. You can communicate with others through computer networks, electronic mail, and fax. Some instructors require their students to turn in their papers on floppy disks instead of printed out on paper or allow students to send in their work through a modem.

Collaborative Writing

Collaboration is working together with others to accomplish a goal or complete a project. One of the great advantages of writing collaboration is that it encourages planning and review among the writers that leads to improved writing performance. You probably already have some experience with **peer editing** sessions where you provide feedback to others and, in turn, receive feedback about your own writing. Your instructor may schedule collaborative learning exercises into your class, especially during the feedback step of the writing phase.

You may also be required to work on a **team writing project** at least once during the course. Participation on project teams in classes is required more now because some academic disciplines and businesses frequently use this approach for many types of projects. On a writing team you usually help write certain sections of the final product, but you also contribute to the team your particular expertise, such as a talent for editing or the ability to produce computer graphics. Almost all college graduates write with co-authors on some projects.

LESSON THREE: *Planning Your Paper*

Discovering a Subject

When students are asked why they are having trouble starting a writing project, one of the most frequent responses is, "I don't know what to write about." The truth of the matter is that fear of failure may be preventing them from being logical, creative, and enthusiastic about what should be an engaging task. There really are so many subjects about which to write! Your problem should not be that you can't find a subject, but, rather, how to choose a subject from several that interest you.

Usually when writers talk about the **subject** they have chosen for a paper, they mean the general category, such as "crime" or "computers." When they talk about the **topic** for a paper, they mean the narrowed aspect of the subject about which they have chosen to write, for example, "the magnitude of the money laundering problem in Florida" for crime or "the impact of computers on the teaching of writing" for computers. Some writers use the terms *subject* and *topic* interchangeably. In *Survival*, however, the term *subject* will refer to the larger category before it is narrowed to a more specific concern—the *topic*. Think of them as two stages in the planning phase: discovering a subject (broad) and narrowing it to a specific, manageable topic (specific).

Select a subject ⟶ Narrow it to a topic

Consider three realms of experience while you are discovering a subject: **personal experience, reading,** and **discussion**. The three realms of experience overlap. In fact, the ideal subject probably involves all three. A personal experience of yours might lead you to seek out some reading material on the subject, and in turn your reaction to the reading material could lead you to a discussion with family, friends, or classmates. Or, to look at the process another way, any time you read something, your reaction to that material is always influenced by your previous experiences as well as by any prior reading and related discussions you may have had.

The Realms of Experience

Searching for a subject is often a skimming-and-scanning exercise—looking through local newspapers, paying attention to the news on television, scrolling through the subjects on the electronic periodical index in the library, or searching through your own memories or your journal if you keep one. What have you read lately that might be the source of a subject? Look through news magazines like *Time* or *Newsweek*. Go to the library and consult the *Readers' Guide to Periodical Literature* or the electronic index, contemplating the different subject categories. Recall recent conversations you have had with family, friends, teachers, classmates, or fellow workers. Tune into a talk show or news program. Look over your lecture notes from an interesting class. Think creatively. For example, if you could launch a campaign to include an initiative on the ballot during the next election, what would it be? Is there something you leave experienced that you could write about, something you have done that your classmates might want to know more about?

Try to select your subject quickly, the one that interests you the most. The best advice anyone can give you at this point is to pick a subject and start working with it immediately. Look over your list of candidates, select the winner, and save the rest for another time. (See Appendix C: "Suggested Subjects," for a list of 350 subjects.)

EXERCISE 2.2

Develop a work schedule for your paper. (Begin with Exercise 2.5.)

Work Schedule

Project Title: Social Problem Paper   **Due Date** _____

Exercise	Project Assignment	Sample Allotment	Your Time Allotment	Date Due
Ex. 2.3	Subject	(1/2 day)	_____	_____
Ex. 2.4	Topic	(1/2 day)	_____	_____
Ex. 2.5	Research	(1 day)	_____	_____
Ex. 2.6	Thesis	(1/2 day)	_____	_____
Ex. 2.7	Outline	(1/2 day)	_____	_____
Ex. 2.8	Opening Sentence	(1/4 day)	_____	_____
Ex. 2.9	Introductory Paragraph	(1/4 day)	_____	_____
Ex. 2.11	Body Paragraphs	(3/4 day)	_____	_____
Ex. 2.12	Concluding Paragraph	(1/4 day)	_____	_____
Ex. 2.15	Feedback on First Draft	(1 day)	_____	_____
Ex. 2.16	Final Manuscript	(1 day)	_____	_____

Have your work schedule approved.

EXERCISE 2.3

Select a social problem as the subject for the paper you will complete by the end of this chapter. Before making your choice, list three to five potential subjects; then choose the one that interests you most.

Possible Subjects

1. _____

2. _____

3. _____

4. _____

5. _____

Subject Chosen _____

    Discuss your subject choice with your instructor.

Narrowing the Subject to a Topic

After you have discovered a subject for your paper, the main problem is narrowing it sufficiently. Most of the papers you will write will be reasonably short—papers from two to seven pages in length (250 words per page, double-spaced). The social problem paper you are writing for Chapter Two will be two to three pages long. Therefore, the topic for any short paper must be carefully limited.

By using various creative and analytical processes, you can narrow your subject to a manageable topic. You may already have your own method for narrowing the subject. If not, you can experiment with a number of widely used techniques until you find the one that works best for you.

Brainstorming

Begin by putting the *subject* you have chosen at the top of your screen or sheet of paper and then listing anything that the original word or phrase brings to mind. Words or phrases that follow may relate to the original or to subsequent items. There is no time limit; however, you should limit yourself at first just to see how productive you can be in a short time—fifteen minutes is a good start. Since this activity is an attempt to release the flow of creative ideas, anything that comes to mind on the subject should be recorded. There is no such thing as a "wrong" response in this exercise. When you are finished, examine your list, looking for a word or phrase that seems interesting and narrow enough in scope to be a good *topic* for a short paper.

Freewriting

Start by putting the *subject* at the top of your screen or sheet of paper. Then write as fast as you can without worrying about correctness of grammar, spelling, and the like. As with brainstorming, there is no set time limit, but you should try limiting yourself to twenty or thirty minutes. Freewriting is a great limbering-up exercise and can start you "thinking in writing" by seeing yourself produce phrases and sentences on the subject. This method works especially well for students who need to actually begin writing a paper before they can do much planning. As soon as you stop freewriting, look over what you have written and decide what your narrowed *topic* will be. Usually you will have written your way into the subject enough to discover the actual topic that you will focus on in your paper.

Clustering

Begin by writing and circling your *subject* in the middle of a page. (You won't be able to cluster on your computer unless you are quite adept at graphics.) Then draw a line with an arrow extending out from it, and write a word or phrase suggested by the first. Continue to build your graphic system of circles with arrows as one thing suggests another. Along the way a word or phrase may give rise to a whole new set of words and phrases. With this graphic system you can quickly and easily see how each word or idea relates to the others that you have developed. Try to limit yourself to fifteen minutes for this exercise. At the end of fifteen minutes, study your clusters to find your narrowed *topic*.

Illustration of Clustering

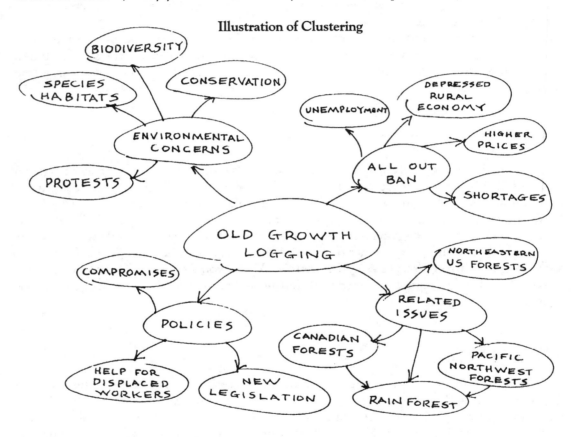

Analytical Questioning

Although many writers rely on the informal discovery techniques of brainstorming, freewriting, and clustering to narrow their subjects, others prefer analytical techniques. One of the most effective is to ask yourself a set of questions about your *subject* in order to decide on a manageable *topic*.

1. Is there a controversial aspect that will allow you to write either for or against something? If so, can you limit your subject by writing about just one side of the controversy, for example, by attacking or defending?

Example

Crime ──────────▶ Lenient sentences for white-collar criminals

2. Is there a good way to narrow a subject by restricting it to a particular time or place?

Example

Water shortages ──────────▶ Growing threat of salinity in Western soils

3. Is there some way to limit the subject through natural divisions?

Example

Pollution ──────────▶ Underground water pollution

Pyramiding

Pyramiding is another analytical technique for narrowing a subject. Writers like this method because it uses a visual aid for moving in the natural order from the general to the specific. Start by drawing a pyramid like the one illustrated below (or use the centering function on your computer without the diagram). Then write your *subject* in the top space, and in the spaces under it, move successively through more specific forms of the topic until you have funneled down to an extremely focused *topic* suitable for a short paper. Notice that as your topic becomes more specific it grows longer. Thus, your narrowed topic forms the base of the pyramid, its foundation.

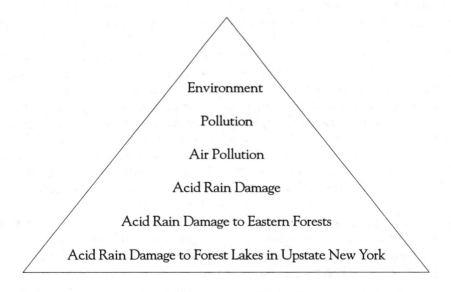

Environment

Pollution

Air Pollution

Acid Rain Damage

Acid Rain Damage to Eastern Forests

Acid Rain Damage to Forest Lakes in Upstate New York

EXERCISE 2.4

Narrow the subject you selected in Exercise 2.3 to a topic suitable for a 500-750 word social problem paper. Use one or more of the prewriting strategies: brainstorming, freewriting, clustering, analytical questioning, or pyramiding.

Narrowed Topic: _____

_____

Have your topic approved.

Researching Your Topic

Before beginning to write, you will probably need to learn more about your topic. By gathering information and analyzing and evaluating it, you become knowledgeable enough to write convincingly. Your need to conduct **research** will vary with the assignment. For this first paper, for example, you will not need to conduct systematic library research. Perhaps all you will need to do is discuss your topic with friends or family members or read a few magazine or newspaper articles to increase your background knowledge. Your textbooks and class notes are another potential source of background information for this first paper. For other assignments you may need to spend many hours in the library conducting an organized search for the information you need.

A simple starting point you shouldn't overlook is an inventory of **your memory** on the topic. Brainstorming, freewriting, clustering, and analytical questioning, and pyramiding are useful in this process, just as they were in narrowing a subject to a topic. After reviewing what you know about the topic, **library research** is usually the next logical step. Chapter Four will explain how to use the library efficiently, including use of the card catalog, bibliographies, periodical indexes, electronic indexes, and other reference works.

Within the library, or wherever available, **computers** have greatly increased your ability to conduct research. Encyclopedias, dictionaries, and other research sources are now routinely installed in computers. Computers can be used to search for bibliographic information in books, magazines, professional journals, government documents, and newspapers. Abstracts and full texts of articles and other printed materials can be obtained by electronic retrieval from computer databases such as the Internet. Searching electronic information services is discussed in Chapter Four along with library research. **Interviews** and **surveys**, research techniques you can use, also are covered in Chapter Seven.

Ask yourself again, what is your purpose in writing the paper, and what will your readers need to know for you to accomplish your purpose? Your purpose may be to inform your readers about something you want them to understand, or to persuade them to adopt a particular point of view or to take action. Aimless browsing in the library or attempting to read everything in print about your topic isn't the way to go. Posing questions to yourself as you prepare to do your research will help you get organized.

1. What background information will I need to include?
2. What don't I understand, and what is it that the readers probably don't understand?

3. Can I explain the problem that needs to be solved? Are there solutions that might work? Is one of them better than the others?
4. What are the alternate points of view on a controversial subject? Which position do I favor? Are most of my readers likely to be in agreement with me, or will they oppose my point of view?
5. What are the arguments I can make? What are the arguments that my readers might raise to counter mine?
6. What evidence can I include to support my arguments and defeat the opposing arguments?
7. How will I give credit to my sources of information? Is any of the information worth quoting?

Finally, take careful notes during your research. Whenever you use the exact wording of one of your sources of information, you are required to enclose the "copied" words in quotation marks. And whenever you quote the exact words of someone else or summarize someone else's ideas or information, you must give credit to the originator and the source. (Notetaking and giving credit to sources are explained in Chapter Four.)

EXERCISE 2.5

Using the questions above as a guide, conduct any research you think you will need to write the first draft of your paper. Keep in mind the time constraints listed in your Work Schedule so that you won't plan more research than is necessary or expected for this first paper. If possible, limit yourself to some brief background reading, perhaps one or two magazine or newspaper articles or some class notes. (Have your research plans approved.)

Basic Essay Structure

Every paper you write must have a beginning, a middle, and an end. The beginning section of any paper is referred to as the **introduction**. Its purpose is to prepare your readers for what is to be explained or argued in the **body** of the paper. The introduction, which may include one or more paragraphs, does this by narrowing from a broad **opening sentence** to a specific **thesis sentence** located at the end of the introduction. The **body paragraphs** follow this introduction. These paragraphs explain and support what is said in the thesis sentence. Finally, a **conclusion** of one or more paragraphs sums up the paper. The conclusion restates the thesis idea or summarizes the entire discussion without sounding redundant and then ends with a generalization that brings the paper to a close.

The number of paragraphs in a paper is not set by a formula, although in some forms of essay writing to be discussed later in this text you will be working within a framework of a set number of paragraphs. The number in any given paper will vary according to how much you have to say and where you decide to break the paragraphs, making them long or short. The diagram on the following page shows how the structure would look in a short paper that might include five paragraphs.

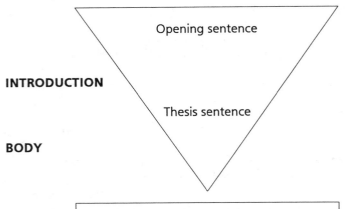

INTRODUCTION

In your opening sentence introduce the subject and capture your reader's attention; then the paragraph should gradually narrow to a very specific thesis sentence.

BODY

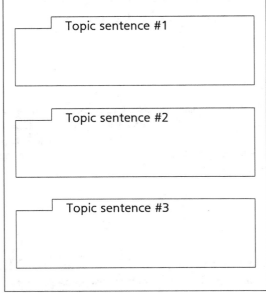

In the body of your paper present whatever is required to support the assertion your thesis makes.

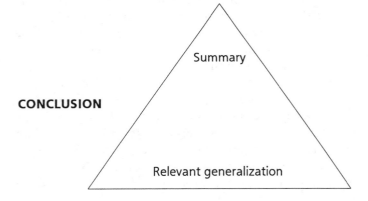

CONCLUSION

The concluding paragraph, in direct contrast to your introductory paragraph, should begin with the specific point and broaden to a general or universal application of your point.

Writing a Thesis Sentence

After you have narrowed your subject to a topic, you are ready to write the **thesis sentence**. The thesis sentence is the most important sentence in any paper you write. It is a single sentence that tells your reader exactly what the paper is trying to say. If the thesis sentence is not clear, the paper cannot possibly succeed. Your thesis has to sum up, in one sentence, the main point that you will explain more completely in the rest of the paper. What is the main idea you want to communicate to your readers in your paper? That is your thesis idea. It underlies all of the discussion that follows it, and everything that is said relates back to it.

Your thesis sentence—that one sentence that states the main idea of your paper—should be the first sentence that you write, but it will not appear at the beginning of your paper. Normally, the thesis is placed at the end of the introduction of your paper. In a short paper, such as the 500-750 word paper you are writing, the introduction will consist of a single paragraph. In such a case, the thesis would usually be the last sentence in that paragraph.

Moving from your narrowed topic to your thesis is not difficult if you can answer that question in a single sentence. Without telling your readers, "I'm going to tell you about . . ." or "The purpose of this paper is . . . ," make the statement, and you have your thesis.

Examples

Computer games now rival television as a recreational pastime for young people.
Unlike television, computer games do not pose a threat to literacy.

The Divided Thesis

Often the surest way to move smoothly from a narrowed topic to a thesis sentence is to read your narrowed topic and ask, "How or why is this so? What are the reasons?"

Example

Narrowed topic:	How farmers and ranchers are threatening the wolf
Question:	How are they threatening the wolf?
Answer:	They are threatening the wolf in many ways.
Select three ways:	They are threatening the wolf
	(1) by using pesticides.
	(2) by converting wild lands into farms and ranges.
	(3) by waging war on the wolf.
Thesis sentence:	Farmers and ranchers have driven the wolf to near extinction by using pesticides, by converting wild lands into farmlands, and by waging open war on this most misunderstood of all wild animals.

The thesis above has refined the answer to the question. The thesis tells exactly how farmers and ranchers have caused the near extinction of the wolf: "by using pesticides, by converting wild lands into farmlands, and by waging open war." This thesis is called a

divided thesis sentence. By narrowing the thesis to these three considerations, all other ways farmers and ranchers have driven the wolf to near extinction are eliminated. For example, the writer developing this thesis could not discuss how fences and roads also helped push the wolf into its present precarious state.

The divided thesis technique is perfect for short papers of 500-750 words in length. It allows the writer to inform the reader openly what to expect in each body paragraph. Here, body paragraph one would be about pesticides; body paragraph two would be about converting wild lands; and body paragraph three would be about waging open war on wolves. Such a technique makes the writing of short papers faster and easier than using any other type of thesis. More examples of divided thesis sentences follow:

Examples

1. Organized groups of city residents are fighting to save their neighborhoods by patrolling with video cameras, documenting the activities of drug dealers and buyers, and reporting to police representatives regularly. (list at end)

2. By patrolling with video cameras, documenting the activities of drug dealers and buyers, and reporting to police representatives regularly, organized groups of city residents are fighting to save their neighborhoods. (list at beginning)

Should You Always Write a Three-Part Divided Thesis?

NO, NOT NECESSARILY.

The three-part thesis works well in many papers, especially papers no longer than 750 words, but it is not mandatory or even desirable in all papers.

1. You may need a four- or five-part thesis.

   Example

   Each of the economic systems in Russia, China, Vietnam, and Cuba is different.

2. A divided thesis may be too long and, therefore, difficult to read. You can write a short version implying that the body of the paper will be divided into sections.

   Example

   Many questions about the Kennedy assassinations remain unanswered.

3. A thesis can assert the main idea of a paper without pointing to divisions in the paper.

   Examples

   Although nuclear energy seems to be the most promising source of energy for the next three decades, only a few experimental nuclear power plants should be allowed during the next ten years.

   OR

   The drought-stricken African countries bordering the Sahara Desert have failed to develop nearby water resources.

EXERCISE 2.6

Develop the thesis you will use for your social problem paper. Try writing different versions of your thesis before you decide which to use.

1. What is your narrowed topic? _____

_____

2. Convert your narrowed topic to a question. _____

_____

3. Write a one-sentence answer to the question (an undivided thesis statement). _____

_____

_____

4. How or why is that so? List three to five reasons for the idea you stated above.

   (1) _____

   (2) _____

   (3) _____

   (4) _____

   (5) _____

5. The next step is to experiment with versions of your thesis that incorporate some or all of the reasons you have listed. After writing several versions, write the one you have chosen for your paper in the space provided. **Note: You are required to use a divided thesis for this paper.**

_____

_____

_____

_____

6. Consider the order in which you have stated the main idea and the reasons in your divided thesis. Do you want to state your main idea before or after listing your reasons? Put your reasons in a logical order—you will usually save the best for last but may arrange your reasons in a time or geographical order. Also make sure your final version is not too wordy.

_____

_____

_____

_____

Developing an Outline

In the last step of the planning phase, you will develop a particular kind of outline known as the **thesis-topic sentence outline.** After you have developed a thesis sentence that expresses the idea you intend to support in your paper, you are ready to begin writing your topic sentences. But before attempting to write a topic sentence, recall what you already know about paragraphs. The construction of body paragraphs differs greatly from that of introductory paragraphs. The most important sentence in the introductory paragraph—the thesis—concludes the paragraph. However, the most important sentence in the body paragraph—the **topic sentence**—usually begins the paragraph. Yet this is only a superficial difference. In the introductory paragraph all sentences except the thesis only serve to give background material for the thesis; consequently, these sentences are more general than those found in the body paragraphs. By contrast, each body paragraph must thoroughly develop the subject introduced by its topic sentence, with detailed explanations and numerous examples.

The topic sentence is to the body paragraph what the thesis is to the essay: the controlling force. The topic sentence controls in three important ways. It focuses on a particular aspect of the subject about which you are writing. In addition, the topic sentence limits what you may include in the paragraph. Finally, the topic sentence makes it easier for the reader to see how your paragraph supports the paper's thesis.

When you begin writing your topic sentences, you will realize how important your thesis sentence is. For instance, if your thesis sentence is divided, you will be able to see at a glance what each body paragraph should cover. The sample thesis sentence about the wolf—a divided thesis—shows clearly how a writer's point can be made. The divisions make it easy to see what to expect in each body paragraph. Consider that thesis and its topic sentences:

Example

Thesis: Farmers and ranchers have driven the wolf to near extinction by using pesticides, by converting wild lands into farmlands, and by waging open war on this most misunderstood of all wild animals.

TS #1: The pesticides farmers have used to control insects and rodents have entered the wolf's food chain since the wolf dines primarily on rodents, and the wolf's offspring and general health have suffered because of it.

TS #2: Every time more wild land has been deforested and converted to farmland, the wolves that once hunted there have been reduced to homeless wanderers, often unable to find enough food to survive harsh winters.

TS #3: Unquestionably, the most serious threats to the survival of the wolf have been the rifle, poison, and the bounty system used by farmers and ranchers who mistakenly blame the wolf for all their dead livestock.

Ideally, the time to write topic sentences is immediately after completing the thesis statement; however, some people prefer to write topic sentences after writing the entire introductory paragraph. The topic sentences help you the most when you can see them in a list before you add supporting sentences for each paragraph. If topic sentences are written before support is added, an outline or framework develops that helps you envision your complete composition. If you can construct a thesis-topic sentence outline of the entire essay, you can often see irrelevant or misplaced material before it becomes a serious problem.

As you write topic sentences, you must incorporate some kind of focus in them. If your topic sentences are too broad, your paragraphs may constantly wander off the subject and cause you and your reader unnecessary frustration. A good way to control your paragraphs is to be sure every topic sentence has a **controlling idea** you can point to. As the phrase suggests, the controlling idea is the word or phrase that limits the content of the paragraph. The following topic sentence would be difficult to develop because it lacks a sufficiently focused controlling idea.

Example

Moving from the parents' home into an apartment or dormitory is an experience few young people forget quickly.

To control the paragraph in this case, you would only need to insert a single word in the topic sentence to focus on the kind of experience it is.

Examples

Moving from the parents' home into an apartment or dormitory is a *liberating* experience few young people forget easily.

Moving from the parents' home into an apartment or dormitory is a *frightening* experience few young people forget easily.

Moving from the parents' home into an apartment or dormitory is a *social* experience few young people forget.

Any one of these controlling ideas would make the paragraph far easier to write. For instance, if you were to write about how moving out on your own is a frightening experience, you could explain how being alone at night for the first time is frightening. In the same paragraph, you could explain how fear takes over when the rent is due and you have spent the money for other things. But with that paragraph so defined, any reference to anything except frightening experiences would clearly be irrelevant.

EXERCISE 2.7

Develop a thesis-topic sentence outline for the final version of your thesis. When you are satisfied that you have a workable outline, copy it here or print a hard copy for your instructor.

Thesis: _____

_____

_____

TS #1: _____

_____

_____

TS #2: _____

_____

_____

TS #3: _____

_____

_____

LESSON FOUR: *Writing Your Paper*

Creating an Opening Sentence

Since you have already written a thesis-topic sentence outline for your paper, you have the thesis, the last sentence of the introductory paragraph. Now you need to write the remainder of that first paragraph—a paragraph that should have a minimum of five sentences in it.

The first sentence of the introductory paragraph is called the opening sentence. Not just any sentence will do for an opening sentence; this sentence must have impact on your reader. Since it is the first example of your writing the reader will see, the reader's opinion of your writing will begin to form at this point. For this reason you must use extreme care as you write it. The opening sentence must accomplish two purposes: It must attract your reader's attention, and it must lead into the subject of the paper. The following opening sentence was taken from an article by a very successful writer:

Example

> Motherhood is in trouble, and it ought to be.

Notice how you immediately wonder where the paper is heading. How could motherhood be in trouble? If it is in trouble, the human race is in trouble. And who would speak against mothers? Creating this type of provocative feeling is important because it pulls your reader into your paper.

The opening sentence above is also good because it is general enough so as not to give away the thesis of the paper, yet it introduces what the writer wants to talk about in the paper: the weakening of society's demand that every young couple have children whether or not they want them. This type of opening sentence is called the **provocative opening**.

Another type of opening sentence is the **rhetorical question**, the question for which no answer is expected. For instance, the following opening sentence is from a paper on politics:

Example

> When are Americans going to learn not to believe the promises of politicians?

In this case the writer assumes the reader shares certain experiences and feelings of frustration regarding politics. There can be no concrete answer to the question—some Americans will always believe the promises of some politicians. Using a quotation from a famous person or authority on your subject is also a good way to begin. If the quotation you offer is powerful, it can be effective. But you must be certain it is so relevant to your thesis that your reader can instantly grasp the significance. For instance, if you were writing a paper on euthanasia, a quote from Shakespeare might work as follows:

Example

> "To be, or not to be—that is the question."

This paper would then go on to relate the thought behind Hamlet's famous soliloquy on suicide to the subject of the paper, euthanasia. The following are other examples of good opening sentences:

Examples

> Play is the work of children. (provocative)
> How many mothers think they are helping their babies when they are actually doing them more harm than good? (rhetorical)
> Paul Tzimoulis has called the Cayman Islands the "Superbowl of diving," and they are just that. (quotation)

You can use other types of opening sentences, but master these three most common ones first. Remember that the purpose of the opening sentence is to get your reader to want to read what you have written. It must be interesting, or your reader may assume the rest of the paper will be boring and stop reading.

EXERCISE 2.8

For your first draft, experiment by writing one of each type of opening sentence. Then mark the one you want to use for your paper with a check mark.

Provocative: _____

_____

_____

Rhetorical : _____

_____

_____

Quotation: _____

_____

_____

Developing the Introductory Paragraph

For a 500-750 word paper like the one you will write in this chapter, a one-paragraph **introduction** will be sufficient. Longer papers such as those in later chapters may need introductions that are two, three, or even four paragraphs long. But however long the introductory portion of your paper, remember that the last sentence of the introduction is always the thesis, unless you have a good reason for placing it elsewhere.

Between the opening sentence and the thesis, writers customarily give some background to prepare the reader for the thesis message. In a short paper the total length of the introductory paragraph is usually no more than five or six sentences, so you must be brief. You should, however, form a smooth connection between the opening sentence and the thesis. This transition can be accomplished by a number of different methods. Perhaps the most popular introduction gives a historical review of the events leading to the current state of affairs on the issue being discussed. The following paragraph was taken from a 750-word paper on the need for a solution to the problem of radioactive waste disposal.

Example

Some scientists and environmentalists fear that in the very near future the state of Washington may become the most unhealthy place on the planet Earth. As a possible storage site for radioactive waste, central Washington may soon be receiving huge amounts of this notoriously unstable substance that has been accumulating since 1944. When considering Washington as a storage site for waste, one must be aware of the December 1957 disaster that took place within the Ural Mountains of the Soviet Union at what was once the city of Kyshtyn in the District of Zapadno. Radioactive waste, stored in mine shafts, percolated into the surrounding soil causing a nuclear chain reaction. The resulting explosion spewed contaminated soil for more than 1,000 square miles, and prevailing winds carried the contaminants even farther. American scientific leaders are confident, however, that this catastrophe will never be repeated and are preparing for testing at Gable Mountain, near the city of Hanford, to determine whether or not the bulk of this country's radioactive waste can be stored safely within the ancient basaltic lava flows of the Columbia Plateau. Unlike the highly fractured Ural Mountains, the great basaltic plateau of the Columbia Basin is a solid formation with an average depth of 3,000 meters; this seemingly ideal formation of dense igneous rock, therefore, will provide the United States with the best possible location for storage of radioactive waste. Viable but costly solutions to the momentous problems of radioactive waste include recycling by means of proton bombardment, storage in space orbit, and deep sea burial; however, at the present there is no workable alternative to a project such as the proposed storage facility at Hanford.

Here the writer goes from a provocative opening sentence to a historical example; the writer tells what scientists hope will not happen in Hanford by telling first what happened in Russia in 1957. After giving this historical example, the writer explains how it compares to the Hanford situation and then leads the reader smoothly into the thesis.

Sometimes writers find it more suitable to give their readers a more complete historical sketch. Consider the following introduction. It contains three paragraphs, so it is an example of the kind of introduction you could use for a longer paper; for example, a library research paper.

Example

"Gold and land abundant," was the persuading call which reached the ears of America's Eastern populace from the new land called California. Storekeepers sold their shops and bought wagons and horses. Farmers packed up their families and farming tools. All made ready for the trip to California. The year was 1849, and the progression of California's population had begun.

In the century that followed, there was much turmoil over the ownership of California's rich soil, impeding many an individual's dream of owning land. The problem lay in the confusion over land holdings by the Southern Pacific Railroad and its stockholders, and those of the land speculators who unscrupulously acquired large parcels of land through the purchase of Spanish land grants. The legal battles were long and complicated, and the courts were sympathetic to the speculators and robber barons. As a consequence, the average squatter was shut out, and the control of California's real property was guaranteed to the beneficiaries of these magnates. The injustice seen in California in those early days appears to have been catapulted through time and into an urban setting as descendants of those squatters can be seen living in the rundown apartment complexes owned by many of these same old families.

Oblivious to the economic distress the renter feels, these owners periodically increase the rent demanded, an action justified by the fact that they themselves continue to pay rising property taxes, increased utility costs and steeper interest rates on borrowed money. Due to an over-inflated economy, the legacy of these land holders and speculators, a housing shortage has been developed, and the building industry has been thrown into a recession. There are ways, however, to help renters and to curtail this downward economic spiral. A well-defined system of rent controls, complimented by tax credits and low-cost loans to property owners and tailored to each of California's economic populations, would not only provide the reasonably priced housing but would also stimulate the sagging building industry economy.

Although this is the introduction for a longer paper than you will be required to write in this chapter, you can easily see how the writer's use of historical material leads from a quote in the opening sentence to the thesis. A shorter paper would require a shorter introduction, of course, so much less material between the opening sentence and the thesis would be included.

EXERCISE 2.9

Draft an introductory paragraph for the thesis you wrote in Exercise 2.6. Use the opening sentence you selected in Exercise 2.8. Then copy your introductory paragraph in the space provided or print a hard copy, either in its "rough form" or in a more polished form, whichever you prefer.

_____

_____

_____

_____

_____

_____

_____

_____

_____

_____

_____

_____

_____

_____

_____

_____

Writing the Body Paragraphs

Once you have written your topic sentences, writing the **body paragraphs** is just a matter of following a standard procedure. Read your topic sentence and ask "how?" and "why?" Every answer is a **primary support sentence,** so-called because it directly elaborates upon the basic idea put forth in the topic sentence. For instance, if you were assigned a history paper on the Battle of Salamis, you would begin by developing a thesis statement and its accompanying topic sentences. Study the following outline. Notice that this thesis is not divided. Although it is an effective thesis, it must be accompanied by strong topic sentences. As a rule, the more general your thesis is, the more specific your topic sentences have to be.

Example

Thesis: The Battle of Salamis in 480 B.C. changed the course of history by demonstrating the importance of a strong navy to a nation's fate.

TS #1: When the battle took place, the Greek armies had already been defeated and the country occupied by the Persian army.

TS #2: Three hundred eighty Greek ships defeated the 1,400 ships of the Persians by employing superior tactics.

TS #3: Xerxes realized his vulnerability if the Greeks controlled the seas and withdrew his army from Greece.

TS #4: Learning from the Greek victory at Salamis, many small nations such as England have won world respect and position through naval strength.

After working up this thesis-topic sentence outline, the next step would be to develop the topic sentences into paragraphs, one paragraph at a time. Suppose you were writing on TS #2.

Your first task would be to write your primary support sentences (PS), for example, as follows:

Example

TS #2: Three hundred eighty Greek ships defeated the 1,400 ships of the Persians by employing superior tactics.

PS #1: The Greek commander, Themistocles, took up position just inside a narrows through which the Persians would have to pass.

PS #2: He had also selected his position because his opponents would have the seas at their backs, thus making maneuverability nearly impossible.

PS #3: Then, after the leading Persian ships came through the narrows to engage the vastly inferior Greek navy, the Greeks attacked.

PS #4: With the seas at their backs, with the other Persian ships at their backs and sides, and with the Greek navy in front, the Persians found themselves trapped.

PS #5: The result of the battle was a loss of over two hundred Persian ships compared with almost no losses by the Greeks.

Obviously, if you joined the above topic sentence and primary support sentences, you would find you had created a paragraph. At first, the paragraph might look good to you, but rest assured that your history instructor would not be impressed. Details are missing everywhere. Details that explain or clarify the primary support sentences are stated in **secondary**

support sentences. The details missing from the resulting paragraph would only be detected by someone who knew something about the battle; to put it another way, the details would only be omitted by someone who had a superficial knowledge of the Battle of Salamis. If you think for a minute, you will realize that the Persian fleet must have been poorly commanded or that some explanations are missing. Missing is any mention that the majority of the Greek fleet was hiding behind an island and that the few Greek warships in sight were retreating. Suddenly, the entire picture changes focus from incompetent Persian officers to an outstanding Greek officer named Themistocles. Notice how different the paragraph looks at the beginning when the first primary support sentence is reinforced by secondary support sentences. (**TS**=topic sentence, **PS**=primary support sentence, **SS**=secondary support sentence)

Example

> **TS** Three hundred eighty Greek ships defeated the 1,400 ships of the Persians by employing superior tactics. **PS** The Greek commander, Themistocles, took up position just inside a narrows through which the Persian fleet would have to pass. **SS** When the oncoming Persian sailors looked through the narrows, they saw only a few retreating Greek warships. **SS** Thinking that the retreating ships were the last of a demoralized Greek navy, the Persians pushed through the narrows into the trap set by the main force of Greek warships that were hidden from sight by an island. **PS** Themistocles had also selected his position because his opponents would have the seas at their backs, thus making maneuverability nearly impossible . . . .

This paragraph would, of course, go on to become much longer. The point is that secondary support sentences are absolutely necessary whenever a primary support sentence does not explain everything with perfect clarity.

Secondary support sentences are especially important in all writing because it is these examples or details that make your paper effective. After all, writing assignments are given to make sure that you truly understand the subject being studied; it is the secondary support sentences that give the information the instructor is looking for. Your instant clue to a paragraph without secondary support—one that every instructor recognizes instantly—is a short paragraph. If you write a paragraph that has fewer than five sentences in it, you can be sure that something is wrong, usually that the paragraph lacks secondary support.

THE FIVE-SENTENCE RULE
Count the sentences in each paragraph you write. A paragraph containing fewer than five sentences is too short and should be expanded.

The following paragraph was taken from a college paper. The sentences have all been labeled to help you recognize them.

Example

> **TS** Space storage of radioactive waste, however, could result in the removal of all living matter from this planet. **PS** The most minute human or mechanical error could result in a shroud of radioactive material that would encircle the earth for as long as 4,000,000 years.

SS Major accidents within the space program have been few; however, ten percent of all space flights have malfunctioned in some way. SS A malfunction aboard a space vessel containing radioactive waste would be the most devastating event the world has ever seen. SS Elements such as plutonium-239 and cesium-246, with a half-life of 250,000 and 2,000,000 years respectively, would be released into the troposphere, causing all life to cease. PS Astroscientists contend that radioactive waste within ceramic containers can be transported into space via space shuttle; they are reluctant to admit, though, that a proven container does not exist. SS The Oak Ridge Laboratory in Tennessee, after years of testing and millions of tax dollars, has yet to produce a ceramic container that will withstand the intense heat produced by radioactive waste. SS Production of a container that will withstand the heat of a premature burnout is not even within the scope of the project. CS Storage of radioactive waste in space orbit is a distinct possibility; however, it is useless to even consider such a concept within the next few decades.

Notice that the paragraph above ends with a **concluding sentence (CS)** that sums up the position taken in the paragraph. Not every paragraph you write will need a concluding sentence, but often you can give a paragraph a more complete appearance by including a sentence like the one above.

You should also be aware that not every primary support sentence needs a secondary support sentence. If a primary support sentence is clear and a secondary support sentence would be so obvious it would bore the reader, you can go on to the next primary sentence. But, as a general rule, try one or more secondary support sentences before making that decision. Observe how the writer omitted the secondary support once in the following paragraph. Some would argue that the unsupported primary support sentence in the following paragraph would have been clearer had some secondary support been offered. But the writer of this paragraph decided it was not needed.

Example

TS Opponents argue rent control would lessen interest in remodeling, refurbishing, and new construction of rental units because the cost of borrowed money would cancel any profit or even throw owners into a negative cash flow position. PS This argument is valid as current circumstances in the money market dictate high interest rates on short-term loans for use in renovation. PS New construction money is equally as difficult to obtain because increased requirements on multiple-unit construction forces the cost of completion beyond a reasonable return on investment. SS The incidental costs of borrowing money, such as appraisal fees, blueprints, title search, pest control inspections, and loan fees, have tripled in the last five years. SS This has made it costly, up front, to get a loan. PS To further complicate the possibility for renovation or remodeling, many new ordinances concerning sewage disposal, pollution control, energy consumption, fire regulations, and restrictions on water usage have been adopted for the good of the community. SS These ordinances almost always require modification of the existing systems. SS Modifications mean more money invested by the property owner with no additional profit realized. CS Thus, rent control combined with high investment costs would discourage investors.

EXERCISE 2.10

Label the sentences in the following paragraph (**TS, PS, SS, CS**). (Answers on page 96)

_____ Aquatic life, especially the anadromous fish, has been adversely affected by the pumping stations at the southwest corner of the Great Delta. _____ Pumping causes fast current flows. _____ Thus, invertebrates on which the fish feed cannot grow properly because of the increase of water flow. _____ In addition, small fish usually drift to their food supply, reaching it at the time their bodies need it. _____ The increased flow often interferes with this cycle, and many of the small fish die. _____ Pumping also changes the direction of the water flow in some Delta channels, causing confusion for migrating fish, especially salmon returning to their spawning grounds. _____ To make matters worse, because the Southern Delta section is a nursery area for striped bass, fish are present there most of the year. _____ The pumping action draws fish to the export pumps, and fish too small to be adequately screened, striped bass in particular, along with the organisms on which they feed, and fish eggs are drawn through the pumps where they are either destroyed or transported south with water. _____ Salmon and other large fish do not go through the pumps, but because they become trapped in the screens, they have to be literally picked out by hand and transported to the Western Delta. _____ This handling is hard on the fish, causing many losses, and it is expensive.

EXERCISE 2.11

Write the body paragraphs for your paper, following the thesis-topic sentence outline you developed in Exercise 2.7. Then, either in rough or polished form, copy one of the paragraphs in the space provided, or print a hard copy of all the paragraphs.

To increase your understanding of your paragraph structure, label each sentence as **TS** (topic sentence), **PS** (primary support sentence), **SS** (secondary support sentence), or **CS** (concluding sentence).

_____

_____

_____

_____

_____

_____

_____

_____

_____

Have your work checked.

Drafting the Concluding Paragraph

After you have written the introductory and body paragraphs, the **concluding paragraph** should be easy. The first sentence of the conclusion sums up everything you have said in the paper, and then the remainder of the paragraph makes a general statement about the significance of the subject. This is also your last opportunity to convince the reader that your position is the correct one. When you have summed up the content of the paper as briefly as possible in the first sentence or two, you should end your paragraph with a few sentences commenting on why anyone should care about the topic. The following paragraph sums up a discussion of the problems of water management in the Great Delta.

Example

> In an age of increasingly scarce resources, careful studies should be made on how best to solve the water problems without destroying fish and wildlife or the environment. There is enough water in the state to provide for everyone's needs. However, water hoarding by a handful of landowners for self-serving reasons does not benefit the population as a whole. Eventually, a limit as to how much water can be removed from the Delta must be set so that rivers can continue to flow. Moreover, preserving the natural beauty of the state is a responsibility that must be accepted for the benefit of future generations.

The following concluding paragraph is particularly effective since it sums up the writer's position briefly and smoothly.

Example

> The task of solving the housing shortage in this state is a tremendous one. It involves taking a comprehensive look at the causes and effects of high interest rates and high rents on the state's economy. It involves establishing government agencies and procedures for rent control and tenant evaluation. It requires restructuring property tax laws and implementing tax credits. Finally, the demand for rehabilitation or new construction money at reasonable interest rates must be met. When all of these plans have been formulated and initiated, there will be no justification for arbitrary annual 10% rent increases for the elderly woman in the decaying house down the street or doubling the rent on the apartment across the street each time new tenants move in.

EXERCISE 2.12

Write a concluding paragraph for the introductory and body paragraphs you wrote in Exercise 2.9 and Exercise 2.11. Copy your concluding paragraph in the space provided, or print a hard copy. If you are writing on a computer, print a hard copy of your entire paper at this point.

_____

_____

_____

_____

_____

_____

_____

_____

_____

_____

_____

_____

_____

_____

_____

_____

_____

_____

_____

Have your work checked.

EXERCISE 2.13

Read the following essay carefully. The author views the avoidance of risk-taking in life as a social problem. Notice how well the writer's ideas flow together. Your paragraphs do not have to be this long, but notice that the reason the paragraphs are long here is because of the student's ability to provide secondary support. It is the abundant secondary support that makes the paper so convincing. When you have finished reading the paper, answer the questions that follow (the sentences have been numbered for the exercise).

Sandra McGaffic

English 1A TTh 9:30

Dr. Guches

28 March 1995

(Expository Essay)

Jeopardy Is the Spice of Life

(1) People squander their talents and relinquish their youth in exchange for an illusion of security that steals their dreams. (2) Early in life they learn to surrender their treasures before they lose them, to lose their dreams before they realize them. (3) Danger, which is implicit in risk-taking, paralyzes them. (4) Yet, danger is the element that will set them free. (5) By providing fresh experience, manifesting courage, and affording exhilaration, danger revitalizes humdrum existence.

(6) Unfortunately, when people should be putting fresh experiences into their lives by taking risks, they attempt to break up the monotony of humdrum day-to-day living by taking a well-planned annual vacation. (7) Yet, often that long-awaited holiday is anticlimactic. (8) The week of preparations is more rewarding: those who hate accidents do the most plotting and plan themselves out of spontaneity and danger. (9) These same people would find fresh experience and would benefit greatly by stealing their parents' or spouse's car and driving to a strange city for an afternoon. (10) By so doing they would be seeking out the danger of unpredictability they habitually avoid. (11) The danger of becoming lost, smashing the car, or being found out intensifies the adventure. (12) For an afternoon timid souls experience life outside of their fearful impotence.

(13) Once they wander into unfamiliar territory, fearful people find

themselves confronted by more and more perceived threats. **(14)** The abnormality of the situation in which they have placed themselves forces them into new behavior patterns. **(15)** They are forced to recognize and to manage danger because paralysis will not save them. **(16)** With each new risk they successfully negotiate, courage and capability are rediscovered. **(17)** Once they have discarded their clothes at a nude beach, they begin to realize that security will not be bought by donning clothes again, that security, perhaps, is irrelevant. **(18)** This perspective helps them to cast away safety-seeking patterns that occlude strengths and capabilities, revealing courage and an inner self-reliance that they had not hitherto suspected.

(19) Thanks to this self-reliance, formerly timid people begin to enjoy danger for its own sake, for the exhilaration it yields. **(20)** A good shot of adrenalin clears the mind and sharpens the senses. **(21)** Danger can be experienced and appreciated on different levels, and people may decide what level of personal risk will reward them sufficiently. **(22)** For some, the thought of an attack on their artistic ego is devastating: a public exhibition of their work would be dangerous enough to offer stimulation. **(23)** Others risk their lives running with the bulls in Pamplona, Spain. **(24)** However people choose to court danger, the rule of thumb is, the larger the risk, the greater the exhilaration.

(25) Once people face danger instead of cowering and name their fears instead of blindly reacting, they will begin to exercise control over their lives. **(26)** They learn to appreciate the ephemeral moment by breaking routine. **(27)** By successfully negotiating risks, they learn to recognize the personal power and courage in their personality they had allowed to lie dormant. **(28)** They begin to live fully by risking all.

(29) Nothing in life is guaranteed to endure; living with danger is a step toward taking responsibility for existence.

EXERCISE 2.14

From the list of terms on the right, select the letter of the term which describes each sentence designated by the numbers in parentheses on the left. (Answers on page 96)

1. Sentence (1)   _____
2. Sentence (5)   _____
3. Sentence (6)   _____
4. Sentence (13) _____
5. Sentence (14) _____
6. Sentence (15) _____
7. Sentence (16) _____
8. Sentence (17) _____
9. Sentence (18) _____
10. Sentence (19) _____
11. Sentence (20) _____
12. Sentence (21) _____
13. Sentence (22) _____
14. Sentence (23) _____
15. Sentence (25) _____

a. Topic Sentence

b. Thesis Sentence

c. Opening Sentence

d. Primary Support Sentence

e. Secondary Support Sentence

f. Concluding Sentence

EXERCISE 2.15

Receiving feedback on your first draft.

1. If you haven't already done so, pull together your introductory, body, and concluding paragraphs in a complete draft so that the draft can be reviewed by others. Also, make any improvements you can think of as a result of reading the sample paper "Jeopardy Is the Spice of Life."

2. Have the first draft of your paper reviewed.

   Option A: Submit a draft of your social problem paper to your instructor for feedback about its content and structure. Revise your paper to make the recommended improvements and corrections.

   Option B: Submit a draft of your social problem paper to one or more of your classmates, requesting feedback about its content and structure. Your instructor may want to organize this class exercise, assigning the procedures to be followed.

   Option C: Review the draft of your social problem paper by yourself, looking for ways to improve its content and structure.

LESSON FIVE: *Editing Your Paper*

The editing phase is the final phase of the writing process. At this point you are ready to produce the final draft—or manuscript—of your paper, and your primary goal is to produce a manuscript that follows the required format, is neatly typed or computer printed, and is error free.

Editing

Part of preparing your paper for presentation involves editing the sentences so that each one will communicate effectively with your readers. Each sentence must be clearly understood by you and by whoever is reading your paper. None of your sentences should wander from the topic, or your readers' minds may wander, too. Furthermore, the sentences within the paragraphs must tie together coherently so that your readers can easily follow your line of reasoning. Also, your choice of words should be appropriate, and the syntax of your sentences should not be awkward or confusing. Syntax is the way words are put together to form sentences, and the grammatical rules for written expression are much more precise than for informal oral communication. Finally, your sentences should be edited so they are concise and clear if you want your readers to quickly comprehend each point you are making.

Proofreading

Because your final manuscript must be free from errors in spelling, grammar, usage, punctuation, and other writing conventions, it must be carefully proofread. Proofreading is the process of reading and marking the corrections that need to be made. If you look at the insides of the front and back covers of *Survival* you will find correction symbols that are commonly used for this purpose. If you are using a computer, it probably has a spell-check feature, and some even have a grammar- or style-check function. Most writers edit for content and structure several times during the drafting phase. Then in the editing phase, they read through the paper again, revising the sentences, and then one more time, proofreading for errors that need to be corrected.

Manuscript Preparation

The manuscript of your paper is the final copy that you submit to your instructor for evaluation. It is often referred to as the "final draft." Its appearance is important because it is the final step in making your paper as easy as possible for your reader to follow and understand. Now your readers' response will be all important, particularly that of your most important reader—your instructor. Your writing during the drafting phase was expected to be less than perfect. Your final manuscript, however, is like a published document. Therefore, you must spend the time and effort necessary to make it as nearly perfect as is possible.

The required format for your social problem paper is illustrated in Sandra McGaffic's paper "Jeopardy is the Spice of Life" (pages 89-91). It shows how to write your heading, where to place the headers (author's last name and page numbers, and the paper's title). You will also notice that the entire manuscript is double-spaced, that each paragraph is indented five spaces, and that it has one-inch margins. Of course, you will not number or label your sentences in your final manuscript unless requested to do so by your instructor. The sentences were numbered in "Jeopardy Is the Spice of Life" as part of Exercise 2.14, and you labeled your sentences in your draft to gain insight into the organization and development of your paper.

EXERCISE 2.16

Prepare the final manuscript of your social problem paper to be handed in to your instructor for grading. Make all the revisions and corrections that are necessary to make your final manuscript as effective and error-free as possible.

FINAL MANUSCRIPT CHECKLIST

1. Does your paper have a strong, effective thesis sentence?
2. Are all topic sentences clearly stated?
3. Are there five or more sentences in every paragraph?
4. Have you used secondary support (details, facts, figures, and examples)?
5. Does your paper have an interesting opening sentence?
6. Is the summary sentence precise and the conclusion effective?
7. Do your paragraphs have an adequate sentence variety and smooth transitions?
8. Have you used third person throughout, except in anecdotes?
9. Is your paper free of awkward or grammatically incorrect sentences?
10. Is the first word of every paragraph indented?
11. Have you checked for fragments, run-ons, and comma splices?
12. Have you checked your spelling, punctuation, and capitalization?
13. Is your paper neatly written or typed?
14. Is your paper double-spaced and on one side only?
15. Did you put the heading in the upper-left corner and center the title of the paper?
16. Are your page numbers and headers correct?

Computer Safety Tips

1. Keep your paper stored on your hard disk until you have received your grade for the course.
2. Back up your hard disk by copying your paper onto a floppy disk.
3. File a photocopy of the hard copy of your paper.

CHAPTER TWO ESSAY PAPER

Name _____   Date _____

Class _____   Instructor _____

Meeting Time _____   Day _____   Circle One: Original Paper

                                                                        Revision

IMPORTANT: REVISED PAPER MUST BE ACCOMPANIED BY THE ORIGINAL!!

CHECKLIST

I. Content
  A. Topic
  B. Logic and ideas
  C. Reader interest

II. Structure
  A. Thesis sentence
  B. Topic sentences
  C. Opening sentence
  D. Primary and secondary support sentences
  E. Concluding sentence
  F. Irrelevant material
  G. Transitions

III. Sentence style and mechanics
  A. Sentence structure
  B. Agreement, pronoun reference, tense, person
  C. Spelling, punctuation, capitalization

IV. Format
  A. Heading and title (like sample on p. 89)
  B. Pagination and margins (like sample paper)
  C. Typing or handwriting (double-spaced)

Grade for Original Paper _____

Grade for Revision (if required) _____

Answers to Chapter Two

Exercise 2.10

TS Aquatic life, especially the anadromous fish, has been adversely affected by the pumping stations at the southwest corner of the Great Delta. PS Pumping causes fast current flows. SS Thus, invertebrates on which the fish feed cannot grow properly because of the increase of water flow. SS In addition, small fish usually drift to their food supply, reaching it at the time their bodies need it. SS The increased flow often interferes with this cycle, and many of the small fish die. PS Pumping also changes the direction of the water flow in some Delta channels, causing confusion for migrating fish, especially salmon returning to their spawning grounds. PS To make matters worse, because the Southern Delta section is a nursery area for striped bass, fish are present there most of the year. SS The pumping action draws fish to the export pumps, and fish too small to be adequately screened, striped bass in particular, along with the organisms on which they feed, and fish eggs, are drawn through the pumps where they are either destroyed or transported south with water. SS Salmon and other large fish do not go through the pumps, but because they become trapped in the screens, they have to be literally picked out by hand and transported to the Western Delta. SS This handling is hard on the fish, causing many losses, and it is expensive.

Exercise 2.14

1. c
2. b
3. a
4. d
5. e
6. e
7. d
8. e
9. a
10. a
11. d
12. d
13. e
14. e
15. f

CHAPTER THREE

Argumentative Structure

Objectives

When you have finished this chapter, you will have

1. used the three-phase writing process.
2. selected a subject and narrowed it to a topic.
3. researched the topic.
4. listed the pros and cons.
5. written and refined the thesis sentence.
6. planned an argumentative strategy.
7. written a thesis-topic sentence outline.
8. drafted a 750-1,000 word argumentative paper.
9. received feedback and revised the paper.
10. produced the final manuscript in the required format.

3

Life is filled with controversies—large and small. Nations make war; politicians debate; theorists argue; concerned citizens write letters to the editors; neighbors quarrel; customers complain. Violence may mark the failure of argumentative rhetoric, a civilized substitute. Persuasion and diplomacy lead to agreement, cooperation, peace, and other kinds of constructive behavior. Therefore, learning to deal with controversy—in an educated way—is important. You should learn to present your ideas in a way that offers you the best chance of persuading your audience that your point of view is worth adopting. The same basic rhetorical principles, once learned, will work well in both oral and written arguments. The persuasive strategies learned here will also help critical thinking skills that will be useful in other courses and in many aspects of your life. In this chapter you will learn to write an argumentative paper, using variations of a time-proven strategy: the **pro-con argument.**

Of the different types of papers you will learn to write, the **argument** is one of the most useful. By writing an argument whenever the opportunity arises, you increase the chances that your reader will be interested in what you have to say, for, as William Hazlitt, the famous essayist, wrote, "When a thing ceases to be a subject of controversy, it ceases to be a subject of interest." In general, instructors place a higher value on argumentative papers than they do on informative reports. They will appreciate the fact that you have the courage to go out on a limb—to venture a debatable position—even if they do not agree with your position. And, by writing an argument, you make your paper easier to read. The basic organization of an argument is straightforward: Assert a position in a thesis and support it with a list of reasons. The several variations you will learn, employing con-pro patterns, are easy to follow. You will also find the argumentative strategy can be used for most writing assignments. Writing is rhetoric, and as Aristotle said, rhetoric is the art of choosing the most advantageous argument in a given situation. Almost any writing assignment will provide you with the opportunity to take a stand and argue your reasons for that position. Use the argumentative strategy whenever possible for papers, research projects, book reports, and essay tests. In this chapter you will learn three ways to organize an argument. And by learning to write these three versions, you will be preparing yourself with rhetorical strategies that should greatly increase your chances for success in college writing.

Lesson One: *Planning Your Argument*

The **planning phase** of writing your argument is especially important because it takes you through the steps crucial to understanding the pro-con argument.

Finding a Controversial Subject

A controversy is a dispute, often conducted in public, during which people speak out, stating opposing views. Use the techniques suggested in Chapter Two's "Discovering a Subject" (page 62) to find a **controversial subject** that interests you. This subject will then be narrowed to the topic you will use for a 750-1,000 word argumentative paper (three to five typed pages).

Sources to Consider

Personal experiences
Differences of opinion among experts in your hobby
Issues in your chosen field or major
Class lecture notes and textbooks
Volunteer work or service-learning projects
Conversations with family, friends, classmates, co-workers
Local and national newspapers, such as, the *New York Times*
Television and radio news and talk shows
National Public Radio's *Morning Edition* or *All Things Considered*
News magazines, such as *Newsweek* and *Time*
The Readers' Guide to Periodical Literature
Pamphlet files in library
Books and professional journals
Computer networks, such as the Internet
Appendix C: Suggested Subjects (page 384)

EXERCISE 3.1

List three controversial subjects of interest and choose one that you will narrow to the topic of your argument. (Your instructor may select your subject from among the three you suggest.)

Possible Subjects:

1. _____

2. _____

3. _____

Subject Chosen: _____

Research

Before narrowing your topic, you may feel the need to do some background reading on your subject. Certainly, you are not expected to engage in the kind of comprehensive library research that will be required in Chapter Four when you write your library research paper. But you may need to visit the library to find articles or other material on your subject so that you know enough to proceed confidently with the planning phase. Several hours' reading about your subject may expand your knowledge to the point where you can more clearly see the possibilities for narrowing your subject. Background reading will also help you see all of the issues involved in the controversy you will discuss in your argument. Furthermore, the reading will be of immense help when you develop your list of pros and cons—the claims of the opposing sides. Finally, this preliminary reading may be of use later during the writing phase when you are looking for a strong quote for your opening or when you need supporting information to include in the body paragraphs.

If possible, make photocopies of the articles or at least the pages from which you are summarizing your information. Your instructor will show you how to give credit to your sources of information.

Library research is not the only source of information needed for developing your argument. Other sources of information, such as classroom lecture notes, journal entries, interviews, small group discussions, and recollections of personal experiences, may also be helpful (refer to the list on page 100).

Exercise 3.2

Briefly record in journal fashion your efforts to increase your background knowledge through your reading and research. Where did you find your sources, how did you locate them, what did you read?

_____

_____

_____

_____

_____

_____

_____

_____

_____

Have your reading notes approved.

Narrowing the Subject to a Topic

Use one of the prewriting techniques discussed in Chapter Two's "Narrowing the Subject to a Topic" (page 65) to narrow your subject to the topic you will develop in your argument. Quite naturally, you may not think you know enough about your subject to engage in the narrowing process yet. Since the writing process is often not a linear process, you may want to wait and narrow your subject after you do some background research. When you feel you are ready, simply employ one of the prewriting techniques to choose your narrowed topic.

Prewriting Techniques

Brainstorming
Freewriting
Clustering
Analytical Questioning
Pyramiding

Examples

Controversial subject chosen: Genetic Engineering

Prewriting technique: Analytical Questioning

> Is there a controversial aspect that will allow you to write either for or against the subject?

Answer: Yes.   (Now go a step further with your questions.)
> What are the related issues? (State them as questions—a form of brainstorming.)
> What are the techniques of genetic engineering?
> What are the differences in food, animals, and humans?
> What are the possible health hazards of genetically altered food?
> Is it ethical to tamper with the reproductive process in humans?
> Do parents have the right to determine their child's characteristics?
> Is genetic therapy a breakthrough for curing life-threatening diseases like breast cancer?
> Should the government include preventative genetic technology in everyone's insurance coverage to ensure equal access?
> Is genetic predisposition a greater factor than environment for susceptibility to disease?
> Could there be abuse of genetic testing by health insurance companies? Is there well-planned regulation that will prevent accidental genetic disasters?
> Is the all-out ban on genetic engineering that many theologians are calling for necessary?
> Why are farmers and some scientists opposed to genetic alterations?
> Should genetic development be driven by profit motives?
> Should human functions be commercialized?
> What safety and security measures, if any, are in place in the United States and other countries to protect against genetic engineering disasters?

Possible Topics:

    A. Ethical issues raised by genetic engineering
    B. Safety and security in biotech companies
    C. Government regulation of the biotech industry

Topic Chosen: The moral dilemma of tampering with human nature

2. Subject category chosen: hate speech

Prewriting technique: Clustering

Topic chosen: School speech codes and the First Amendment

EXERCISE 3.3

Use one of the prewriting techniques to narrow your subject to the topic you will develop in your argument. Then write in the information requested below.

Subject chosen: _____

Prewriting technique: _____

Topic chosen: _____

Have your topic approved.

EXERCISE 3.4

Develop a work schedule for your paper.

Work Schedule

Project Title: Argumentative Paper   **Due Date** _____

Exercise	Project Assignment	Sample Allotment	Your Time Allotment	Date Due
Ex. 3.5	Pros and Cons	(1/2 day)	_____	_____
Ex. 3.6	Thesis	(1/2 day)	_____	_____
Ex. 3.7	Strategy	(1/2 day)	_____	_____
Ex. 3.8	Outline	(1/2 day)	_____	_____
Ex. 3.9	First Draft	(1 day)	_____	_____
Ex. 3.10	Feedback	(1 day)	_____	_____
Ex. 3.11	Revised Draft	(1 day)	_____	_____
Ex. 3.12	Final Manuscript	(1/2 day)	_____	_____

Have your work schedule approved.

Listing the Pros and Cons

Any statement in your paper that raises arguments against the position you have taken in your thesis is **con**, or against your argument. Thus, if you are in favor of capital punishment, any statement against it is a con. But if you are opposed to capital punishment, any statement that favors it is a con. Any statement that supports the position you have taken is **pro**. Before writing your thesis, you must complete three preliminary steps that will help you organize your thoughts on what is pro and what is con.

First, pose your topic as a question, as you did in selecting your topic. This time, however, focus on your own opinions about the topic. Are you for or against building more nuclear power plants? Do you support or oppose the existing smoking ordinances in your community? Should a government agency be allowed to use potentially dangerous pesticides in residential areas to control insects harmful to agriculture? Should women be allowed (or required) to serve in combat roles? What measures should be taken to protect women from sexual harassment in the military? Should private militias be subject to government supervision and regulation? Should the purchase of assault weapons be prohibited? Do you support current affirmative action policies in education? Any controversial issue can be stated as a question, and when you are able to answer that question, you will know what your basic position will be.

Second, compile a list of pros and cons that should be considered before answering your question. There are two good reasons for making a list of the pros and cons. The list will help you become more open-minded about the topic, seeing both sides of the issues. You might even change or modify your position as a result. The list will also enable you to anticipate opposition to your position. Therefore, you will see more clearly which points should be covered in your argument to counter that opposition.

Now, write down the main question to be decided.

Example

Should a person found guilty of first-degree murder be executed?

Next, list in two columns all of the pro and con reasons that come to mind. For instance, in the first column—the pro column—list reasons supporting capital punishment. In the second column—the con column—list reasons against capital punishment. Usually you can think of a con for each pro, but not always. At this point you are not concerned about your position, but rather, you are trying to determine what in general are the pros and cons of the issue.

Capital Punishment

Pro	**Con**
1. Revenge should be granted friends and relatives of the victim.	1. Revenge is an outmoded concept of justice, incompatible with modern concepts of psychology and law.
2. The death penalty acts effectively as a deterrent to would-be murderers.	2. Statistics show that the death penalty is not an effective deterrent against murder.
3. Especially despicable and atrocious crimes warrant extreme punishment.	3. Especially horrible murders are committed by insane people, and insane people should be cured, not executed.
4. Those who are against capital punishment are naive about the horror and savagery murderers perpetrate on their victims.	4. Opponents of the death penalty are well informed through the media.
5. The Old Testament supports the death penalty. "Who so sheddeth man's blood, by man shall his blood be shed: for in the image of God made he man." (Genesis 9:6)	5. The Bible opposes capital punishment: "Thou shalt not kill."
6. Hardened criminals cannot be rehabilitated.	6. Murderers can be rehabilitated.
7. Convicted murderers given life sentences may be paroled and murder again.	7. Convicted murderers are rarely paroled.
8. The death penalty deters potential armed robbers, rapists, and hijackers who realize that they might inadvertently murder their victims.	8. Armed robbers, rapists, and hijackers rarely anticipate murdering their victims.
9. Prison guards are not safe if convicts serving life sentences do not have the threat of the death penalty preventing them from murderous attacks on the guards.	9. The threat of the death penalty has not kept convicts from murdering guards and one another in the past.
10. A few innocent people may be executed, but most convicted murderers are guilty.	10. Innocent people may be executed by mistake.

EXERCISE 3.5

1. State the topic you have chosen for your argumentative paper as a question. (Remember, you may not use capital punishment as a topic.)

_____

_____

_____

_____

2. Make a list of the pros and cons. Number your list, and for every pro try to think of a corresponding con.

Pro	Con
_____	_____
_____	_____
_____	_____
_____	_____
_____	_____
_____	_____
_____	_____
_____	_____
_____	_____
_____	_____
_____	_____
_____	_____
_____	_____

_____   _____

_____   _____

_____   _____

_____   _____

_____   _____

_____   _____

_____   _____

_____   _____

3. Briefly answer the question posed at the beginning of this exercise. This answer is your basic position. From this point on, any statement that supports this position is a pro, and any statement against this position is a con.

_____

_____

_____

_____

Have your work checked.

Writing and Refining Your Thesis

The position statement formulated in the previous exercise is actually your thesis in rudimentary form. You may be tempted to use this statement as the final thesis in your paper because it may be powerful and dramatic.

Examples

> The poor are not blessed.
> Murderers should be executed.
> The President should be impeached.
> Welfare is a huge swindle.
> Income tax laws are unfair.
> Mixed marriages are good.
> UFOs are real.

Each of these statements dogmatically asserts a debatable position. And your thesis must be a debatable declaration—a statement with which your reader can agree or disagree. But none of these statements is developed enough for a well-written argument.

After having decided upon your basic position statement, you should transform it into a more refined thesis statement. This transformation can be accomplished easily in progressive stages.

Refinement #1—Add a phrase or clause summarizing the reasons you will use to support your basic position. The easiest way to connect this summary is to use the word *because*.

Examples

> Affirmative action hiring policies should be continued *because* without them organizations tend to continue racially exclusive hiring patterns and *because* we need to create a workforce that mirrors the ethnic mix of the community.

> OR

> *Because* they are no longer needed, *because* they embarrass minority employees, and *because* they create reverse discrimination, affirmative action programs should be dismantled.

You do not have to use the word *because* to add the summary of your reasons. The *because* can be implied but not stated.

Examples

> Affirmative action policies should be continued to prevent organizations from repeating racially exclusive hiring patterns and to create a workforce that mirrors the ethnic mix of the community.

> OR

> An embarrassment to minority employees and potentially the cause of reverse discrimination, affirmative action programs are no longer needed and should be dismantled.

If possible, revise your thesis so that it will outline the argument that follows it. Often the body of the argument will develop three to five reasons supporting your position. By listing these reasons in the same order they will appear in the argument, you make your line of reasoning easy to follow.

Examples

> Racial segregation in schools is unjustifiable because it generates feelings of inferiority and magnifies the sense of inequality; furthermore, it violates both the due process clause of the Fifth Amendment and the equal protection clause of the Fourteenth Amendment.

> OR

> Racial segregation in schools is unjustifiable because it is unconstitutional and psychologically detrimental to minorities.

Refinement #2—Consider the advisability of tempering your thesis statement. Your thesis assertion may be overstated, too dogmatic, or overgeneralized, and, consequently, vulnerable to attack. You may have to qualify your position so that it will seem reasonable after the reader has read your entire argument. For example, the previous thesis statements about affirmative action could be tempered to read as follows:

Examples

> Affirmative action policies should be continued only if an organization keeps repeating racially exclusive hiring patterns and experiences difficulty creating a workforce that mirrors the ethnic mix of the community.

> OR

> Embarassing to minority employees who oppose affirmative action and potentially the cause of reverse discrimination, affirmative action policies should be re-examined with the aim of either abolishing them or changing them significantly.

Refinement #3—After all of your dividing and refining, your thesis may be too long and too complicated, making it unwieldly and difficult to comprehend. If you think your thesis is long or awkward, ask your instructor if a shorter, simpler version would be more effective. Then revise your thesis, if necessary.

Long Version

> When a student contemplating his or her first purchase of a computer considers cost, power and speed, screen size and clarity, keyboard size, ease of using the mouse, need for peripherals and batteries, and security from theft, the small Notebook or laptop may not be the best choice compared to a desktop.

Short Version

> For a number of reasons, the small Notebook or laptop computer may not be the best choice for a student buying his or her first computer.

If you decide to stay with the longer version of your thesis, edit it for wordiness. Often you can say the same thing in fewer words, making your thesis easier to read. Study the following examples; the wordy version appears on the left and the edited version on the right.

WORDY

EDITED

A correctly administered and adequately funded law for handguns would substantially lower the number of deaths from criminal activity and would also considerably lower the number of accidental homicides. (29 words)

A correctly administered and adequately funded handgun law would substantially lower the number of criminal and accidental homicides. (18 words)

Although some politicians and scientists have made the commitment to continue work on the development of "Star Wars" weapons after the end of the Cold War, the need for the system now is questioned along with its tremendous cost when other priorities seem more important and there is strong sentiment to balance the national budget. (55 words)

Although some politicians and scientists are still committed to developing "Star Wars" weapons, others question the need now that the Cold War is over and other funding priorities seem more important. (31 words)

Because the school's computer registration system used now discriminates unfairly against students who transfer from other schools and against students who attend part-time days and evenings, and because the current system produces schedules of classes at times students will not take them, the system should be replaced by a fairer and more efficient system for online computer registration. (58 words)

Because the school's computerized registration discriminates against transfer and part-time students and schedules classes at times student refuse to take them, a fairer, more efficient online system should be implemented. (30 words)

EXERCISE 3.6

1. Repeat the basic position statement for your argument, the answer to the question that you wrote in Exercise 3.5.

_____

_____

_____

_____

2. Refinement #1—Add a clause or phrase that summarizes the reasons you will use to support your basic position. Select the reasons you want to use from those in the list of pros and cons you compiled in Exercise 3.5. As a general rule, use at least three but no more than five reasons.

_____

_____

_____

_____

3. Refinement #2—If necessary, write a qualified version of your thesis.

_____

_____

_____

_____

4. Refinement #3—If your thesis seems too wordy, write a shorter version.

_____

_____

_____

_____

Have your work checked.

Planning a Strategy

This section explains three strategies you can use whenever you write an argument. Accompanying each of the three explanations is an argumentative paper written by a student that demonstrates the strategy.

Plan One

When using Plan One to organize an argument, write a series of body paragraphs explaining why your thesis should be believed. The easiest way to do this is to begin with a list of at least three but no more than five reasons you want to include. Then devote a paragraph to each reason. Because each paragraph should be at least five sentences long, however, you may want to include more than one reason in a paragraph. Organize the paragraphs so that your least important reason is explained first and your most important reason is explained last. As you write your paragraphs, remember what you have learned about topic sentences, primary support sentences, and secondary support sentences. Explain your points thoroughly, and use examples frequently.

PLAN ONE (PROS ONLY)

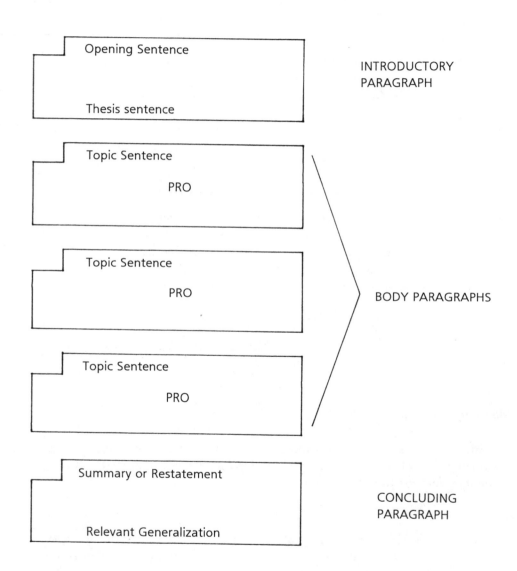

Read the sample paper that follows:

Sandra McGaffic

English 1A TTh 9:30

Dr. Guches

16 February 1995

(Argumentative Essay)

Emphasizing Creativity Over Gender Role Conformity

Introduction   Frustration is the usual result of having a good idea and not being able to put it into motion. Most people have had a glimmer of inspiration that failed because they were not able to follow through with it. People do not realize that there is more to the creative process than "Eureka!" Insight does come out of nowhere but is preceded by preconditioning and experience and followed by stubborn hard work. Many people with ideas have neither the background nor the perseverance to coax their ideas into reality. Furthermore, traditional child rearing, with its emphasis on adhering to socially defined gender roles, limits creativity by its restrictions. Creativity requires fertile surroundings and flexibility to thrive, and this requirement calls for a change in approach to child rearing. Experimentation with gender roles should be encouraged if parents want their children to develop resources that enhance creativity. Children who are encouraged to experiment with gender roles increase their capacity for creativity by developing a realistic sense of their own capability, resourcefulness, and integrity through assuming responsibilities, through gaining diverse experience, and by exercising independent judgment.

Pro   Families that have traditional views concerning sex roles are not intrigued by any experimentation with gender roles by their children. They have entrenched ideas on proper conduct and divide household tasks and family responsibilities accordingly. As a result, their children develop behavior patterns and internalize restrictions which dull creativity. For example, boys often have only token household duties and are to a certain extent expected to slough responsibilities. Their sisters, however, are burdened with household tasks such as doing laundry, preparing dinner, and taking care of younger children. This work is often taken for granted while much is made of projects and tasks the boys accomplish. This attitude will not bring a positive approach toward learning: unrewarding work diminishes the girls' drive to excel while inflated praise gives the boys a false sense of adequacy. Children who are thus restricted have their capacity for creativity impaired by their pessimistic or unrealistic attitudes. On the other hand, children who are encouraged to tackle all kinds of work without regard to gender role tradition develop a relaxed attitude and a more realistic sense of their worth. Work is considered a valuable pastime because it is productive, and there are no stigmas attached to household tasks. By assuming and upholding responsibilities, children develop confidence in their capabilities. Furthermore, children who are accustomed to hard work are better able to work through the frustrations of trying to solidify creative effort.

Pro   Diverse experience is another condition that benefits the creative process. Children who have tried many types of activities without regard to gender role restrictions have more resources at hand than children who stay within the restrictions. Traditionally children are steered away from interests that are considered inappropriate for their gender. This restrictive approach is unnecessary and wasteful. For a more positive effect, emphasis can be placed on benefits that can be wrought from the activity. For example, clothing construction is a valuable endeavor. It is obviously creative and productive in and of itself, yet is an activity from which boys are diverted. Conceivably, background in working with fabrics could give boys a familiarity with textures, colors, and patterns that would give them advantages in artistic design. Resources that are gained from a myriad of experiences may be drawn to an advantage in any situation: creative people are better at recognizing their strengths, and they are always devising ways of using their talents.

Pro   In addition to resourcefulness, productive creativity requires the essential characteristic of strong independent judgment. Children who move freely between socially defined gender roles develop independent judgment as an outgrowth of their emphasis of quality over conformity. They will have encountered the inevitable tacit disapproval from teachers, parents of friends, and other adults made uncomfortable by creativity demonstrated in untypical gender role identification, They will have learned to dismiss this disapproval. Society is stability-seeking in nature, and creativity, which is motion-seeking, cannot survive society's impositions. Resilience to criticism is a vital characteristic of productive creativity. It allows creative people to maintain energy levels by focusing on the solution to their projects rather than the defense of them. Independent judgment preserves their integrity and the integrity of their work.

Conclusion   Progress has assumed a dizzying pace in the information age, and creativity, the ability to look ahead as well as explore in new directions, is becoming increasingly vital. Creativity does occur naturally, but certain traits and conditions are necessary to make it productive. Children who are raised conforming to gender role stereotypes are hampered by their internalized, gender-correct attitudes. By developing a capacity for work, gathering background experience, and developing independent judgment, children who transcend the stereotypes stand a better chance of becoming the creative thinkers the world needs.

Plan Two

The order in which you admit and refute opposing arguments is important. Always acknowledge that a point of the opposition exists first, and then reason against it. In other words, if you make a **con statement,** make it before an accompanying **pro statement.** Your strategy, always, should be to end up on your own side. Do not weaken your position by following a statement supporting your thesis with a statement raising objections to the statement. Briefly summarize the point of opposition, and then refute that point as persuasively as possible.

When using Plan Two to write an argument, you do not simply support your thesis with a series of body paragraphs explaining why your thesis should be believed. Instead, you insert a *con* paragraph before the pro paragraphs, just after the introductory paragraph, at the beginning of the body of the paper. In this con paragraph you summarize the arguments against your position. The idea is to anticipate the objections to your argument and show the reader that you are aware of them and that you can deal with them honestly and openly in the pro paragraphs that follow this con paragraph. This paragraph must be worded in such a way, however, that readers will make no mistake about which side you are on. They must realize immediately that you are merely summarizing the opposing point of view. Otherwise, readers may mistakenly think that you are using Plan One and that the arguments of your opponents are really yours.

The way to signal clearly to your readers whether they are reading a con or pro paragraph is to use traditional **argumentative transitions** effectively. For example, *but* or *however* placed at the beginning of a sentence in an argument is a traditional signal that a writer is turning from the con to the pro side of the argument. If you use one of these transitional words to introduce a con point, you could send a false signal to readers.

Basically, there are two ways to lead into a con section in an argument. The first way is to acknowledge only that your opponents claim something is true. You do not concede that the opponents are right; you just show your readers that you are informed enough to know what your opponents think.

Examples

Opponents of increased funding for space programs argue that the money would be better spent in programs providing more jobs for people.

Those who argue against gun control like to quote slogans, like "Guns don't kill, people do" and "Control criminals—not guns."

Some environmental scientists contend that the increased level of carbon dioxide in the earth's atmosphere will raise global temperatures until the mid-latitudinal regions become steaming jungles.

A second way to lead into a con section is to concede, or admit, that your opponents are correct, or at least partially correct, in some claim they make. You can make this admission knowing that in the end you will win your argument.

Examples

> Granted, air pollution in the area has increased noticeably in the last ten years.
>
> Opponents of the no-smoking law are correct when they argue that providing separate facilities for smoking and non-smoking workers will be tremendously expensive.

Here are some commonly used **con** transitions:

CON

Opponents argue that	Doubtless,
Proponents claim that	To be sure,
Some people believe that	Granted,
One argument commonly raised is that	It would seem that
Although [Jones and others] found that	Apparently
One must admit	[Jones and others] are partially correct
Of course,	when they say that
No doubt,	

Your turnaround to the pro side should be bold and definite. Having made your concession to the opposing points of view, signal your readers that they are now seeing what you believe.

Examples

> But many of the technological advancements that will soon result in new commercial applications, and therefore more jobs, owe part or all of their development to previous space programs.
>
> Yet, the slogans of the pro-gun people, in spite of being catchy and popular, do not hold up under logical analysis.
>
> However, in spite of the fears of these scientists, it is also quite possible that the increase in carbon dioxide will produce a new ice age.
>
> But the proposal that automobile traffic can be cut 35 percent to combat this air pollution is unrealistic.
>
> Nevertheless, any expense is worthwhile if it will prevent nonsmokers from risking serious health problems.

Here are the most commonly used **pro** transitions:

PRO

But (no comma)	On the contrary,
However,	Surely, however,
Yet,	Still,
Nevertheless,	

By using the proper transition when you begin the concluding paragraph of your argument, you can reinforce the idea that your basic position is the logical culmination of your reasoning.

Examples

> Therefore, increased funding for the space program is crucial.

> Thus, handgun control is needed and can work.

> Hence, the initial increase in the mean temperature of the earth will cause an eventual lowering of the mean temperature and, as a result, the return of the glaciers.

> So one can only conclude that future proposals to curb automobile pollution will have to be more attractive to the general public.

> Obviously, therefore, the anti-smoking regulations should be strictly enforced.

Here are some of the most often used **concluding transitions**:

Concluding Transitions

Therefore,	Hence,
Thus,	And, therefore,
Consequently,	Obviously, therefore,
So	

When using Plan Two, your con paragraph can summarize more than one objection to your position. Try, however, to limit yourself to no more than two or three. Plan Two works best when you have just one con point you want to develop thoroughly or when several con points can be summarized succinctly. Consider this plan when you want to summarize briefly the opposition's point of view before you go on to argue your position. (Note: Many variations of Plan Two are possible. Check with your instructor if you want to adapt that basic plan.)

PLAN TWO (CON SECTION FIRST)

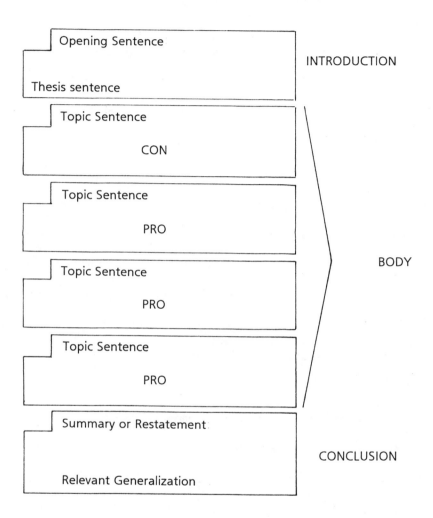

Read the sample paper that follows:

Hui-Wu-Johnson

English 1-A TTH 9:30

Mrs. Mehaffy

April 17 1995

Affirmative Action: We Aren't There Yet

Introduction Critics of affirmative action in education are full of bitter tales of reverse discrimination, all about deserving whites or Asian-Americans losing out to relatively less deserving African-Americans and Hispanics benefiting from an unjust system of racial preferences. Opponents have focused upon the perceived advantages given African-Americans and Hispanics in highly competitive college admissions, leading to complaints about these two groups being granted admission despite having lower gradepoint averages and/or SAT test scores than whites or Asian-Americans denied admission. These concerns reflect a serious misunderstanding of what really happens in the affirmative action college admission process. The situation is further exacerbated by the secrecy surrounding admissions policies. In fact, there are many misperceptions and misunderstandings about affirmative action, and the story of its triumphs, and of the continuing need for such programs in education, is too often ignored. Affirmative action in college admissions is a vital means of assuring that graduating classes reflect the diversity of the nation as a whole, and as such they should be retained, and even broadened to include economic criteria.

Con Critics, most vocal in the Republican Party, have mounted a campaign to scrap affirmative action in college admissions. They argue that affirmative action programs, originally meant to be temporary, are no longer needed. Twenty-five years ago they seemed necessary to many but something to be rid of as soon as they were no longer needed. Opponents of affirmative action in college admissions argue that racial and gender biases have subsided and that colleges are firmly committed to diverse enrollments. College admissions officers, if left on their own without the guidelines of affirmative action, would be objective and open-minded and would not, as in earlier years, automatically give preference to white males. The biggest gripe of opponents is that current admissions practices are unfair to some students who are denied admission in spite of higher academic qualifications than those of minorities admitted through affirmative action. Among the dissatisfied students and parents are Asian-Americans who, as a group, have earned higher grades and scored higher on admissions tests than white students, the next best performing group. Moreover, opponents contend, affirmative action undermines the principle that the opportunities of America's melting pot society are open to anyone who is smart enough and works hard enough to reap its rewards. Frustration seems to be widespread, too, because college admissions officers are secretive in how they go about granting preference to minority applicants, creating false impressions about minority candidates who are admitted without special consideration. The controversy has split roughly along political party lines, with the Republicans calling for an end to affirmative action and the Democrats promoting the need to retain preferential admissions.

Pro   In spite of the opponent's concerns, however, scrapping affirmative action programs in college admissions now would seem premature. Institutional inertia and sometimes subtle prejudice have in the past and could continue to shut minorities out. According to political columnist William Raspberry, "Affirmative action, an idea of the Lyndon Johnson era, was based on the observable fact that institutions tend to re-create themselves, unless acted upon by some outside force. It was this self-perpetuation, and not discrimination alone, that [Johnson thought] accounted for the underrepresentation of African-Americans and other minorities in the more desirable venues of society" (Sacramento Bee, 25 February 1995, B7). Academic affirmative action programs are intended to promote equality of opportunity because, prior to their existence, preferences based on race, sex, and ethnicity too often were given to white males. A real danger still exists, in spite of opponents' assurances to the contrary, that without preferential admissions, enrollment patterns would revert to earlier ones that excluded African-Americans and Hispanics. As the nation's population grows more ethnically diverse, common sense dictates that the makeup of its college graduating classes should mirror those changing demographics. Critics of afffirmative action need to adjust their notion that affirmative action programs are temporary remedies. Prejudices that were once so blatant, while not nearly so obvious now, still lurk in the wings threatening minorities and women.

Pro   However, admissions officers will need to be more candid about their processes if critics of affirmative action are to accept preferential admissions programs. The applicants and their parents are usually not told how affirmative action works. Typically, more than two-thirds of the freshman slots are filled strictly on the basis of grades and test scores without any consideration of race, and most of the students in those slots are whites and Asian-Americans. Almost all African-American and Hispanic students are admitted through a second route, in which the university considers race and family economic status. Being up front about the weight given to race may not put an end to criticism, but more people could see that only a portion of admissions are set aside for acceptance based on criteria other than grades and test scores. For years colleges have set aside slots for athletes, students with artistic talent, children of alumni, and the economically disadvantaged, looking beyond their academic qualifications for other achievements and qualities that showed signs of promise. With affirmative action, schools have merely expanded the criteria for this pool of special admissions. The basic premise is that we can look beyond conventional measurements to create a diverse student population, which in a democratic society is a desirable goal.

Pro   In fact, it may be time to take the concept of expanded criteria for special admissions further. More attention should be paid to the economic status of the applicants. Within the pool set aside for afffirmative action, both race and economic status should be considered. Conceivably if two applicants have the same grades and test scores, but one is from an affluent background and the other from a background of poverty, the low-income student's record may reflect a greater achievement. Marilyn McGrath Lewis, admissions director for Harvard and Radcliffe explained:

> Although College Board achievement and SAT scores are good predictors of freshman grades, she said, they become less reliable later. Furthermore, a study of three classes of Harvard alumni over three decades found a high correlation between 'success'--defined by income, community involvement and professional satisfaction--and two criteria that might not ordinarily be associated with Harvard freshmen: low SAT scores and a blue collar background" (Shipler, <u>New York Times</u>, 5 March 1995).

Research needs to be done to see how economic admissions criteria, which might be more palatable to critics of affirmative action, would affect the percentages of the different ethnic goups admitted because the goal should still be to achieve diversity.

Conclusion   Affirmative action programs are definitely in danger. Vocal opponents are mounting campaigns to abolish preferential admissions programs. Their stated goal is to return the nation to the original purpose of the U.S. Civil Rights Act of 1964, which they assert forbade discrimination against any individual on the basis of race, sex, or ethnicity. Thus, college admissions formulas would be administered equally to all with no special preference given to any racial group. If, however, such a course would result in the virtual exclusion of African-Americans and Hispanics or any other group from enrollment in the country's more sought after universities, the long term effect could be undesirable social stratification with white and Asian-American graduates at the top and African-Americans and Hispanics less well equipped to compete for desirable jobs, and to lead the fuller, richer lives that should be available to all. Therefore, the battle to preserve affirmative action must continue because a richly diverse nation needs a diverse group of college-educated citizens if democracy is to prevail.

Plan Three

When using Plan Three, alternate cons and pros. Argue back and forth, admitting that arguments against your position do exist, but always turn around to refute these opposing points. Do not weaken your position by following a statement supporting your thesis with a statement raising objections.

You may devote an entire paragraph to a con point and a separate paragraph to the pro point refuting it, or include both the con and pro in a single paragraph. An easy way to organize the body of an argument using this plan is to write a con paragraph and its corresponding pro paragraph, then another con paragraph and its accompanying pro paragraph, and then at least one strictly pro paragraph—a full body of five paragraphs.

Ideally, the paragraphs should be ordered so the paper becomes more interesting as it progresses from argument to argument. Plan Three works best when your opposing points are formidable, complex, and difficult to refute.

PLAN THREE (ALTERNATING CONS AND PROS)

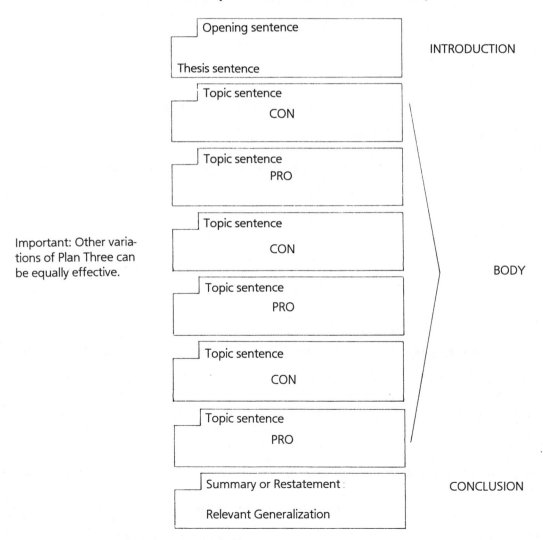

Important: Other varia-
tions of Plan Three can
be equally effective.

Daniel Nota

English 1A M 5:30

Mr. Mehaffy

17 May 1995

(Argumentative Paper)

Computers: Will the Real Frog Please Stand Up

Introduction   In the 1960's Marshall McLuhan proclaimed that television would revolutionize communications in the modern world, driving print into obscurity and eventual obsolescence. Now, similar predictions are being made for computers: they are expected to revolutionize business, entertainment, medicine, and education, boosting power and efficiency in these and many other areas of our lives. In many ways, computers have satisfied these expectations and show even greater promise for the future. In education, vast financial resources are expended in hopes that computers will fulfill a variety of educational needs. It is important to recognize, however, what computers can and cannot do in the classroom. In teaching critical thinking, reading and writing, and social skills, they have definite and sometimes little-realized limitations.

Con   Many parents and teachers bemoan the fact that television is a passive activity; it usually does not encourage critical thinking and often induces a sort of waking sleep as mindless images flicker across the screen. Computers are different. Some computer games, such as Tetris and SimCity, encourage critical and creative thinking to identify problems, propose solutions, and create new worlds within the parameters of the game. Many schools are offering such software to students as a means of developing analytical and creative thinking skills. Other kinds of educational software claim to help elementary or high school students master challenges such as the rigors of scientific method. Nicholas

Negroponte claims:

> Since computer simulation of just about anything is now
> possible, one need not learn about a frog by dissecting it.
> Instead children can be asked to design frogs, to build an
> animal with frog-like behavior, to modify that behavior, to
> simulate the muscles, to play with the frog (On Being
> Digital, 199).

This computerized way of learning about frogs suggests dazzling benefits to educational software: it can help students master scientific methods, think creatively, and learn about the world all through an exciting, interactive engagement with computers.

Pro   However, we should be skeptical about attempts to elevate computer software to the status of an all-powerful teaching tool enabling students to learn critical and creative thinking. Any computer user must work within the limitations of the program he or she is using; student writers using word processing programs often find that the spell-check systems give them a "right" answer that is not right at all within the context of the particular sentence they are writing. Although computers have many scientific applications, the rigors of scientific method are best taught by engagement with the real, not the virtual world. Negroponte's celebration of learning science by software suggests the limitations of the software. Exploring frogs in this way may be entertaining and of some benefit, but it is difficult to see how such a "computer simulation" will help students discover the characteristics of the real frog lying ignored on the dissecting table. Students and teachers should be aware that software can constrain rather than encourage critical and creative thought; students may be harmed by squeezing imagination and free-ranging critical thinking into the limiting demands of a computer simulation guiding them through a programmed world.

Con   Every year there is a growing drumbeat of concern that reading and writing skills are declining among the student population. It is conceivable that the trend to teach reading through hypertext (linking text with pictures) will aid slow readers or those with certain learning disabilities. Certainly reading through software and CD-ROMs, immersed in a flashing kaleidoscope of music, pictures and words, can be more engaging than struggling with the unadorned printed word. Furthermore, some software may be of use in teaching some writing skills, such as basic grammar and sentence writing. A growing number of teachers also believe that students can enhance their research and writing skills on the Internet, an interactive medium that helps students communicate with others through the written word.

Pro   Nevertheless, educators should view the entertaining, audio-visual enhanced reading and writing software as just that: entertainment that can actually have an adverse effect on learning. Clifford Stoll quotes a high school English teacher in California: "Computers are lollipops that rot your teeth. The students love them. But when they get hooked, they get bored with all the whoopee stuff. It makes reading a book seem tedious. Books don't have sound effects and their brains have to do all the work" (Silicon Snake Oil, 140). Although computers have some invaluable time-saving features, original ideas still come from people, and their real world experiences.

Con   Granted, computers can be used to teach social skills such as cooperation and communication between students. Schools have always been an important place to develop social skills; the daily, face-to-face contacts in the classroom are a vital training ground for communicating and working cooperatively. Computers are touted as an exciting means of promoting communication between students. Some programs allow students to edit or review one another's written work online. The Internet and software programs may help promote learning and communication within a school, or even between cities and other countries.

Pro   However, computers are a very expensive meanse of accomplishing what can be done using more traditional methods. Student team projects (co-writing and editing, peer review) can be pursued face-to-face in small groups, or by letter writing campaigns between schools. Also, one of the most important social skills, conflict resolution, is not aided by computer enhancement. Software can teach students to overcome programmed obstacles or chat online, but computer programs cannot help with the messy, unpredictable tensions and frustrations of everyday social interaction. Indeed, someone isolated behind a computer may be learning how not to deal with social life.

Conclusion   Should computers be used in the classroom setting? Absolutely. Students should know how to handle a word-processing program and, depending on grade level, use a spreadsheet or some of the other information systems computers do so well. But computers are not an educational panacea. Edutainment software is not the only or best means for teaching students to think, to read and write, or to develop social skills. Computer technology is a part of the learning experience, but we should not forget there are real frogs in a real world demanding attention.

Other Strategies

Not all writers follow Plan One, Two, or Three when they write arguments. Many professional magazine and newspaper writers, for example, seem to violate advice given in *Survival,* and yet their arguments are interesting and persuasive. Employing the journalistic style, they often do not include explicit thesis statements; they frequently write very short paragraphs; they often use first and second person; they sometimes use unorthodox punctuation. But they do usually follow basic argumentative rules, for instance, that a con always be followed by a pro and that an organized line of reasoning be used. These writers are using different strategies than you are asked to use in this course—and they are doing so much like musicians who play extemporaneous jazz piano only after they have mastered the basics of classical or traditional piano style.

The sample paper that follows was written by a student, not a professional writer. The paper is included to show how a writer can creatively adapt one of the three plans, in this case Plan Three. The introduction contains two paragraphs instead of one, with the thesis placed at the end of the second paragraph. Paragraph three presents statistical arguments on the pro side. Then paragraph four works back and forth in a series of con-pro arguments. The remainder of the paper beginning with paragraph five presents pro arguments based on the author's personal experience after her husband's motorcycle accident. This anecdotal quality along with the use of the first person makes the argument particularly persuasive.

Sandra Huit

English 1-A TTH 12:30

Mr. Schneider

2 October 1994

(Essay #2: Argument)

Helmet Laws: Requiring Motorcyclists to Use Their Heads

"No brains to save," my husband would murmur whenever he saw a bareheaded motorcyclist. Carl did not come by this dictum naively or with rancor. After 22 years of safe and cautious "biking," his own helmet saved his life when he broadsided an automobile that was making an abrupt U-turn on a steep foothills road. Although he sustained a serious head injury which left him hemiplegic and subject to chronic motion sickness for the rest of his life, we know that without a helmet, he would have been killed, and his passenger, his 16-year-old son, would have suffered more than a light concussion.

In 1991 California enacted legislation mandating that all motorcyclists wear helmets. Claiming that their individual freedoms were being abridged, a vocal minority of riders vehemently protested the new law. They continue to lobby loudly to repeal the helmet law despite overwhelming statistical evidence that helmets save lives. California should continue to require that all cyclists wear helmets because the social costs incurred by unhelmeted motorcycle riders are not only monetary, but misery for the victims and their families.

According to the Department of Motor Vehicles, only 2.8 percent of the vehicles registered in California are motorcycles. However, motorcycles are disproportionately involved in 7.2 percent of all vehicular fatal and injury accidents. The National Highway Traffic Safety Administration calculates that, per miles driven, a motorcyclist is 20 times more likely to die in a crash than an automobile driver. The leading cause of death and injury in motorcycle crashes is head injury, and unhelmeted riders are six times as likely to suffer fatal or critical head injuries. Following an accident, unhelmeted motorcyclists usually have longer stays in the hospital with treatment costs ranging from 44 to 72 percent higher than for helmeted drivers. In 1992, the first year the California helmet law was in effect, motorcycle injuries were reduced 27 percent, from 16,739 in 1991 to 12,195. Thirty-six percent fewer motorcyclists died from their injuries—only 326 killed compared to 509 deaths in 1991.

Still there are some who feel that the freedom of choice to ride a motorcycle without a helmet is a valuable freedom which has been lost. When asked why they prefer riding with their heads unprotected, they often respond that they enjoy feeling the wind blowing through their hair and follow with a discussion of the dangers inherent in helmets. Motorcycle helmets are said to impair visibility by limiting peripheral vision. Actually, legal helmets are designed with a range of 210-degree visibility, exceeding the 140-degree minimum limit required of all motorists by the California DMV. Eyeglass and sunglass frames inhibit peripheral vision more than helmet screens. Motorcyclists are still free to turn their heads to survey traffic. Some claim that helmets muffle sound and prevent riders from hearing traffic noise which may be critical to avoiding accidents. According to Lieutenant Mike Nivens of the CHP Motorcycle Safety Program, at any speed over 15-20 miles per hour, the stream-lined design of a helmet reduces the sounds of wind blowing by the ears and the roar of the cycle's motor and enhances the ability to hear ambulance sirens, horns, and other nearby engine motors. As for the argument that helmets cause neck injuries, researchers at Michigan University have shown that helmets prevent neck injuries by protecting the head and neck in an accident. The cause of neck injuries is the impact of the crash, not the cushioning of the helmet.

For every motorcyclist killed in vehicular accidents, many more are injured. Although broken bones and crushed spleens are painful, head injuries are the most devastating result of motorcycle accidents. The brain-damaged frequently linger in comas for hours, days, or months. When they awaken, if they awaken, the very qualities of mind and personality which made up their unique personhood may be altered, perhaps permanently. Brain injury can impair motor skills and cause paralysis that limits walking or even use of hands, just as in stroke victims. Speech impairment is another noticeable result, as head trauma victims often must entirely rebuild their vocabularies and search for appropriate words. The search can be hampered by a stalling in the thought processes, making it impossible to process thoughts quickly or even to handle simultaneous thoughts. Questions, if even understood, may require 10 to 20 minutes for the brain to send a reply to the mouth. Occupational therapy is often required to relearn the sequencing of mundane tasks, like dressing (socks first, then slacks, and then the shoes). Short-term memory loss interferes with everything; the sequence of dressing is lost when we forget that we are dressing, so the process can become interminable. In the worst instances, bright, urbane men and women become cheerful dullards, with rare interests beyond their present needs, with logical thinking frustratingly scrambled, but with a memory of who they used to be. Although the frustration can indirectly lead to depression or other personality disorders, major personality changes, including violent temper, are often a direct result of head injury. Wives find themselves married to strangers; young children are more mature than their brain-damaged parents; understandably, 90 percent of marriages end when one partner suffers brain damage. Employers can find no place for formerly competent workers. The consequences are more than disabling.

My husband and I were lucky because his intelligence and wonderful sense of humor survived his head trauma. But while we were in the "survivor" community, we witnessed families destroyed and lives wasted by the head injuries sustained by unhelmeted motorcyclists. Whenever I see a bumper sticker proclaiming that "Helmet Laws Suck," I am reminded of the alternative. Whenever I hear a rider bemoaning his loss of freedom to choose, I wonder what choices his loved ones would have if he were to become another unhelmeted motorcycle injury statistic. To reduce that possibility, California should retain its current helmet law and even consider sentencing violators to community service with head-trauma families and organizations.

EXERCISE 3.7

Which of the three strategies seems best for your argumentative paper? (Circle one)

PLAN ONE   PLAN TWO   PLAN THREE

Briefly explain your decision:

_____

_____

_____

_____

Outlining Your Argument

After the preliminary planning work you have already completed, writing a **thesis-topic sentence outline** will be relatively easy. The exercise that follows will guide you through the process.

EXERCISE 3.8

Using your list of pros and cons in Exercise 3.5, select the two or three points against your position that you will include in your paper if you use either Plan Two or Plan Three.

(1) _____

_____

_____

(2) _____

_____

_____

(3) _____

_____

_____

List the three to five points you will use to support your position.

(1) _____

_____

_____

(2) _____

_____

_____

(3) _____

_____

_____

(4) _____

_____

_____

(5) _____

_____

_____

Using the strategy you decided upon in Exercise 3.7—Plan One, Two, or Three—convert the con and pro points listed earlier in this exercise into the topic sentences you will use for the body paragraphs in your argument. (You are not required to include con points unless you use Plan Two or Three.)

Move the thesis you have developed from Exercise 3.5, and write your thesis-topic sentence outline. Double-check your thesis first. Does it cover the points you plan to include, or do you need to revise it in light of the work you have done in this exercise?

Thesis: _____

_____

_____

_____

_____

1. _____

_____

_____

_____

_____

2. _____

_____

_____

_____

_____

3. _____

_____

_____

_____

_____

4. _____

_____

_____

_____

_____

5. _____

_____

_____

_____

_____

6. _____

_____

_____

_____

_____

7. _____

_____

_____

_____

_____

8. _____

_____

_____

_____

_____

Have your work approved.

LESSON TWO: *Writing Your Argument*

First Draft

Write a first draft of your argument. A first draft is a preliminary version that will be improved and proofread later. It is your first attempt to expand your thesis statement and integrate topic sentences in a detailed discussion. Although every writer develops an approach to first-draft writing unique in some respects, two general techniques seem to be used most frequently. Some writers develop their first drafts slowly, painstakingly writing and rewriting almost every sentence. They cannot begin a new sentence until the previous one is as perfect as they can make it. For these writers first-draft writing is an exhausting ordeal. Most writers, however, work as rapidly as possible, revising very little as they write their first drafts. They need the satisfaction of immediately putting their most important thoughts down on paper, reorganizing, refining, and correcting their paragraphs in subsequent drafts. Try to use the rapid-write method when you write your first draft, but if that does not work, develop a method that does.

Begin your introductory paragraph with an interesting statement. Then add three or four sentences building up to your thesis, which should be placed at the end of the paragraph. See that the sentence leading into your thesis makes a smooth transition. You may need to add a sentence to prevent the connection from being awkward. But spend as little time as possible on this paragraph for now. Unless you are a compulsive reviser, try to be content with your first or second version temporarily. Return to your introductory paragraph later; you will find it much easier to revise the paragraph after you have written the rest of the paper. By then the creative thoughts needed for a good introductory paragraph will more easily flash into mind. Furthermore, you will have the advantage of knowing what you have written in the body and conclusion; thus, you will be able to avoid writing sentences that would be repeated in other sections. You have already written your thesis; moreover, you have written an outline of topic sentences to guide you as you develop your thesis. Concentrate on the body paragraphs, refer to your list of topic sentences constantly, and write!

> *Suggestion:*
> Print your thesis and list of topic sentences on a poster and tape it to your desk or wall.

Follow your outline, and stay on the subject in each body paragraph. Every sentence should flow smoothly into the next. Envision each body paragraph as a well-organized network of primary and secondary support sentences that makes it impossible for your reader not to know what you are saying in the topic sentence. Think ahead. Plan the sequence of sentences—this forethought only takes seconds when your writing faculties are working well. Of course, writing is not entirely a mechanical process: it is also a creative, evolving process. Planning does not always work. Good writing is basically mechanical, but it is an art, too—the result of creative inspiration, the communication of thoughts magically conjured up by your brain. Writing one idea often inspires another, an idea not thought of before and, therefore, not in your plan. Adapt your paragraph plan and use these ideas if they will help the paragraph and the paper. Then double-check the topic sentence for two problems. It should still cover the content of the entire paragraph, and any modifications in the topic sentence must not prevent the smooth progression of ideas from topic sentence to topic sentence. The paragraph must make the thesis of the argument clearer.

How long should a body paragraph be? Any body paragraph in your argument that does not have five or more sentences should be expanded. As pointed out in Chapter Two, very short paragraphs belong in newspapers and magazines where the columns are narrow, not in academic papers. Occasionally in a long paper you can use a very short paragraph for transitional purposes when you are linking major sections within the body of the paper. But short transitional paragraphs are not needed in your argument and other papers you will write in *Survival*.

In general, long paragraphs are better than short ones, but paragraphs can be too long. For example, a paragraph that runs two or three pages in a handwritten paper may be difficult to read, just as a paragraph more than a page long in a typed paper can be hard to follow. If a paragraph seems too long, you can usually find a natural break where it can be divided into two paragraphs or places where it can be divided into three paragraphs if it is extremely long. After dividing a long paragraph, you may have to rewrite the original topic sentence and reword the first sentence of each new paragraph in order that each one will begin with a strong topic sentence. You also may have to add sentences, either to provide topic sentences or to extend any new paragraph that as a result of the dividing may be too short. These changes can be made as you write your first draft, or they can be made in later revisions.

More than anything else, every body paragraph needs pertinent details. Your instructor expects detailed discussion, not a series of unsupported ideas and aphorisms. You may know what you mean when you make a generalization, but you cannot be sure your reader will know what you are thinking unless you explain your ideas thoroughly. Of course, easy-to-follow organization helps.

Begin each body paragraph with a topic sentence, and support it with a clearly organized pattern of primary and secondary support sentences. To write detailed paragraphs, you must make a special effort to include enough secondary support sentences. When you add explanations, examples, quotations, statistics, anecdotes, and other kinds of specifics, you make it easier for your reader to understand what you are trying to say. As your argument is evaluated, your instructor will study the body paragraphs to see if you have supported your primary support sentences with secondary support sentences and to look for specifics in those sentences. Where do you go to find these specifics? You can find the information you need in books, magazines, pamphlets, lecture notes, television programs, movies, interviews, and discussions. However, the best source of supporting information may be your own experiences. You have read; you have listened to others; you have lived and worked. Through all of this experience you have been gathering ideas, opinions, and facts about controversial issues. If you take the time to think, you can probably come up with most of the specifics you need to support your argument without consulting other sources. Many appropriate examples and other supporting details will occur to you as you write your first draft. Write them in your paper or on your outline before you forget them. In subsequent revisions you can examine your paragraphs closely in a more organized effort to add specific secondary support.

If you incorporate researched material in your paper, you must give credit to your sources of information. With your instructor's permission, you may use a simplified version of parenthetical documentation (for this paper only). Note the source of the quoted, summarized, or paraphrased passage in parentheses at the end of the passage. Use a lead-in, if possible, as in the following examples.

Passage Quoted from Newspaper

Organizations that have failed to integrate their workforces are not necessarily guilty of hiring discrimination. According to columnist William Raspberry, "Affirmative action, an idea of the Lyndon Johnson era, was based on the observable fact that institutions tend to re-create themselves, unless acted upon by some outside force. It was this self-perpetuation, and not discrimination alone, that (Johnson thought) accounted for the underrepresentation of

African-Americans and other minorities in the more desirable venues of society" (<u>Sacramento Bee</u>, 25 February 1995. B7).

Information Paraphrased from Book

In spite of what the ads say, milk may not be a healthy food for everyone. According to D.D. Metcalf, the majority of the world's people cannot digest milk. Up to one in every five whites and more than eight of ten non-whites lack the enzyme lactase that is needed to digest milk and milk products (Kronhausen, Kronhausen, and Demopoulous. <u>Formula for Life</u>, 1989: 329).

In the first example above, the actual wording of the columnist is quoted. Consequently, the passage us enclosed in **quotation marks**. The passage was found in his column on page B7 of the February 25, 1995, edition of the newspaper. In the second example, the actual wording from the book is paraphrased. That means that the authors' observations have been restated in different words. As a result, no quotation marks are used. The information was found on page 329 of the book, copyrighted in the year 1989.

When you have written your body paragraphs, begin your concluding paragraph with a restatement of your thesis or a summary of the major points developed. Whatever you write, avoid the same wording used in your thesis or body paragraphs. If you do not change the wording of your reiteration, you will likely bore the reader, and your instructor may comment that your conclusion seems redundant. Also remember not to end your paper with your restatement or summary. Add two or three sentences, wise generalizations, perhaps an apt quote, affirming the relevance and importance of what you have argued. Take time with these statements because the wrong thing said at the end of a paper can invalidate the effect of everything written previously.

EXERCISE 3.9

Write the first draft of your argument.

Feedback about Your First Draft—Suggestions for Revision

By the time you finish your first draft, you will be ready for some feedback about its content and organization, either from your instructor or from your classmates. Most important, you will want to know if the points you are making are clear and whether your arguments seem logical and are affecting your readers the way that you thought they would. Through this feedback you will learn what works well and what could be improved. Your readers will probably also comment about sentence construction problems, punctuation, and spelling errors. But, most likely, these concerns won't be addressed in earnest until the Editing Phase—when you clean up your paper for formal presentation and evaluation.

Time may not permit your instructor to read and comment on everyone's draft or to set aside a class period for peer editing by your classmates. If that is the case, you will have to look elsewhere for constructive criticism. After laying the draft aside for awhile, you will find upon rereading it that you will see a number of improvements that can be made. The Checklist that follows on page 143 has been provided to guide you through the feedback process.

EXERCISE 3.10

After you have completed your first draft, choose one of the following options for receiving feedback. Use the Checklist that follows or other guidelines provided by your instructor.

Option A: Submit your draft to your instructor for his or her comments.

Option B: Engage in a peer editing exercise with your classmates, either in pairs or in small groups. Your instructor will organize this activity.

Option C: Seek feedback from a tutor, friend, or family member. (Your instructor must give you permission; it may be required that you choose Option D.)

Option D: Reread your draft, searching for improvements you can make.

CHECKLIST

Introductory Paragraph

1. Does your introductory paragraph begin with an effective opening statement? (See Chapter Two, page 76.)
2. Is your introductory paragraph at least five sentences long?
3. Do you have a thesis statement?
4. Is your thesis a debatable statement located at the end of your introductory paragraph?
5. Is your thesis a miniature outline of your argument? Would your thesis be more effective if it were divided, or if it is divided, would a shorter, undivided version work better?

Body Paragraphs

6. Have you successfully employed Plan One, Two, or Three, or an adaptation of one of those plans?
7. Does each body paragraph begin with a topic sentence that covers the content of the entire paragraph and supports the thesis?
8. Does each body paragraph contain all the primary and secondary support sentences it needs? (At least five sentences in each paragraph?) Is each paragraph free from irrelevant sentences? Have you included enough examples? Are they interesting?
9. Have you used enough transitional words and phrases, especially to signal pro and con sections? Have you used the pro and con words correctly? Does each sentence flow smoothly into the next?

Concluding Paragraph

10. Does your concluding paragraph begin with a summary or restatement of the thesis? Have you rephrased to avoid redundancy?
11. Have you added a thought-provoking generalization to your summary or restatement?
12. Is the concluding paragraph at least five sentences in length?

Overall Considerations

13. Have you successfully supported your thesis? Is your argument logical and persuasive?
14. Have you given credit to other sources of information (parenthetical documentation)?
15. Will your paper hold your reader's interest? If not, how can it be improved?

As an example of how the basic structure of your paper can be improved, read question 8 on the checklist. Perhaps you did not include enough detail in your first draft. Search for places where generalizations can be made clearer by adding specifics—more secondary support. Add details! Add facts and figures; include comparisons; rely on personal observations and anecdotes you have heard or read about; use common sense and logic to develop your arguments. Most important, add examples—too many are better than too few.

Use Examples

> For example, clothing construction is a valuable endeavor. It is obviously creative and productive in and of itself, yet as an activity from which boys are diverted. Conceivably, background in working with fabrics could give boys a familiarity with textures, colors, and patterns that would give them advantages in artistic design.

Use Facts

Marilyn McGrath Lewis, admissions director for Harvard and Radcliffe explained, "Although College Board achievement and SAT scores are good predictors of freshman grades, they become less reliable later. Furthermore, a study of three classes of Harvard alumni over three decades found a higher correlation between 'success'—defined by income, community involvement and professional satisfaction—and two criteria that might not ordinarily be associated with Harvard freshmen: low SAT scores and a blue collar background" (Shipler, <u>New York Times</u>, 5 March 1995). (See page 123.)

Use Figures (Numbers)

According to the Department of Motor Vehicles, only 2.8 percent of the vehicles registered in California are motorcycles. However, motorcycles are disproportionately involved in 7.2 percent of all vehicular fatal and injury accidents. The National Highway Traffic Safety Administration calculates that, per miles driven, a motorcyclist is 20 times more likely to die in a crash than an automobile driver. (See page 132.)

Use Comparisons

In 1992, the first year the California helmet law was in effect, motorcycle injuries were reduced 27 percent, from 16,739 in 1991 to 12,195. Thirty-six percent fewer motorcyclists died from their injuries—only 326 killed compared to 509 deaths in 1991. (See page 133.)

Include Personal Observations as Generalizations

Short-term memory loss interferes with everything; the sequence of dressing is lost when we forget that we are dressing, so the process can become interminable. (See page 134.)

Any computer user must work within the limitations of the program he or she is using; student writers using word processing programs often find that spell check systems give them a "right" answer that is not right at all within the context of the particular sentence they are writing. (See page 127.)

Include Narrations You Have Heard or Read About

"No brains to save," my husband would murmur whenever he saw a bareheaded motorcyclist. Carl did not come by this dictum naively or with rancor. After 22 years of safe and cautious "biking," his own helmet saved his life when he broadsided an automobile that was making and abrupt U-turn on a steep foothills road. Although he sustained a serious head injury which left him hemiplegic and subject to chronic motion sickness for the rest of his life, we know that without a helmet, he would have been *killed*, and his passenger, his sixteen-year-old son, would have suffered more than a light concussion. (See page 131.)

Use Common Sense to Develop Your Arguments

As the nation's population grows more ethnically diverse, common sense dictates that the makeup of its college graduating classes should mirror those changing demographics. (See page 122.)

Revising Your Draft

Begin work rewriting your argument as soon as you have received suggestions from your readers or as soon as you have completed your self-check. It is important to work on the revisions while the suggestions are fresh in your mind. Of course, you will need to consider each suggestion carefully before you decide to make the change. You will find, too, that you may need further clarification about a suggested change. If so, check further with the reader who made the suggestion to better understand that person's perception of the problem and how a revision might improve the paper.

EXERCISE 3.11

Rewrite your argumentative paper, making all of the changes that you think will improve your paper. It is highly unlikely that your instructor will provide feedback about this revised draft. As soon as this second draft is completed, you will be moving into the editing phase. (If required, have your revision approved.)

LESSON THREE: *Editing Phase: Preparing the Final Manuscript*

Stylistic Improvements

Your argument, perhaps after considerable struggle, is down on paper. You have asserted a thesis and supported it with an organized line of reasoning (Plan One, Two, or Three). Furthermore, you have made improvements in the basic structure of your argument. But you still must make the revisions and corrections that will make your writing articulate, persuasive, and easy to read.

For suggestions, turn to Appendix B: "A Guide to Stylistic Revision" at the back of the book (page 366). Study each section, attempting to find stylistic improvements you can make in your argument. You may discover, for example, that some sentences lack parallel construction or that many of your sentences are unnecessarily wordy; you may find a few sentences lack energy because they are built around passive verbs.

Even if you do not consider yourself to be a skillful writer—at least not this early in the course—you can learn to make desired improvements in your writing. You can practice these new skills on your Chapter Three argument and perfect them as you write other papers—both for this course and for your other courses.

While evaluating your argument, your instructor may make comments referring you to specific sections in Appendix B. These comments will be of great help to you in rewriting your paper.

Final Proofreading and Format

Before you submit your argument for evaluation, give your sentences some last-minute attention. Slowly proofread your paper for errors. If you need help, ask for it. On later papers, however, you will be expected to do your own proofreading. Correct mistakes in agreement, pronoun reference, tense, and person; check for sentence variety and proper use of coordinating conjunctions and transitions; repair all run-ons, comma splices, and fragments. Double-check your punctuation.

Reminder: Never use the phrases **In my opinion, I believe, I think,** or **It seems to me.**

Finally, correct any misspelled words. (Check for capitalization errors, too.) Use the spell-check on your computer or consult a dictionary for the preferred spelling of any words that might be misspelled. Your instructor expects only an occasional misspelling and no uncorrected typographical errors. Allow time to proofread your paper carefully.

FORMAT FOR FINAL MANUSCRIPT

1. Key in or type your argument, double-spacing the entire manuscript. Your instructor may give you permission to write in blue or black ink, skipping every other line.

2. Print, type, or write on one side of the page only.

3. If you are using a computer, make corrections right up until you print your final manuscript. If you are typing or handwriting your paper, last-minute corrections can be made on the final manuscript. Neatly draw a single line through the portion to be revised or corrected, and then print the correction above the crossed-out portion. Additions should be inserted above a caret mark($\wedge$). Whenever time permits, however, retype or rewrite the page or the entire paper.

4. Use the sample papers in this chapter as a guide in format matters: heading, headers, title, spacing, margins, and page numbers.

5. If you are including a graphic, such as a chart, a table, or an illustration, ask your instructor for advice regarding its acknowledgment and placement.

EXERCISE 3.12

Prepare the final manuscript of your argumentative paper. Submit it for evaluation.

Computer Safety Tips

1. Keep your argumentative paper stored on your hard disk until you have received your grade for the course.
2. Back up your hard disk by copying your paper onto a floppy disk.
3. File a photocopy of the hard copy of your paper.

CHAPTER THREE ARGUMENTATIVE STRUCTURE

Name _____   Date _____

Class _____   Instructor _____

Meeting Time _____   Day _____   Circle One: Original Paper

Revision

IMPORTANT: REVISED PAPER MUST BE ACCOMPANIED BY THE ORIGINAL!!

CHECKLIST

I. Content
   A. Logic and ideas
   B. Reader interest

II. Structure
   A. Introductory paragraph
      1. Opening statement
      2. Length (at least five sentences)
      3. Thesis statement

   B. Body paragraphs
      1. Basic structure (Plan One, Two, Three, or adaptation)
      2. Topic sentences
      3. Primary and secondary support sentences
      4. Use of transitional words and phrases
      5. Concluding sentences

   C. Concluding paragraph
      1. Summary sentence
      2. Concluding generalization

III. Sentence style and mechanics
   A. Sentence structure
   B. Agreement, pronoun reference, tense, person
   C. Spelling, punctuation, capitalization

IV. Format
   A. Appearance
      1. Heading
      2. Title
      3. Page numbers and headers
      4. Margins
      5. Neatness

   B. Documentation (if needed)
      1. Lead-ins
      2. Parenthetical references

Grade for Original Paper _____

Grade for Revision (if required) _____

CHAPTER FOUR

The Library Research Paper

Objectives

When you have finished this chapter, you will have completed

1. a topic proposal
2. a library orientation
3. a working bibliography
4. research notes
5. a thesis and an outline
6. a first draft of the paper
7. Notes and Works Cited
8. the final manuscript
9. a revision (if assigned)

4

In this chapter you will learn a step-by-step approach to writing a **library research paper**. The skills you practice will be useful when you write papers for this course and future courses. This systematic approach to gathering information, shaping it into a paper, documenting your references, and preparing a manuscript can be used now and on through graduate school. Being organized and attentive to details will reduce your chances of encountering problems that often bewilder and frustrate students working on research projects.

STEPS IN WRITING A LIBRARY RESEARCH PAPER

1. Proposing a topic
2. Familiarizing yourself with the library you will be using
3. Compiling a working bibliography
4. Taking research notes
5. Writing a final thesis and outline
6. Composing the first draft of the paper
7. Writing the Notes and Works Cited
8. Preparing the final manuscript
9. Revising the paper (if required)

To make certain you have mastered the skills being taught, you are required to have your work for each step approved before you proceed to the next. (See the cover sheet on page 224.) By the time you have completed all five lessons in this chapter, your library research paper will be written and ready for evaluation.

LESSON ONE: *Proposing a Topic*

Unless instructed otherwise, you will be allowed to propose your own topic for your library research paper. Choose your topic thoughtfully, and do not hesitate to consult with your instructor and others about the advisability of pursuing a particular subject.

FACTORS TO CONSIDER

Your interests
A proper-sized topic
Availability of material
Time limitations
Minimum requirements
Your instructor's advice

Your Interests

Select a general topic that interests you. Consider the assignment an opportunity to study an issue that concerns you, to reach a conclusion about the issue, and to communicate your findings in a paper. Being interested in your topic is of paramount importance.

Examples

Alternative energy sources
Computer technologies
"Hate Speech" codes for schools
Homeless people
Logging of old-growth forests
Overpopulation

See the comprehensive list of general topics in Appendix C.

PRELIMINARY READING

Browsing in the library may help you find a topic. Look through current magazines that appeal to you. Study recent newspapers, both local and national, such as the *New York Times*, the *Wall Street Journal*, and the *Christian Science Monitor*. Search through the card catalog drawers or the electronic card catalog. One of the best places to look is the *Readers' Guide to Periodical Literature*. In minutes you can skim through hundreds of general topics, noticing which ones look interesting and also which ones have the most magazine articles listed under them. Just wandering slowly through the shelves of books in the library, stopping here and there to examine some of the books, may lead to the discovery of an interesting topic. Most library staffs prepare lists of current issues suitable for library research papers. Some libraries distribute starter bibliographies on frequently researched topics. See if there is an index for the pamphlet file; this index will list hundreds of potential topics. Finally, look for the two-volume *Library of Congress Subject Headings*, usually located in the card catalog or reference area. Spending some time with these potential sources of topics may be productive.

A Proper-Sized Topic

Working with your general topic until it is the proper size is of utmost importance. You have already spent considerable time in previous chapters learning to narrow topics. However, the problems that can arise if the topic is too large become especially frustrating while you are writing a library research paper. If the topic is too large, you will probably not be able to gather all of the information needed in the time allocated; you will also encounter difficulty when it comes time to organize an outline. Thus, by narrowing your topic before beginning your research, you can avoid being swamped by an unwieldly mass of information. Also, if your topic is not narrow enough, your paper may end up being too long.

Most electronic indexes are programmed to help you narrow the field of your research, but some are not. Consequently, if you attempt to research a topic that is too broad like "abortion," you might find yourself faced with a list of several hundred sources. Such a long list would require you to spend an excessive amount of time eliminating irrelevant sources. A long list would indicate from the start that your topic should be further narrowed before you proceed.

A topic that is too broad will almost certainly lead to a superficial paper, lacking detail and in-depth discussion. The library paper that reads as if it is from an encyclopedia is generally a poor idea. Instructors do not want papers that summarize everything there is to know about a topic. Likewise, they do not want a biography paper that deals with the entire life of a person. Keep in mind, too, that the older a topic is and the more that has been published about it, the more specific and creative you have to be in choosing some particular aspect about which to write.

Availability of Material

You must consider whether or not sufficient material will be available in the library you will use. Narrowing your topic too much can lead to serious problems. The most common problem that students encounter when their topics are too narrow is that they are unable to find enough source material to write their papers. Watch out for topics that have just become big news, too. A brand-new controversy may be prominently featured in the media when it breaks, catching your interest, but it takes several months for most libraries to accumulate and index materials on new subjects. Beware of local issues, also; many topics dealing with your own community may be best left for Chapter Seven where you will write an investigative paper.

Do not abandon an interesting topic too hastily. The fear that the library does not contain enough information may be unfounded. Perhaps the information is there, and you simply have not figured out how to find it. For instance, you may be looking in an index under "Nuclear Weapons" when the articles are actually listed under "Atomic Weapons." Talking to your librarian and instructor is important before deciding whether or not a topic will work.

Time Limitations—Four Weeks

Time is another important consideration. At the most, you should spend no more than four weeks gathering your information, planning, and writing your library research paper.

LENGTH—1,500 Word Minimum

The minimum requirements of the library research paper will influence your choice of topics, too. For this paper you are to write at least 1,500 words of text. If you prepare your paper using a computer or a typewriter, plan on averaging 200-250 words per double-spaced page. Thus, you will need at least six pages, plus one page for the Notes (if included—see pages 212-213), and one or more pages for the Works Cited. If your instructor allows handwritten papers and you write on every other line of 8 1/2-by-11-inch notebook paper, you can plan to average 100 words per page of text—15 pages of text and the accompanying pages mentioned above.

REQUIRED REFERENCES—A Minimum of Ten Sources Cited

At the end of your library research paper, you will include a Works Cited page. In the Works Cited you will list in **alphabetical order** all of the research sources referred to in your paper and in the Notes (see pages 212-213). To fulfill the requirements for this chapter, your Works Cited must contain at least ten research sources actually cited in the final version of your paper. You may include more than ten sources, but you must obtain your instructor's permission to include fewer than ten. As you prepare your research paper, you will use the Modern Language Association format (MLA).

EXERCISE 4.1

As always, you must begin this writing project by developing a work schedule. Review the section on developing a work schedule in Chapter Two (page 61) if you need to, and then prepare your work schedule for completing your research paper on time. Use the chart you develop on the next page to keep control of your project and track your progress. As you complete the work schedule, begin by considering how much time you have to research and write your essay. Column three offers a suggested work schedule based on a four-week time allotment. You should use column four to write down your schedule after you find out what your actual time allotment will be. This schedule assumes that your class meets three days a week.

Work Schedule

Project Title: Research Paper

Due Date _____

Exercise	Project Assignment	Sample Allotment	Your Time Allotment	Date Due
Ex. 4.2	Topics	(1 day)	_____	_____
Ex. 4.3	Proposal	(1 day)	_____	_____
Ex. 4.4	Library	(1 day)	_____	_____
Ex. 4.5	Bib Cards	(2 days)	_____	_____
Ex. 4.6	Guide	(1 day)	_____	_____
Ex. 4.7	Note Cards	(3 days)	_____	_____
Ex. 4.8	Thesis	(1 day)	_____	_____
Ex. 4.9	First Draft	(1 week)	_____	_____
Ex. 4.10	Final Manuscript	(1 week)	_____	_____

Have your work schedule approved.

Your Instructor's Advice

Be positive and creative in approaching your instructor with a proposed topic. Sometimes an instructor experiences renewed interest in a worn-out topic if the student proposes a fresh approach. An instructor who has read too many papers on the pros and cons of nuclear power may be interested in a paper on the risks involved in transporting nuclear wastes. A paper outlining the causes of divorce would be dull, whereas one explaining the unique problems of divorced male parents might be interesting. Discuss your topic with your instructor before you commit yourself to it.

Writing the Topic Proposal

The *topic proposal* is a brief report, usually a paragraph, explaining what you hope to accomplish in your research paper and your research strategy. Although research paper proposals can be very formal in nature, yours will be informal. Thus, you may use first person ("I" and "my") in your proposal, and there is no required format. You should, however, try to include the following information:

TOPIC PROPOSAL
1. Your narrowed topic
2. Any tentative thesis, research questions, or working outline you have developed
3. An assessment of the availability of materials
4. An assurance that the topic can be researched in one week

Sample Proposal

My general topic is foreign investments in the United States. I will concentrate on agricultural purchases by foreign investors. The main research question I want to answer is, "Are the increasing purchases of U.S. agricultural land going to result in a foreign takeover of our farms?" I have read that whole farms are being purchased by wealthy investors from other countries. My tentative thesis is that if large-scale purchases of prime agricultural land continue, the farm-belt economy will be dangerously undermined in the future. However, I need to do more research before I can form a final opinion about the seriousness of this threat. A quick check in electronic and printed indexes showed that a number of recent articles on the topic are available in our library. Although I could not find a book directly related to my topic in the card catalog, the librarian told me I could find books and reference materials dealing with agriculture in the United States that would provide good background material. I believe my topic is limited enough to allow me to complete my note taking in three days.

If you are unfamiliar with the library you will be using, you may want to read Lesson Two (page 158) before you visit the library to look for a topic.

EXERCISE 4.2

List three potential topics for your library research paper. Then after making a preliminary investigation in the library—skim through the next lesson if necessary—consult with your instructor and the librarian.

Finally, choose the topic that seems best for your topic proposal (to be written in Exercise 4.3).

Potential Topic #1

_____

_____

_____

Potential Topic #2

_____

_____

_____

Potential Topic #3

_____

_____

_____

EXERCISE 4.3

After having one of the potential topics in Exercise 4.2 approved, write a topic proposal for your library research paper. Prepare your proposal on a computer or typewriter, or you can prepare it on notebook paper if your instructor will accept handwritten copy. Submit the final, edited copy to your instructor.

_____

_____

_____

_____

_____

_____

_____

_____

LESSON TWO: *Library Areas*

For you to be successful at research paper writing, you need to develop the knack of rapidly finding your source material and taking notes, leaving plenty of time to write your paper. You will need to become familiar with the areas and services provided by the library used. Think of the library as an information bank made up of a number of areas, each specializing in certain types of materials and services. Most libraries have at least seven areas:

1. **Card Catalog**—The card catalog, a listing of all books owned by a library, has changed from drawers filled with 3-by-5-inch cards in many libraries. Modern libraries have their card catalogs on computers. Since not all libraries have replaced their card catalogs with computers, you may find that the library you use may still have cards. When you work in a library that has a computerized card catalog, it will probably be referred to as an "online catalog," rather than a card catalog. Generally, online catalogs are given a name, such as OPAQ or LOIS. These names are usually just acronyms that stand for the company that developed the system or the school district that owns the system.

   While card catalogs traditionally only list the books and records owned by the library, online catalogs now contain not only that listing of books but also Internet (which allows you to communicate electronically with other institutions) and indexes for many newspapers, magazines, and journals stored in your library.

2. **Stacks**—Books are kept on shelves called stacks. After you find the call number of a book which you would like to examine, go to the stacks to find the volume. If the library does not allow you access to the stacks, it has "closed stacks," and you simply ask a librarian to obtain the book for you. Many libraries that have open stack areas have some closed areas, such as

the "reserve stacks," where instructors place special materials to which students have controlled access.

3. **Checkout Counter**—Information, reserve books and materials, library cards, and checkout services are available at this counter.

4. **Reference**—Encyclopedias, almanacs, maps, biographical indexes, dictionaries, and other reference materials are kept in the reference area or room. Often these materials can be used only in the library.

5. **Serials**—Commonly referred to as the periodicals area, the serials area contains all of the magazines and professional journals in the library. Most libraries use a combination of stacks and microfilm and microfiche for their periodicals. Newspapers are also found in this area, in piles and on microfilm. The indexes for the periodicals may be found in the general vicinity of the periodicals or in the reference area. Indexes may be computer programs such as *InfoTrac* and *MAS*, or they may be bound volumes such as the *Readers' Guide to Periodical Literature*, the *Social Science Index* or the *Educational Index*. Large libraries may have these indexes both online and in bound volumes on tables in the serials area.

6. **Pamphlet File**—Often referred to as the vertical file, the pamphlet file is normally found in or near the reference area. It contains pamphlets, newspaper clippings, government bulletins, and reprints on most current topics.

7. **Microforms**—Almost every library now has a collection of microfilm and microfiche materials. National newspapers (*New York Times, Wall Street Journal, Christian Science Monitor*), current and back issues of periodicals, and *Dissertations Abstracts International* are commonly stored on microforms. The microfilm or microfiche copies of some periodicals, for example, for older issues of magazines and journals, may be the only ones available in the library. The microform copies, in other cases, may duplicate the printed copies shelved in the stacks. As you familiarize yourself with the library, take the time to learn what is available on microforms and whether indexes for those materials are provided.

LIBRARY SERVICES

Librarians

You will sometimes need help to locate materials. The librarian who specializes in the area where you are working will be your best source of information. If you need general orientation, inquire about scheduled library orientation tours or any orientation packets that may be available to assist students unfamiliar with the library or some of its materials.

Interlibrary Loan

You will often find that the library you are using does not have a particular book you need. Through the librarian, Interlibrary Loan may be able to borrow the book from another library for you. (Allow a week or two for transit time—the failure of a book to arrive on schedule is not a valid excuse for handing in a late paper.)

Libraries also keep lists of the magazines and journals located in other libraries in your area. If your library does not have a periodical you need, ask your librarian for the serials lists from other libraries. To read these periodicals, however, will require you to obtain them through Interlibrary Loan or to visit the libraries where they are housed.

Microfilm and Microfiche Readers

Most libraries have at least one microfilm and one microfiche reading machine. Although directions for their use are usually displayed, a librarian will show you how to operate any machine you may wish to use if you have difficulty.

Photocopy Machines

Modern libraries also provide equipment that can assist you with the task of collecting the information you will need to write your paper. To save time, you can make photocopies of periodical articles, portions of books, and other materials. These photocopies can then be studied more carefully at home. You can use the photocopy machine for a small fee. Most larger libraries also have coin-operated copiers that will produce copies of articles on microfilm or microfiche.

Electronic Aids: Media Materials

Many libraries lend students record and tape players, film viewers, and other audio-visual equipment. More and more libraries are providing computers and word processors for student use. Ask at the checkout counter for the equipment you need. (Make it a point to inquire about recordings, films, computer software, and other media materials housed in the library.)

Computer Database Searches

Most libraries have replaced or will be replacing their traditional volumes of indexes with computers that are connected to mainframe systems or CD-ROM readers. These computer software programs enable you to find the same information you were able to find previously in the printed volumes. These computers are often connected to printers that will provide you with a printout telling you where to get a copy of the book or article you need. This makes your research much faster. Some of these programs will offer you the option of a computer printout of the newspaper or magazine article you wish to read thereby saving you even more time than you would have spent searching the stacks for the article and then copying it.

Computers will also enable you to conduct research electronically. You can be connected to an online database via a modem on a library computer and a telephone. Such online research can be remarkably helpful when investigating some topics. Be aware, however, that such database searches can be expensive. You can quickly run up a bill of many dollars on such searches. If you determine that such database searches would truly help your research project, ask your librarian to estimate the cost before you proceed. Some of the information from these database searches will be available quickly; sometimes, however, the information will take days or weeks to arrive at your library. Discuss your research needs with your librarian to determine if database searches are available to you and if they would be helpful.

Another online database that you may find useful as you research your topic is the Internet, and it may not be necessary to go to the library to use this source. More and more students have access to Internet at home, in the dorm, or at work. Thousands of live databases offer information on virtually every subject on which you may wish to write. Before you invest too much time into online research, however, you should check with your instructor to find out what your school's policy is on the use of online sources in research papers. Some schools limit the number of online sources students may use in research papers.

If you do use online sources in your paper, remember that it is just as important to document electronic sources as printed sources. Your reader must be able to find every source you refer to in your essay from the information you provide. If your reference is to a book, your reader must be able to find the book on the shelf; if your reference is to an online source, your reader must be able to find it as well. You are required, therefore, to provide documentation that will allow your reader to go directly to that source and read the entire original document. In order to allow your reader to find an electronic source, therefore, you must give an exact path that will lead your reader to each electronic source without fail. If you are not confident that a source can be found, don't include it in your paper.

Sample Portion of Printout

```
ED180332  HE012062
   Climbing  the Academic Ladder:   Doctoral Women Scientists in
Academe.
   National Academy of Sciences - National  Research  Council,
Washington, D.C. Commission on Human Resources.
   1979   176p.
   Available from: Office of Publications, National Academy of
Sciences, 2101 Constitution Avenue, NW, Washington, DC 20418
($8.00)
   EDRS Price - MF01 Plus Postage. PC Not Available from EDRS.
   Language: English
   Document Type:  RESEARCH REPORT (143);  STATISTICAL MATERIAL
(110)
   Geographic Source: U.S.; District of Columbia
   Journal Announcement: RIEMAY80
   The status of women scientists in academic  institutions  is
examined  as well as women's current situation in postdoctoral
training and their role on national science  advisory  boards.
Obstacles  that  women  must  overcome  to become professional
scientists are discussed in Chapter I,  focusing  on  cultural
and structural factors. Characteristics, educational patterns,
and supply of women doctorates in the sciences are examined in
Chapter II. Men and women were found to be similar in quality,
length of time spent to earn a degree, and in proportions that
are trained at highly rated institutions. Chapter III examines
sex  differences  in  postdoctoral  training patterns.  Recent
developments  in  the  academic  employment  of  men  and women
scientists  are  discussed in Chapter IV.  Changes in numbers,
rank,  tenure,  and salary are investigated.  It is noted that
the  increase  in  women Ph.D.'s that began in the 1960's has
been  followed  by an increase in their presence among science
faculties. Participation of women in three major groups within
the national science advisory system is reviewed in Chapter V.
Figures  from  the National Academy of Sciences,  the National
```

EXERCISE 4.4

To familiarize yourself with the library you will be using during your library research project, choose one or more of the following options:

1. Attend a library orientation arranged by your instructor.
2. Complete a library orientation exercise distributed by the library staff.
3. Arrange for someone familiar with the library to give you a walking tour.
4. Conduct your own library orientation. Explore the library you will use, locating the areas mentioned in this lesson and inquiring about the services offered.

Answer the following questions:

1. Which of the above options did you complete? _____
2. Have you obtained a library card? _____
3. What are the library hours? _____

LESSON THREE: *Using the Library to Compile Your Working Bibliography*

After completing your library orientation, the next major step in your library research paper project is to compile a **working bibliography.** A researcher uses the working bibliography while gathering information and writing the first draft. It is not the final list of references called "Works Cited" that will be included in the final manuscript of your paper. The list of works cited shows the sources actually referred to in the final version of the paper. But the working bibliography is compiled before the books, magazines, and other sources are actually studied.

Taking the time to list potential sources before you check them out will save you time because your search will be more organized. Less time is needed to compile your working bibliography all at once than to stop and read each promising source as you discover it.

Take your time as you prepare your working bibliography. As you list your potential sources on index cards, place only one source on each card. List three times as many sources as you think you will need because you will not be able to find some, others will be checked out or missing, and some will not contain any information you can use. Since you will need a minimum of ten sources for the Works Cited in your final manuscript, *prepare thirty working bibliography cards.*

Investigate a Variety of Library Sources

To make certain you have conducted a thorough investigation of the library, make a serious attempt to list at least **five** of the following kinds or sources:

1. Magazine articles listed in the *Readers' Guide to Periodical Literature* or *InfoTrac*
2. Newspaper articles listed in *NewsBank*

3. Books listed in the card catalog or online catalog
4. Newspaper articles listed in the index to the *New York Times*
5. Books shelved in the Reference Area of your library
6. Materials from the pamphlet files
7. Recordings, video cassettes, and CD-ROMs
8. Information gathered from information services and databases
9. Journal articles listed in *Education Index*, *Nursing Index*, etc.

Working Bibliography Cards

Use one 3-by-5-inch index card for each source. Separate cards are better than a single list for a working bibliography because they can be shuffled, sorted, and matched to your note cards, outline, and Works Cited as you write your paper. Each time you discover a potential source of information, fill out a card, listing all of the information you will need to identify and locate the source. Although you may include a brief note about the content of the source on a working bibliography card, these cards should not be confused with note cards. The main purpose of the working bibliography cards is to guide you to the sources.

Keep your working bibliography in order at all times. Every time you locate a new source, take the time to make a working bibliography card, even later in the project. You will need your working bibliography cards to assemble your Works Cited, which will be placed at the end of your final manuscript. The format used for your working bibliography cards is the one you will use for the entries in your Works Cited. Samples of the most common kinds of entries are included in this lesson. For examples of other types, study the sample entries in Appendix A.

Some students enter working bibliographies on computers so they can organize all of their information in one place. These students worry about losing their stack of 3-by-5-inch cards if they write them out and carry them with them. This is a realistic concern, but putting the working bibliography on a computer takes more time and creates other problems. When you have completed your working bibliography, if you keep it on a computer, you will need to print out and cut the working bibliography into separate entries in order to proceed. The time-tested practice of writing out working bibliography cards will most likely save you time.

BEGIN YOUR WORKING BIBLIOGRAPHY

> **Note!** Resist the temptation to start finding and reading the articles and books as you assemble your working bibliography. If your paper must have a minimum of 10 sources listed in the Works Cited, you should make at least 30 working bibliography cards before you begin locating and reading the sources. If you can't find enough sources for your working bibliography, you will need to change your topic. If you have begun finding and reading articles and then have to change your topic, you will have wasted considerable time.

Encyclopedias

The most frequently used encyclopedias are the general encyclopedias, which are often good sources of background information for library research papers. These encyclopedias are usually stored together in the reference section of the library.

Examples

> *Encyclopaedia Britannica*
> *Encyclopedia Americana*
> *Collier's Encyclopedia*
> *Columbia Encyclopedia*

You should also be aware that a number of encyclopedias are currently available on CD-ROM. If you have access to a computer with a CD-ROM, you should check to see if an encyclopedia has already been installed. Those libraries that have made computers available to students have also begun installing encyclopedias, so check with your librarian, too.

Most libraries also contain many specialized encyclopedias (e.g., *Encyclopedia of Educational Research, Encyclopedia of World History, Catholic Encyclopedia, McGraw-Hill Encyclopedia of Science and Technology*). Agriculture, art, education, history, religion, science, social science, biography, and literature all have one or more specialized encyclopedias. These encyclopedias are ordinarily found in the reference section of the library, or they can be located by using the subject cards in the card catalog. Be careful, however, that the information you use from these encyclopedias is not out of date. The *Encyclopedia of Social Sciences*, for example, was published from 1930 to 1935.

Do not rely upon an encyclopedia for anything more than general background information, however. Some instructors, particularly those teaching English, prefer that you not use encyclopedias for cited sources at all. They believe that you should be investigating a subject in considerably more depth than an entry in an encyclopedia can possibly provide. Thus, an encyclopedia may well be the source with which you begin; it contains the information you should have before you begin your major research.

Study the sample working bibliography card on the next page.

SAMPLE WORKING BIBLIOGRAPHY CARD FOR ENCYCLOPEDIA

Mast, Gerald. "Motion Pictures, History of."
The New Encyclopaedia Britannica
Macropaedia, 1981 ed.

See "Age of D.W. Griffith": 515-16.

Undergrad. Lib.

Electronic Indexes

Many libraries have installed electronic indexes, and and an increasing number of students use them to begin their research. The concept of an electronic index has changed so rapidly the last few years that few people can keep up with the changes. You will have to search for answers and work your way through problems as you proceed, but your rewards will make it worth your effort.

The electronic indexes will be found on the computers situated around the library. These indexes will have various titles, so try them all. All, however, serve the same function: to provide you with the information needed to locate articles and books that will help you write your paper. These reduce your research time considerably, of course, but be aware that few libraries have many of these programs because they are very expensive. The following are some of the most common indexes you might find as you research your paper:

> *InfoTrac*
> *MAS (Magazine Article Summaries)*
> *NewsBank*
> *Magazine Index*
> *Business Index*
> *Academic Index*
> *Medline*

These indexes will guide you through your search, and most have printers attached that allow you to receive a printed copy of the sources you have found. You can take these printed copies home or to a quieter section of the library to make your working bibliography cards. Most indexes will also inform you if the materials listed are in your library or if you must travel to another library to find them.

Few libraries will have more than a few electronic indexes, but you should find and use those that are available in your library. When you have exhausted the electronic possibilities, move immediately to the printed indexes of periodicals.

Do not confuse the purpose of electronic indexes. Their only purpose is to help you find magazine, journal, and newspaper articles, and to help you decide if those articles will be helpful to you. Do not assume that you can use summaries you find in electronic indexes as sources in your paper. A few of these indexes contain the entire article on CD-ROM, and you can get a copy by simply pushing a button on the keyboard. These are convenient, but they often present problems as you attempt to write up entries for your Works Cited. Remember the basic rule is that your entry must be complete enough so your reader can go to your source without difficulty.

You may, in fact, want to begin with the printed indexes to speed up your research. If you find the computers too busy, move on to the printed indexes. You can always come back to the electronic indexes later.

Printed Indexes

The Readers' Guide

The *Readers' Guide to Periodical Literature* lists every article published in the 166 most commonly read magazines in the United States. Articles that appear in *Time, Newsweek, Psychology Today, Science Digest,* and other popular magazines are all listed in the *Readers' Guide* by subject and author. There is a volume for each year since 1900, except for the current year. The bimonthly supplements for the current year are shelved right next to the bound volumes.

If your research topic is of current interest, begin by looking in the most recent volumes of the *Readers' Guide*. Resist the temptation to grab older volumes just because someone is using the recent ones, except when earlier volumes would be more appropriate. Check through all the volumes that might prove useful, unless, of course, you find after checking several that you have enough promising article titles. Be aware that many libraries discard most publications (magazines and newspapers) that are more than five years old to make room for newer ones. For this reason, you should avoid using *Readers' Guide* volumes that index publications published more than five years previously.

To use *The Readers' Guide*, look in the alphabetically arranged listings for the subject or author you need. In each volume the article titles are grouped under general headings that are arranged alphabetically. Try looking for the general topic you are researching, "Sports," for example. You may have to think of other headings for your topic. If, perhaps, you find nothing under "Mercy Killing," try "Euthanasia," or if you find nothing under "Gun Control," try "Firearms." Imagine all of the related headings that might lead you to the articles you need.

Each general category may be divided into subcategories. For example, under the general heading "Women," the subheadings "Aging," "Anatomy," "Education," "Employment," and "Equal Rights" are listed. Cross references may be listed too, for instance, under "Women" in the subsection "Employment," "See also, 'Married Women—Employment,'" (For further directions, for a list of the periodicals indexed, and for the meaning of abbreviations, see the front of each volume.)

After locating the general category or subcategory you are looking for, search for article titles that seem worth investigating. Then list the complete information for each article on a separate 3-by-5-inch index card.

Later, when you actually have checked out each magazine and are ready to take notes, recheck all of the information listed on the corresponding working bibliography card. Add any missing information such as the author's full name or the article's subtitle. The use of a + to indicate "and other pages" (e.g. 17+) is acceptable; however, if notes are taken from any of these additional pages, you must list the exact pages referred to on your note cards. Since your Works Cited will be compiled from your working bibliography cards, make certain that you include all of the information on them to avoid having to return to the library.

READERS' GUIDE TO PERIODICAL LITERATURE

GREEK COOKING *See* Cooking, Greek
GREEK ORTHODOX CHURCH *See* Orthodox Eastern
  Church
GREEKS
Georgia (Republic)
  Caught in the ethnic crossfire [Greeks living in Abkhazia
    caught in the middle of a civil war with Georgia]
    P. Glastris. il *U.S. News & World Report* v116 p24
    Je 13 '94
United States
  See also
  Greek Americans
GREELEY, ANDREW M., 1928-
  Priests should make preaching their number one job
    [with readers' comments] *U.S. Catholic* v58 p13-17
    D '93
GREEN, BARBARA
  about
  Shadows and light. E. Agar. il *American Artist* v58 p38-43
    F '94
GREEN, BENNY
  about
  Green with gusto. M. Johnson. il por *Down Beat* v60
    p21-4 N '93
GREEN, DANIEL ANDRE
  about
  Reasonable doubt. S. Raab. il pors *Gentlemen's Quarterly*
    v64 p240-7+ Mr '94
GREEN, FREDERICA MATHEWES- *See* Mathewes-
  Green, Frederica
GREEN, GEORGE DAWES
  about
  An early verdict on 'The juror' is unanimous. G. Feldman.
    il por *Publishers Weekly* v241 p20-1 Ap 25 '94
GREEN, OGGIE
  about
  NY granny collects cans to educate grandkids. il por
    Jet v85 p37 Ap 25 '94
GREEN, WILLIAM
  Health crimes: why are so many Americans breaking
    the law for medical reasons? il *American Health* v12
    p58-62 D '93
GREEN
  How green was my kitchen. R. Deen. il *Commonweal*
    v121 p31 Je 17 '94
GREEN DAY (MUSICAL GROUP)
  Green Day: Dookie [sound recording] Reviews
    Time il v143 p72 Je 27 '94. C. J. Farley
GREEN FLASH *See* Sunset phenomena
GREEN HOUSEKEEPING SEAL OF ENVIRONMEN-
  TAL LEADERSHIP AWARDS
  Saving the earth starts here. L. J. Brown. il *Good
    Housekeeping* v217 p51-2+ N '93
GREEN PARTY (CANADA)
  Green relief for forest defenders [Green Party to pay
    fines for jailed protesters at Clayoquot Sound] K.
    Goldberg. il *The Progressive* v58 p13 Mr '94

GREENE, ANN E., AND ALLISON, RICHARD F.
  Recombination between viral RNA and transgenic plant
    transcripts. bibl f il *Science* v263 p1423-5 Mr 11
    '94
GREENE, GAEL
  The insatiable critic. See occasional issues of New York
GREENE, GAYLE, 1943-, AND RATNER, VICKI
  A toxic link to breast cancer? *The Nation* v258 p866-9
    Je 20 '94
GREENE, GRAHAM, 1904-1991
  about
  A life in the margins. R. McCrum. il *The New Yorker*
    v70 p46-9+ Ap 11 '94
GREENE, LEONARD M.
  about
  Ending welfare as we know it. G. P. Brockway. il *The
    New Leader* v77 p12-13 Mr 14-28 '94
GREENFELD, KARL TARO
  Generation [X] il *The New York Times Magazine* p36-41
    Je 26 '94
  The making of a prime minister. *The Nation* v258
    p828-30+ Je 13 '94
GREENFIELD, JERRY
  Anecdotes, facetiae, satire, etc.
  I've seen the lite [Ben & Jerry's ice cream factory]
    J. Queenan. il *Gentlemen's Quarterly* v64 p216-22
    Ap '94
GREENFIELD, MEG, 1930-
  [Column] See occasional issues of Newsweek
GREENFIELD COMMUNITY COLLEGE
  A tale of two colleges [financial inequity between students
    at Amherst College and Greenfield Community College]
    R. Dizard. il *Change* v25 p27-31 S/O '93
GREENHOUSE EFFECT
  See also
  World climate review
  Climate forecast: unsettled. C. A. White. il *Canada and
    the World* v59 p10-12 My '94
  Global warming: why is the planet feverish? [research
    by Michael E. Schlesinger and Navin Ramankutty]
    R. Monastersky. *Science News* v145 p134 F 26 '94
  Iron fertilization: a tonic, but no cure for the greenhouse.
    R. A. Kerr. il *Science* v263 p1089-90 F 25 '94
  Methane increase put on pause. R. A. Kerr. il *Science*
    v263 p751 F 11 '94
  New findings in paleoclimatology and astronomy provide
    a wider context for our natural disasters. R. M. Adams.
    Smithsonian v24 p10 Mr '94
  No global warming? [declining CO_2 emissions] K. Leutw-
    yler. il *Scientific American* v270 p24 F '94
  Political science [W. Happer dismissed from post at
    DOE after opposing views of A. Gore concerning
    ozone depletion] R. Bailey. por *Reason* v25 p61-3
    D '93
  The potential impact of global warming on agriculture.
    il *Scientific American* v270 p39 Mr '94

SAMPLE WORKING BIBLIOGRAPHY CARD FOR *READERS' GUIDE*

White, C.A. "Climate Forecast: Unsettled." (ANADA and the WORLD May 1994: 10-12.

ARC Library

Magazine

The Periodical List or Cardex

Every library compiles an index of the periodicals it collects. Some libraries provide a computer printout list, others a printed list, and many use a Cardex file. These lists or files are kept in the vicinity of the *Readers' Guide to Periodical Literature*. After filling out a working bibliography card for a magazine (or any periodical you hope to locate), check the periodical index to see if the library has the particular issue you need. The periodical index will also tell you whether the periodical you want is in the stacks, on microfilm, or on microfiche.

Most libraries also carry the periodical lists for other libraries in the region. You may, for example, discover periodical lists for the community colleges, the state colleges and universities, the city and county libraries in the area and, sometimes, for all the libraries belonging to a regional association. Then, provided you have the time and transportation, you can go to another library to obtain the needed periodicals. Be sure to note the location of the periodical on your working bibliography card. Also ask for the *Union List of Serials in Libraries of the United States and Canada*, which lists periodicals from 1963 to date.

The New York Times Index

Another good place to look for potential sources is the *New York Times Index*. This index is similar to the *Readers' Guide to Periodical Literature* except that it only lists *New York Times* articles, and these articles are summarized. These summaries will help you determine whether or not articles are worth reading. Keep in mind that any entry may refer only to part of an article, the portion relating to the subtitle under which the entry is listed. As is the case with the *Readers' Guide,* you may have to use some ingenuity to think of the topic heading that will work best. Each entry begins with a summary and ends with a date, page, and column reference. Directions for interpreting the index are found at the beginning of each volume.

Use a separate working bibliography card for each promising *New York Times Index* entry. Some of the information you will need will not be listed in the index citation, so you will need to find it later when you read the article and take notes on it.

> "Seasonal Hole in Ozone."
> New York Times 8 Oct. 1994:
> I 7.

Working Bibliography Card for *New York Times Index*

The *New York Times* provides excellent source material for your research paper, but check with your librarian before using the index to be certain your library has facilities that will enable you to access the articles you need. Because the *Times* is so large, most libraries purchase the back issues on spools of microfilm and store them in file cabinet drawers. Many libraries, unfortunately, no longer have the machines you will need to read the spools of microfilm. Since articles in the *Times* are among the best written and the coverage the most complete, however, you should use them whenever you write a research paper if you can.

> Notice that part of the information in the sample card above is missing: author? title of article? edition (e.g., natl. ed.)? Any missing information should be added when you actually read the article.

Card Catalog

As you read earlier in this chapter, on page 158, the card catalog has changed from drawers filled with 3-by-5-inch cards to online computer programs in many libraries. Not all libraries have yet been able to convert to the electronic catalogs, however, so you can expect some libraries to still have the card catalog in drawers. Be flexible; both will serve you equally well.

1. **Author Card**—These cards are alphabetized according to the author, or the name of the first author if a book has more than one author. Names beginning M' and Mc are alphabetically filed as if they were spelled *Mac*. Thus, *McFarland* would be considered *MacFarland*, *M'Coy* as *MacCoy*.

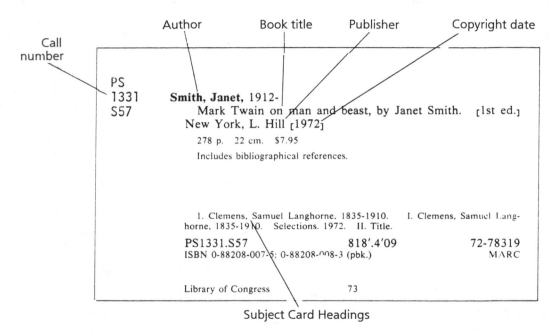

2. **Title Card**—For each book filed in alphabetical order, there is a card headed by the title of the book. Although the titles are in alphabetical order, some oddities about the alphabetizing should be known. Noun determiners at the beginning of titles, such as *A, An, The,* and *Les* (French) are ignored. Thus, the book *The Hidden Persuaders* would be filed under *H* for *Hidden*, and the book *Les Miserables* would be found under *M*. Furthermore, abbreviations at the beginning of titles are treated as if they were spelled out. Thus, *Mr.* would be considered *Mister* and *St.* would be considered *Saint*. And titles containing numbers are filed as if the numbers were spelled out. George Orwell's *1984*, for example, is listed under *N*, as if it were spelled *Nineteen Eighty-Four*.

Author · Book title · Publisher · Copyright date

Call number

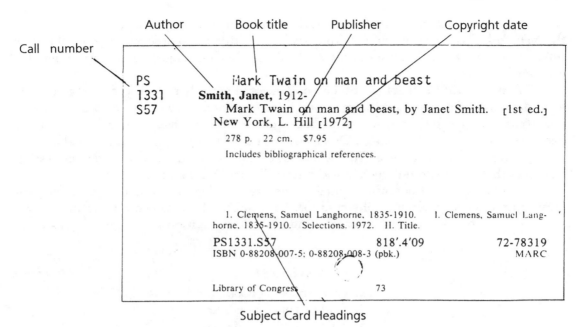

PS
1331
S57

Mark Twain on man and beast

Smith, Janet, 1912-
    Mark Twain on man and beast, by Janet Smith.   [1st ed.]
New York, L. Hill [1972]

278 p.   22 cm. $7.95

Includes bibliographical references.

    1. Clemens, Samuel Langhorne. 1835-1910.   I. Clemens, Samuel Lang-
horne, 1835-1910.   Selections. 1972.   II. Title.

PS1331.S57   818'.4'09   72-78319
ISBN 0-88208-007-5; 0-88208-008-3 (pbk.)   MARC

Library of Congress   73

Subject Card Headings

3. **Subject Card**—Books may also be located by referring to the subject cards in the card catalog. Suppose, for instance, you are writing a research paper on sexual discrimination against women. By looking under the general subject heading "Women," you would find relevant titles, for example Margaret Mead's *Male and Female: A Study of the Sexes in a Changing World* and Susan Faludi's *Backlash.* Subject headings for some historical subjects are filed chronologically. For example, under "World War" the books dealing with World War One are listed before those about World War Two.

Author · Subject · Publisher · Copyright date

Call number

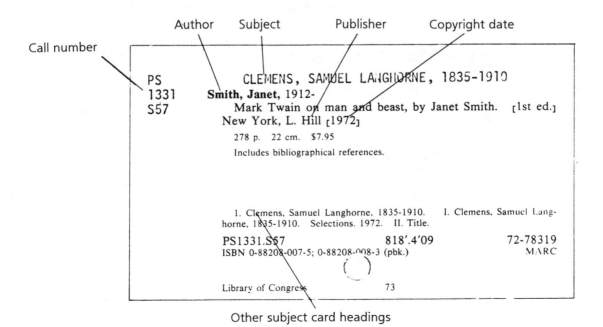

PS
1331
S57

CLEMENS, SAMUEL LANGHORNE, 1835-1910

Smith, Janet, 1912-
    Mark Twain on man and beast, by Janet Smith.   [1st ed.]
New York, L. Hill [1972]

278 p.   22 cm. $7.95

Includes bibliographical references.

    1. Clemens, Samuel Langhorne, 1835-1910.   I. Clemens, Samuel Lang-
horne, 1835-1910.   Selections. 1972.   II. Title.

PS1331.S57   818'.4'09   72-78319
ISBN 0-88208-007-5; 0-88208-008-3 (pbk.)   MARC

Library of Congress   73

Other subject card headings

If you are searching for useful books, the same advice given for the *Readers' Guide* and the *New York Times Index* holds true. You may have to think of synonyms for your subject or subcategories that may be listed in the card catalog. Several subject cards may be filed for each book.

Often you will be unable to find a book devoted entirely to your topic. Again, be a good detective. You may find information buried in a book that relates only generally to your topic. For example, there are whole books about vitamins, but each book on nutrition has at least a chapter on vitamins. Or suppose you are writing a paper on political corruption. Searching through some American history books might lead to some interesting examples that you could use, such as the famous Teapot Dome scandal.

After you locate a potential source in the card catalog or online computer file, you must write a working bibliography card for that source. The information you include on your card will be the same whether you find the information on printed catalog cards or online.

ALWAYS LIST
1. Call number of book
2. Author's or authors' names
3. Title and subtitle of book
4. Place of publication
5. Publisher's name
6. Copyright date
7. Library (if you are working in several libraries)

LIST IF GIVEN
8. Edition (e.g., 4th ed.)
9. Volume number
10. Reprint information (e.g., 1907; rpt. 1951)

SAMPLE WORKING BIBLIOGRAPHY CARD FOR CARD CATALOG

> Kraljic, Matthew A. *The Greenhouse Effect.*
> New York: Wilson, 1992.
>
> QC 912.3
> G 69
> 1992
> c. 1

From a practical standpoint, whether a library uses the Library of Congress system or Dewey Decimal system of filing books matters little. What matters is that you write down the call number.

> **Note:** For locating essays in books, the *Essay and General Literature Index* may be more helpful than the card catalog.

Other Periodical Indexes

Consulting encyclopedias, the *Readers' Guide to Periodical Literature*, the *New York Times Index*, and the card catalog should be routine—first stops in your library rounds as you compile your working bibliography for any library research paper. But most libraries contain a number of other useful periodical indexes, too. They index professional journals and other publications containing articles of interest to experts in the various subject areas represented. These articles are valuable sources of information for your library research paper. A few are listed below:

SOME PROFESSIONAL PERIODICAL INDEXES

Applied Science and Technology Index
Art Index
Bibliographic Index
Biography Index
Biological and Agricultural Index
Book Review Digest
Bulletin of the Public Affairs Information Service
Business Periodicals Index
Congressional Quarterly Index
Education Index
Humanities Index (formerly *Social Science and Humanities Index*)
Index—Annals of American Academy of Political Science
International Index
[London] Times Index
Psychological Abstracts
Social Sciences Index (formerly *Social Science and Humanities Index*)
Vital Speeches Index

Remember—to make sure the library has the periodical you want, check in the periodical index or the Cardex file listing all periodicals available in the particular library you are using.

The format for working bibliography entries for these professional publications differs slightly from that used for the general periodicals listed in the *Readers' Guide*. After the journal title the volume and issue numbers are listed; instead of the complete date of issue, only the year is listed in parentheses unless the complete date is needed to prevent confusion. Study the two sample cards that follow.

SAMPLE WORKING BIBLIOGRAPHY CARDS FOR PROFESSIONAL JOURNALS

Kerr, R.A. "Iron Fertilization:
a tonic, but no cure for the
greenhouse." *Science*
263(1994): 1089-90.

Central Lib.

Pages Numbered Continuously through Year

Miner, Thomas. "You Never Hear
the One that Hits You."
The Forum (1994): 10-11.

APC - TRC

Pages Numbered Separately in Each Issue

Pamphlet Files

Investigate the pamphlet files (sometimes called the vertical files). These are the filing cabinets filled with pamphlets, news clippings, bulletins, and a variety of other types of materials on frequently researched subjects. These files are a very good source of information about important contemporary problems.

Again, the trick is to think of the different categories under which your topic may be listed (consult the pamphlet file index if one is available). Be sure to note on your working bibliography card the exact location of the potential source. In case your library does not have a copy of a pamphlet that you must have, consult the *Vertical File Index to Selected Pamphlet Material*. You will have to order any material from this index at your own expense. Brief descriptions of the materials, prices, and ordering addresses are included in this index.

Pamphlet materials are often difficult to list in standard working bibliography format. In many cases there is no one right way to list an entry. Some of the materials will not have the proper identifying information on them, for example, dates and page numbers that will be needed later in your Works Cited. On your working bibliography cards, use **N.p.** to indicate that no place of publication is given, **n.p.** to show that the publisher is not listed, **n.d.** to indicate that the date is missing, and **N.pag.** to show that the page number is missing. Sample cards for local newspaper articles and pamphlets are shown below. If you are unable to decide how to list a pamphlet or some other material from the pamphlet file, ask your instructor for assistance.

SAMPLE WORKING BIBLIOGRAPHY CARDS FROM THE PAMPHLET FILE

> Petit, Charles. "Satellite Records Rising Sea Levels." *San Francisco Chronicle* 8 Dec. 1994: n. pag.

Newspaper Article

```
Lilley, John and Calvin Webb.
Climate Warming? Exploring
the Answers. Alberta, Canada:
Environment Council of Alberta,
1990.
```

Pamphlet

Other Sources

All libraries contain many valuable reference materials that have not been mentioned in this lesson. Books, periodicals, indexes, encyclopedias, almanacs, dictionaries, catalogs, bibliographies, theses, dissertations, recordings, tapes, microfilms, films, computer software, maps, atlases, electronic information retrieval services, and other references may be needed at one time or another. Your job is to be resourceful enough to locate and use them. The most important source of information when you are confused is the librarian. Do not hesitate to ask the librarian for help.

Many reference materials are available other than encyclopedias and pamphlets. If, for instance, you need statistics for your paper, you can consult one of the **almanacs** or one of the statistical publications, such as the *Statistical Abstract of the United States*. **Recorded materials** should not be overlooked; your library may have a collection of recordings of campus speakers and others. Look for **special book collections**—art, history, literature, education, and so on. If you are attending a large school, each department or separate college may have its own library in addition to the main campus library.

Materials for your paper may be obtained from **public and private agencies** in the community. Some libraries provide a *Guide to Community and Government Services*. You may want to interview people who are knowledgeable about your research topic.

Whenever you discover one of these sources, fill out a working bibliography card. For the proper entry format to use, for example, for a recording, a television program, or an interview, consult Appendix A.

EXERCISE 4.5

Compile your working bibliography (approximately thirty 3-by-5-inch index cards from at least five different kinds of sources). Consult with your instructor or librarian whenever problems arise. When your working bibliography is finished, have it checked by your instructor.

LESSON FOUR: *Taking Notes*

Why Take Notes?

Often students admit that they do not bother to take notes systematically when engaged in a library research project. Reasoning that they are too busy or that they do not need good notes because they are writing a short paper, many students will jot down notes haphazardly on looseleaf paper, photocopying only references that seem especially important. Worse yet, many simply surround themselves with all of their materials and begin writing, extracting a quote from one source, summarizing a paragraph from another, and so on, depending mainly on adrenalin and quick thinking to see them through their projects.

But those students who do develop the habit of using note cards experience less difficulty writing their papers. They are able to complete short research papers rapidly, and they find themselves well prepared for the demands of difficult, extended research projects assigned in upper division and graduate courses. Bad habits are hard to break, and the habit of not taking careful notes is one of the hardest to break. Until you are familiar with the pitfalls of gathering information in the library, use the traditional note-taking system explained in this lesson.

Some students have begun taking notes on computers. They photocopy the articles that appear useful to them, check out books that are available, sit in front of a computer, and begin keying in the quotes, paraphrases, or summaries that they think they will need when they begin writing their papers. They carefully identify the author and page number of each source as they work. These students prefer using their computers to take notes, insisting that they can key in hundreds of words in the same time it would take them to write out eighty or one hundred. The disadvantage is that notes stored on a computer's hard drive or on a diskette are of limited usefulness when writing the paper. The notes taken on a computer must be organized and printed out, or printed, cut into individualized slips, and sorted to be useful in outlining and writing your paper.

Keep Your Research Guide Handy

When you are ready to begin taking notes, use your research proposal to develop a research guide. On a 4-by-6-inch (or 5-by-8-inch) index card, write your tentative thesis, research questions, or working outline. You may want to combine two types, for example, a tentative thesis and a working outline. Since you should avoid compulsively taking notes on everything you read, you can use the research guide to help you make decisions about when to take notes.

—The research guide helps you make sure you find all of the information you need.

—The research guide saves you time by allowing you to confine your notetaking to the information you will actually need to write your paper.

—It makes arranging your note cards in the order you will use them easier.

You can key each note card to your research card with a designation in the upper-right corner (e.g., *PRO* or *CON*, 3 for research question three, or *IV, C.* from your working outline). Alter your research guide as the need arises, but keep the designations on your note cards updated. Note the following examples:

TENTATIVE THESIS

```
      Tentative Thesis: A growing body of evidence
    shows that UFOs have been reconnoitering Earth.
```

RESEARCH QUESTIONS

Acid Rain

1. What is acid rain?

2. Where does it come from?

3. What are the environmental effects?

4. Which areas are having problems?

5. What are the U. S. Regional disputes about?

6. Why is Canada involved in the controversy?

7. What is being done to stop acid rain?

8. What steps need to be taken in the future?

9. What is my overall conclusion (potential thesis)?

WORKING OUTLINE

ACID RAIN--U.S. FORESTS

I. Primary Sources
   A. Factories
   B. Power Plants
   C. Automobiles
   D. Other
II. Effects on Forests
   A. Areas Affected
   B. Atmospheric Conditions
   C. Trees
   D. Soil
   E. Streams and Lakes
III. Placing the Blame
   A. Disagreement among Experts
   B. Dependence on Fossil Fuels
   C. Government and Private Industry
   D. International Ramifications
   E. Huge Costs

EXERCISE 4.6

Develop your research guide (tentative thesis, research questions, or working outline) and copy it on a 4-by-6-inch (or 5-by-8-inch) note card. You may want to have your research guide checked.

Note Card Headings

If you are taking notes from a book, write the following information at the top of the first note card used for that book: (1) the author's or authors' complete names and (2) the book's title.

**SAMPLE NOTE CARD HEADING
FOR FIRST REFERENCE—BOOK**

PROULX, E. ANNIE. THE SHIPPING NEWS.

If you need more than one note card for a book, abbreviate the heading on subsequent cards. Repeat the author's or authors' last names and the title of the book—in case you later take notes from another book by the same author(s).

**SAMPLE NOTE CARD HEADING
FOR SUBSEQUENT CARD—BOOK**

PROULX. SHIPPING NEWS.

If you are taking notes from a periodical, for example, a magazine, write the following information at the top of the first note card you use for that particular source: (1) the author's or authors' complete names and (2) the article title and subtitle. If no author is given for an article, write just the article title and subtitle.

SAMPLE NOTE CARD HEADING FOR FIRST REFERENCE—PERIODICAL

On any additional note cards for the same article, abbreviate the original heading, taking care not to abbreviate so completely that confusion could arise if you later took notes from another article by the same author or another article with a similar title.

Check Your Working Bibliography Cards

As soon as you actually have a source in your hands, recheck to make certain that your working bibliography card for the source contains all of the information you will need later when you write your Works Cited. Your working bibliography cards must be legible, accurate, and complete. You may, for example, have to replace authors' intitials with full names, which may be listed in the actual magazine article but not on your original working bibliography entry. Or you may discover that a book is a reprint of an older edition and you need to add the reprint information. Furthermore, you may not have been able to list the exact page numbers of an article when you first wrote the bibliography card.

Limit Yourself to One Point per Card

As you take notes, limit yourself to one point per card so that the cards can easily be put into the order they will be used for the paper. While you read and take notes, refer to your research guide (thesis, questions, or outline) frequently. If you find that the source you are reading includes information that can be used in a section of your paper, write a note card and label it in the upper-right corner with the appropriate outline or research question number.

Write on One Side of the Note Card

Experienced researchers agree that it is better to write on just one side of each note card. This procedure makes it easier to study the note cards later and eliminates the problem of forgetting to look on the back of a card and missing important information. Writing on one side does create a minor problem—the second card and any subsequent cards must be identified and numbered so that they will be kept with the front card when the cards are rearranged. This problem is solved by stapling the cards in sets.

SUMMARIZING, PARAPHRASING, QUOTING

Summary Cards

In your notes you may summarize, paraphrase, or quote from your sources. When you summarize, condense what you are summarizing, stating the essential ideas in your own words. You may include specifics—statistics, details, and examples—but the basic idea is to detail briefly what the author has said. Summaries are always shorter than the original passage.

SAMPLE NOTE CARD—SUMMARY

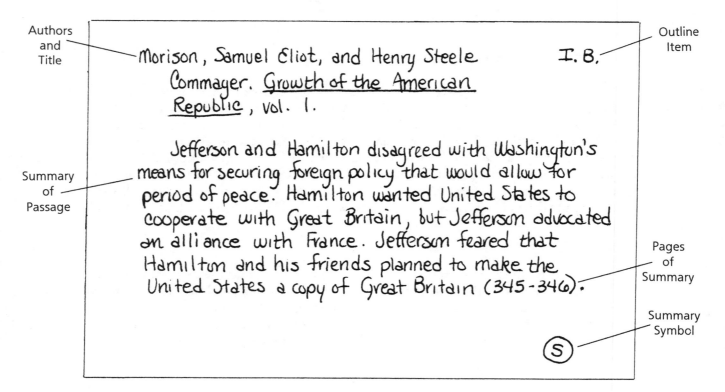

Authors and Title

Outline Item

Summary of Passage

Morison, Samuel Eliot, and Henry Steele Commager. Growth of the American Republic, vol. 1.

I. B.

Jefferson and Hamilton disagreed with Washington's means for securing foreign policy that would allow for period of peace. Hamilton wanted United States to cooperate with Great Britain, but Jefferson advocated an alliance with France. Jefferson feared that Hamilton and his friends planned to make the United States a copy of Great Britain (345-346).

Pages of Summary

Summary Symbol

Ⓢ

The sample note card succinctly summarizes six paragraphs from Morison and Commager's history of early America. Note that the exact page numbers are stated in parentheses at the end of the summary. This information is necessary for preparing the parenthetical references in your paper. Also note the ⑤ in the lower-right corner of the note card. This symbol will remind you that the note is a summary and that it will require a lead-in when integrated in the text of the research paper. The "I.B." in the upper-right corner keys the note card to the your working outline.

Paraphrase Cards

When paraphrasing, you must rewrite the original passage in your own words. More is required than just changing the order of the words a bit and inserting several synonyms. If you decide to keep some of the key words or phrases, be sure to enclose them in quotation marks. Paraphrases are frequently longer than the original passage. Note how the following statement is handled on the paraphrase card.

"Epcot designers have focused on a series of themes that are intended, through example, to inspire people to apply modern technology responsibly to develop solutions to human kind's problems."

SAMPLE NOTE CARD—PARAPHRASE

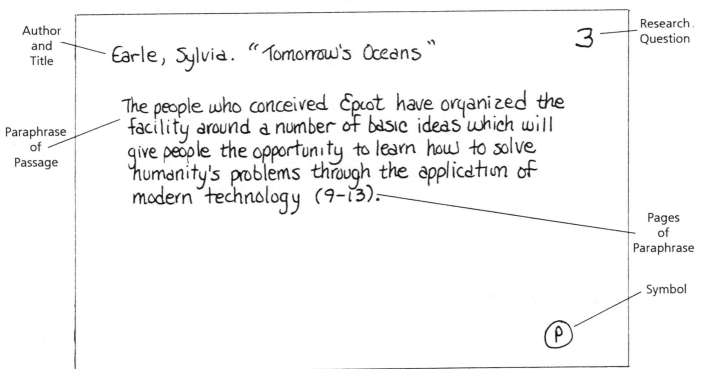

Note again that the exact page numbers of the reference are cited in the parentheses after the paraphrase. This information is needed for the parenthetical references in your paper. The symbol (P) in the lower-right corner of the card is to remind you that the material is paraphrased and will need a lead-in when used in the paper. The "3" in the upper-right corner keys the card to one of your research questions.

Quotation Cards

When you use quoted material, copy the passage exactly as it is written—word for word. Note the following example:

SAMPLE NOTE CARD—QUOTE

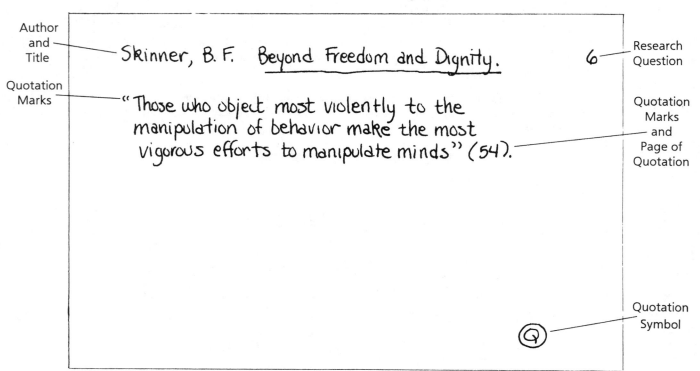

Author and Title

Quotation Marks

Skinner, B. F.   Beyond Freedom and Dignity.   6

" Those who object most violently to the manipulation of behavior make the most vigorous efforts to manipulate minds" (54).

Ⓠ

Research Question

Quotation Marks and Page of Quotation

Quotation Symbol

Quotation marks placed at the beginning and end of the quoted material and the (Q) in the lower-right hand corner of the note card remind the writer to write a lead-in for the passage, to use quotation marks, and to include a parenthetical reference. Forgetting to use quotation marks around a quoted passage creates the appearance that you have plagiarized the material—even if you have documented the passage. Recheck to make certain that the quotation marks and the (Q) appear on your note card of the quoted passage.

Idea Cards

As you take notes, ideas will occur that you want to remember for your paper. Possibly you will react to something you have read, or you will see a connection between what several sources have to say. Or you may have an idea for changing the organization of your paper, or perhaps you will realize suddenly what your final thesis should be. You will not want to lose these thoughts, so record them on **idea cards**. Each time such an idea occurs, simply fill out a notecard and label it appropriately with a short reminder. Place an ⓘ in the lower right-hand corner of the card.

SAMPLE IDEA CARD

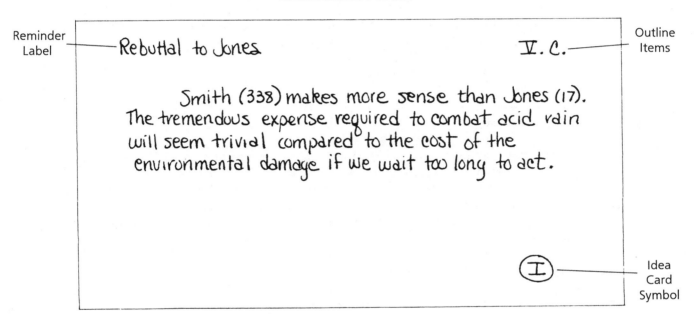

Reminder Label —— Rebuttal to Jones   V. C. —— Outline Items

Smith (338) makes more sense than Jones (17). The tremendous expense required to combat acid rain will seem trivial compared to the cost of the environmental damage if we wait too long to act.

Ⓘ —— Idea Card Symbol

Photocopies

By photocopying library materials, you can spend less time in the library, but later you must take notes from the photocopies. When you write your paper, you should be working from your note cards, not directly from your photocopies. Make sure that the photocopied material is accurately identified, and keep it all together in a folder.

A Warning about Plagiarism

If you intentionally steal another person's thoughts, ideas, words, or data and use them as your own, you are plagiarizing. Plagiarism is absolutely not condoned, and being caught plagiarizing may result in your failing a course, or worse. Anything **summarized, paraphrased,** or **quoted** must be properly acknowledged with a lead-in, quotation marks around a quote, properly used ellipsis marks, and accurate documentation. Study the following example of plagiarism.

Here are two sentences from an article by Wally Wyss, "Rotary Round-Up, Part 1," in *Motor Trend* magazine:

> For every booster, however, there's a detractor, among them [sic] environmentalists who won't settle for anything but complete obliteration of the internal combustion engine. . . . The announcements of "breakthroughs" will continue . . . in gas turbines, Stirling engines, steam hybrid/electrics, or—SHAZAM!— even atomic power.

Now read the last two sentences of a student's paper:

> For every booster, however, there is a detractor, among them environmentalists who won't settle for anything less than the complete obliteration of the internal combustion monster. The announcement of "breakthroughs" will continue . . . gas turbines, steam, hybrid/electronics, or even—SHAZAM—atomic-powered engines.

Be honest! Do your own work, and give credit where credit is due.

Accuracy Is Essential

Accurate note taking is your responsibility. Clear comprehension of what you are reading and clear communication of that meaning in your notes is a must. Be aware that it is highly unethical to change the meaning of original material to achieve a certain point of view when you summarize, paraphase, or quote. Also, you must not carelessly mix summary and quotation or paraphrasing and quotation. Anytime that you use the exact wording of the original passage, you must enclose the original wording in quotation marks.

EXERCISE 4.7

Complete all of the note cards you will need for your research paper. Remember to follow your research guide, and include a variety of different kinds of cards—summary, paraphrase, quotation, and idea cards. Have your note cards approved by your instructor.

LESSON FIVE: *Writing the Paper*

Now that you have finished your research notes, the task of completing your library research paper can be broken down into the following steps:

1. Title page or heading
2. Final outline
3. First draft of paper, including parenthetical documentation
4. Notes (if needed)
5. Works Cited
6. Final manuscript

Read the sample library research paper that begins on the next right-hand page. On left-hand facing pages accompanying the paper, you will find detailed advice explaining the steps listed above.

Study these explanations so you will know what is expected as you write your own paper. After you have studied the sample paper and the facing pages, complete the exercises at the end of the lesson. Then your library research paper will be completed.

Appearance of the Paper

The appearance of the final manuscript is especially important. Use a computer or type in black, making certain the typeface is clean before beginning. Your instructor may allow you to handwrite your paper if you do not type; however, you must write legibly. Use blue or black ink, skipping every other line, and write on one side of the paper only. Although either college-rule or wide-lined notebook paper is acceptable, never use ragged-edge spiral notebook paper. Also, never use paper that is undersized.

Unless errors are discovered at the last minute, there is no excuse for not retyping or rewriting pages that contain even minor errors. Correcting errors at the last minute instead of redoing an entire page or more, however, is preferable to submitting a research paper containing errors (so-called typos, or typing errors, are just as wrong as errors made by the paper's author). Emergency corrections can be made by neatly drawing a single line through the portion to be revised and printing (in ink) the correction directly above the crossed-out portion. Additions should be inserted above a caret mark ($\wedge$).

Corrections are obviously much more easily accomplished when you use a computer than when you use a typewriter or when you write out your paper. For just that reason, if you don't yet know how to use a computer, you should take a computer class soon so you can take advantage of the time and energy saving features of these electronic aids.

Binding the Final Paper

Most instructors want you to fasten the final manuscript together with a paperclip or a single staple (at a 45° angle) in the upper-left corner. Many instructors consider cardboard or plastic covers to be a nuisance. Do not include art work on the title page or fasten the paper with pins, fasteners, rings, rawhide, ribbon, or colored yarn.

> **NOTE:** Protect yourself in case your paper should be lost or not returned by making a photocopy of the final manuscript before you submit it for evaluation.

Title Page

Your instructor may require a title page. If the instructor provides no format to follow, set up the title page according to the following directions:

1. Center the title four inches from the top of the page. Use standard capitalization rules for titles (see page 194); do **not** place your title in quotation marks or underline it.

2. After the title, quadruple-space and center the word *by*.

3. Then quadruple-space and key in or type your name, centering it.

4. Center the course title and number two and one-half inches, approximately fifteen spaces, below your name.

5. Skip two spaces and center the meeting time for the course.

6. After double-spacing, key in the instructor's name. Use the appropriate title, for example, *Professor, Dr., Ms.,* or *Mr.*

7. The name of the school may be included (double-space after the instructor's name).

8. Last, after double-spacing, include the date of submission either with the month first and a comma after the day or with the day first and no comma (e.g., May 11, 1995 or 11 May 1995).

9. Do not place a page number on the title page.

Note: Before composing a title page, see "Heading" on page 194.

The Greenhouse Effect and the Erosion of Antarctica

by

Patrick B. Bell

English 1A

MWF 10

Professor Weaver

American River College

11 May 1995

Outline (Thesis and Topic Sentence)

Many instructors require an outline page listing the thesis and either the topic sentences for the paper or the topics and subtopics that are covered in the paper. A sample *thesis-topic sentence outline* is presented on the facing pages. If your instructor prefers that you use a *topic outline*, see pages 285-286.

Note: Before preparing an outline for your final copy, see "Heading," page 194.

1. In the upper-right corner, one-half inch from the top (approximately four spaces) and one inch from the right edge of the page, set a header if you are using a computer or type if you are using a typewriter. The header consists of your last name and the page number, the lower case Roman numeral **i.** Subsequent pages of the outline would be numbered **ii, iii, iv,** and so on. You must put your last name in front of the page number, leaving one space before the number.

2. Center the word **Outline** one inch (approximately six spaces) from the top of the page.

3. Then double-space and type or key in the title of your paper, centering it and capitalizing properly.

4. Quadruple-space after the title and type or key in your thesis. Precede your thesis sentence with the word **Thesis:** (including a colon and followed by a single space). If your thesis is more than a single line, use double-spacing.

5. Next, quadruple-space and write a topic-sentence outline: a consecutively numbered list of all the topic sentences that will appear in your paper. Be sure to list the first sentence of the introductory and concluding paragraphs. Remember to make changes in your outline if you make any revisions in the topic sentences as you write your paper. Double-space the entire outline.

Outline

The Greenhouse Effect and the Erosion of Antarctica

Thesis: Although controversy remains over the amount of warming that will take place and the effects of that warming, the prevailing conclusion of scientists is that serious erosion of West Antarctica will occur.

1.   Significant additions of carbon dioxide to the earth's atmosphere caused by increased fossil fuel consumption and forest denudation may produce a warming trend that will result in the melting of much of the western portion of Antarctica.

2.   In recent years observers have noted a slight wearing away at the edges of the West Antarctica ice sheet, a marine ice sheet flanked by two ice shelves attached to the ocean floor by a partially submerged chain of islands.

3.   Geologists Arthur N. and Alan H. Strahler point out that the amount of atmospheric carbon dioxide prior to 1860 stood at about 0.021%, or 210 ppm.

4.   Many scientists contend that the warming trend will not be all that bad.

5.   Most researchers in this field, however, disagree.

6.   The remote possibility exists, of course, that Idso and those who agree with him may have a point even though Idso's research procedure seems faulty.

7.   Dust particles come from two major sources: volcanic activity and industrial pollution.

8.   One possible explanation for the temperature rise in the Southern Hemisphere may be sunspot cycles.

9.   But as the warmer air reaches the South Pole, could the subsequent increased moisture both cause more snowfall and contribute to the melting of the West Antarctic ice sheet?

10.   What this could mean is that if, in fact, an increase of carbon dioxide does cause a general upturn in the earth's temperature, an increase in the snowpack of Antarctica is imminent.

11.   While attempting to determine the influence of increased atmospheric carbon dioxide on the earth's climate, researchers have taken into account other factors.

12.   Roger Revelle shares the belief of some climatologists that if the warming trend continues along predicted lines, eventually the West Antarctica ice sheet could disintegrate at a rate of as much as 20 kilometers a year (43).

13.   With the ice sheet's disintegration, the consequences for the rest of the world would be devastating.

14.   Researchers are currently at work on a new project to validate the work done by scientists over the past two decades.

15.   Therefore, on the basis of a review of the literature published thus far, it seems apparent that as atmospheric carbon dioxide increases so will the earth's temperature; as this phenomenon occurs, the West Antarctica ice sheet will gradually disintegrate.

Heading (No Title Page)

The *MLA Handbook for Writers of Research Papers* recommends that a heading be used rather than a title page. (With this format no outline page would be included either.) The format for the first page of a research paper with a heading is as follows:

1. **Header:** Beginning with page two, key in a header that will identify you as the author, in case your reader mixes up your pages with someone else's. In the upper-right corner, one-half inch (approximately four spaces) from the top of the page, place your name, leave a space, and then insert the page number. Never place any punctuation after the page number; do not place "page" in between your name and the page number, and don't underline the page number, enclose it in hyphens, or parentheses. Most computer software packages will help you create a header, automatically inserting your name and the appropriate page number on each page of your paper. This header should be located in the upper-right corner, one-half inch (approximately four spaces) from the top of the page; it should also be one inch from the right side of the paper. (The margin default on your computer may make it necessary to place this header one inch from the top of the page.) Be aware that the *MLA Handbook for Writers of Research Papers* suggests that you should also have a header at the top right of page one. Some instructors, however, prefer that you not put the header on page one, since the complete heading of your paper is at the top left of the page. Check with your instructor.

2. **Heading:** Begin your heading in the upper-left corner, one inch (approximately six spaces) from the top of the page and one inch from the left edge of the page (the normal margin). Double-space the entire heading—your name; then the course title, number, and meeting time; then your instructor's name; then the date it is to be submitted; and finally, in parentheses, the type of paper assigned. While indicating a paper's type is not required by the *MLA Handbook,* many instructors find this designation useful for identifying and evaluating a composition.

3. **Title:** After the heading, double-space and center the title. Use the standard conventions for capitalizing titles. Always capitalize the first and last words of the title and any word after a hyphen or colon. Capitalize the first letter of all words in the title except for articles (*a, an, the*), coordinating conjunctions (*and, nor, but, for, or, yet, so*), prepositions (e.g., *in, on, with, before, to*) and *to* in infinitives (e.g., *to Learn*). Do not capitalize the entire title, place it in quotation marks or underline it. However, any portion of the title that would be placed in quotation marks or underlined if it were in the paper (e.g., the title of a poem or book) would be an exception and should be punctuated appropriately.

If more than one line is needed for the title, use double-spacing. To separate a subtitle from the main title, place a colon after the main title, followed by a single space.

4. **Spacing:** Double-space before beginning the first line of the text, and double-space between each line of text. Use the same double spacing between paragraphs in your paper. To avoid errors and to make the keying in of your paper as convenient as possible if you are using a computer, set your machine on single-space until you have completed your essay and then double-space it when you print it out.

Patrick B. Bell

English 1A MWF 10

Professor Weaver

11 May 1995

(Library Research)

The Greenhouse Effect and the Erosion of Antarctica

Significant additions of carbon dioxide to the earth's atmosphere caused by increased fossil fuel consumption and forest denudation may produce a warming trend that will result in the melting of much of the western portion of Antarctica. The possible consequences are making many people nervous and are sparking heated debates on local, national, and international levels. Assuming that global warming is as serious as some scientists predict, something must be done because global warming will mean global disaster. The possibility of drastically reducing fossil fuel consumption and forest clearing, especially in the tropical regions, does not seem feasible at this time. As it stands now, each year approximately five tons of carbon dioxide are released into the atmosphere for every man, woman, and child in the United States (Katz B11). If a significant portion of Antarctica does in fact melt, it is possible that the sea level will be raised by as much as six meters. According to one researcher, a sea level rise of this magnitude would cause the submergence of coastal cities and island states:

> Among the long list of disaster sites: Bermuda would mostly disappear; Venice, Italy, with its system of dikes and lagoon passes, couldn't hold back the flooding; sewage plants and pipes along New York City's shoreline would be overwhelmed; vast areas of Southeast Asia would become submerged. (David 16)

Although controversy remains over the amount of warming that will take place and the effects of that warming, the prevailing conclusion of scientists is that serious erosion of West Antarctica will occur.

Margins and Spacing

All margins—top, bottom, and both sides—should be as close to one inch as possible. Your instructor will not expect you to adhere to this rule without exception, however, because some computer programs may not allow you to change the margin settings. Therefore, if they are a little too wide or narrow, you might ignore the margins, but if they are noticeably different, discuss the problem with your instructor. The heading on the first page, subsequent pages of the paper, the Notes, and the Works Cited all begin one inch from the top of the page. If you prepare your paper using a computer, use a ragged right margin; do not use a justified right margin. Justified right margins are fine in magazine articles, but they make student papers difficult to read. The computer will automatically hyphenate words as it wraps from one line to the next; however, you must not hyphenate at the end of a line—even if the computer does it automatically. If you use a typewriter for your paper, remember you are responsible for doing what the computer does automatically. That is, you are responsible for correct spacing, correct hyphenation of words, and correct margins.

Double-space all lines in the paper, including long quotations. Never leave additional space between paragraphs as is customary in some business writing. Indent each new paragraph five spaces.

Citations

When you borrow ideas or quotes from other sources, you must tell your reader where you found that information. The notes you place in the text of your paper that show the origin of those ideas or quotes are called citations. Refer to the text of Patrick Bell's paper on the facing page.

In recent years observers have noted a slight wearing away at the edges of the West Antarctica ice sheet, a marine ice sheet flanked by two ice shelves attached to the ocean floor by a partially submerged chain of islands. Its counterpart, East Antarctica, is a true continent of bedrock sitting above sea level and covered by a 2,000-meter layer of ice. The British Antarctic Survey has noted that the retreat corresponds roughly with a rise in global temperature of almost two degrees Celsius since the turn of the century (Begley, Dallas, and Givens 72). This rise in temperature has been linked to a widely known increase in the atmospheric carbon dioxide of about 50 parts per million (ppm) since the late nineteenth century. Atmospheric carbon dioxide constitutes the amount that has not been absorbed by the oceans, which act as sort of a sponge for almost all carbon dioxide emitted. Richard A. Kerr notes that microscopic plants and animals in the oceans use the carbon dioxide to frame their skeletons and to build their tissues ("Carbon Dioxide" 1053). Carbon dioxide is also absorbed by soils and fauna, but not nearly to the degree it is absorbed by oceans. Roger Revelle estimates that about 42 trillion tons of carbon dioxide resides in the oceans, atmosphere, and soil, and that most of it is in the oceans. Currently, the atmospheric carbon dioxide content stands at about 700 billion tons (35). Unfortunately, the oceans absorb carbon dioxide at a relatively slower rate.[1] Because of the inability of the oceans to absorb increasing amounts of carbon dioxide quickly, researchers worry that the earth's temperature will rise in accordance with a condition known as the greenhouse effect. According to Edward S. Ayensu:

> As with a glass-walled terrarium, literally all of the planet's energy comes from the sun. As this short-wave radiation—raw sunshine—heads earthward, it passes through the ozone layer which absorbs most of the ultraviolet rays. Atmospheric water vapor absorbs the infrared rays, and the sun's energy is transformed into long-wave energy, or heat, and eventually radiated back into space. Since carbon dioxide at the earth's

What Must Be Documented?

Whenever you include information in your paper from another source, you must give credit to that source in a reference in the text of your paper and in the Works Cited at the end of the paper. Information that is general knowledge may not need to be documented. Note, however, that instructors' opinions differ as to what is "general knowledge." So check with your instructor in case you are in doubt.

DOCUMENT THE FOLLOWING

1. All quoted material
2. All paraphrased sentences
3. Most summarized information

Lead-Ins

Integrate the researched information from your cards smoothly and concisely. Because anyone reading your paper should be able to tell where a quotation, paraphrase, or summary begins, you should use lead-ins to signal that you are including borrowed material.

Examples

Researchers found that
According to Richard D. Smith,
Bertrand Russell argues that
In *Civilization and Its Discontents*, Sigmund Freud writes,
Brenner found the opposite to be true:
In an interview with Doris Jones, historian Kenneth Ramirez learned that
A 1984 study conducted by University of Iowa psychologists showed that
Roueche explains further that
Morris, Suber, and Bijou note that
A few critics of the proposal (e.g., Margery Gumper and Wilson Worley) have disputed
    the figures.
Computers and word processors, writes Alan Toffler, will revolutionize the office (202-09).

surface absorbs long-wave radiation, the more carbon dioxide in the air

the more heat the planetary atmosphere can retain and the warmer our

living space can become. This phenomenon is popularly known as the

"greenhouse effect." (134)

Geologists Arthur N. and Alan H. Strahler point out that the amount of

atmospheric carbon dioxide prior to 1860 stood at about 0.021%, or 210 ppm. Since

then it has risen to approximately 0.035%, or 350 ppm. If current fossil fuel

consumption and forest clearing continue to rise at the present rate, that amount would

reach about 0.055%, or 550 ppm, by the year 2000, and increase of about 25% since

1860 (78-79). Furthermore, Paul R. Ryan foresees atmospheric carbon dioxide passing

the 600 ppm level by the end of the next century (63). Coupled with that, Roger Revelle

adds that, "If carbon dioxide is indeed altering climate, an unmistakable warming trend

should appear in the 1990s," as a result of the increased atmospheric carbon dioxide

(38). Revelle (39) concludes that this trend would not reverse itself for hundreds of

years (see Figure 1).

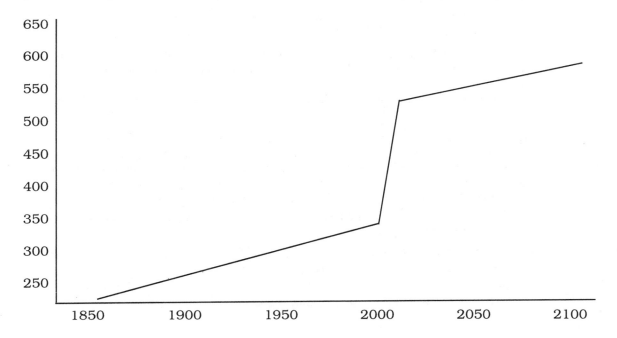

Fig. 1. Projected Increase in Atmospheric Carbon Dioxide.

Parenthetical References

At the end of any quotation, paraphrase, or summary, use a parenthetical reference to indicate the exact source of the material. In the parentheses include any part of the reference that has not been made in the lead-in that introduces the researched material (see "Lead-Ins"). Since readers will learn the complete information needed to locate one of your sources by turning to your Works Cited, you need only to cite the author(s) and page number(s) of the reference or, if no author is given, a shortened title of the article or book and the page number(s). Refer only to the exact page number(s) of the reference.

Examples

As Andrew Sinclair points out, "It was one of the first cases in the American market of scandal being used to push the sales of a book" (102).

The above example shows a quotation with a lead-in and page number separated.

Jack London's separation from his first wife, Bess, became a great help to him in an unexpected way. "It was one of the first cases in the American market of scandal being used to push the sales of a book" (Sinclair 102).

In the example above, the author's name and page number are placed together in the parentheses.

According to Claudia Caruna, years of photographic experience and expensive equipment are not required to take good photographs (69-71).

In the above example, several pages are summarized.

Smith doubts that nuclear missiles could destroy a large incoming meteorite in time to spare the earth from catastrophic damage (Henick 328).

Note that in the above example the article was written by Henick who reports what Smith thought.

Sociologist John B. Purnell believes that children who grow up in suburban neighborhoods mature more slowly than children raised in urban and rural environments (78-80, 93-95).

The above summary came from the pages listed; the Works Cited entry would read 78-80+.

However, it is also possible that the earth will encounter an ice age. The controlling factors are the following: continental drift into warmer or cooler latitudes as suggested by Miller and Thompson (210); solar radiation, the movement of solar systems through interstellar dust as proposed by Fodor (111); or mountain building processes that lift land masses to higher elevations that are cooler, as explained by Strahler (350).

By using multiple references a great deal of information can be condensed in a short space as shown in the above example.

Recent studies on the effect of marijuana on driving skill (Brooks 9; Conrad, Elmore, and Stodetz 123; Klonoff 317) have linked overestimation of the passage of time to the deterioration of driving ability.

Each of the sources above is separated with a semicolon.

Many scientists contend that the warming trend will not be all that bad. They assert that an increase in atmospheric carbon dioxide will be beneficial to plant life. Sylvan Wittwer, director of the Michigan State University agricultural station, points out that increased amounts of carbon dioxide will stimulate plant growth and enhance leaf, root, and flower growth and also fruit yield (Revelle 40). The most recent research by Dan Feldstein shows that if global warming does occur as predicted, the growing seasons in Texas would be extended, which "could increase the growth rate of barley, wheat, cotton, rice and soybeans by up to 40 percent" (D5). Sherwood Idso, a research physicist at the United States Conservation Laboratory in Phoenix, Arizona, not only agrees but also claims that current models for predicting the effects of increased atmospheric carbon dioxide are erroneous. Idso's 12-year study of the greenhouse effect revealed that doubling atmospheric carbon dioxide would not only be beneficial to plant life, but would cause a global temperature increase of about only 0.26 degrees Celsius, far less than the natural variation in climate of approximately two degrees Celsius (Meredith 64).

Most researchers in this field, however, disagree. They believe that a doubling of atmospheric carbon dioxide would raise the global temperature by about three degrees Celsius. Richard Kerr reports that a National Research Council panel sided with the majority and stated that Idso's conclusions were based on imprecise models. Previous models were designed to mirror the physical world; Idso produced models based on the effects of temperature in natural changes of radiation ("CO_2" 620). It is well known among climatologists that temperature changes produced by an increase in atmospheric carbon dioxide have not been observed yet.[2] Idso's models were obtained by taking two substitutes—dust particles and water vapor—and determining a connection between them and changes in temperature. A glaring drawback with one of those substitutes, dust particles, is that their presence in the atmosphere tends to cause cooling trends. Moreover, Idso used specific geographical locations, Phoenix and the Pacific Coast in the

Researchers have found that people between the ages of twenty and fifty are most likely to become victims of rheumatoid arthritis ("How to Cope" 16).

No author is listed in <u>Consumers Research</u> magazine, so a shortened version of the article title has been used. The complete title for the article is "How to Cope with Arthritis."

Alan Toffler observes that the meaning of punctuality is changing. As the country moves out of the industrial age and into the computer age, strict punctuality is giving way to "situational punctuality" (<u>Third Wave</u> 270-71).

If more than one work by an author is listed in the Works Cited, refer to the title, as in the example of the book cited above.

Quoted Passage Enclosed in Quotation Marks

When you copy the exact words someone has spoken or written, you are quoting, and you must copy the passage precisely as it appears in your source. You must use the same spelling, inside punctuation, and capitalization as in the original, even if it contains errors.

When you are quoting fewer than five lines, connect the quoted portion to its lead-in with quotation marks (" "). Capitalize the first word of the quoted passage if it starts a complete sentence, and continue the double-spacing you are using for the rest of the text. Signal the end of the quoted passage with the proper punctuation—commas and periods are placed inside quotation marks. However, if the quotation marks are followed by a parenthetical reference, the period follows the parentheses, as in the examples above.

[Sic] or (Sic)

Errors within quotations may be designated by the word *sic* in square brackets or parentheses, i.e., [*sic*]. Any error found in quoted material will be considered yours unless you designate it. Never correct an error in a quotation, however. Instead use the [*sic*], placing it immediately after the error.

Brackets

Brackets [ ] are used to insert additional information in quoted material or missing information in Works Cited entries.

Virgule

When quoting poetry or song lyrics in your text, use virgule marks (/) to indicate where one line ends and another starts.

United States, to determine the effects of what is really a global phenomenon (Kerr, "CO_2" 620). Thus, to skeptics, Idso's modeling procedures seem suspect.

The remote possibility exists, of course, that Idso and those who agree with him may have a point even though Idso's research procedure seems faulty. The earth may not, in fact, experience a general warming trend. Other factors are involved in the overall climate picture, and some of them may very well cancel out the effects of an overabundance of carbon dioxide in the atmosphere. In order to gain a more complete picture concerning any rise in atmospheric carbon dioxide and the possibility of a subsequent melting of West Antarctica, other variables must be examined. Dust particles, both human-made and volcano-induced, have to be considered as well as the relationship between climate and solar flares.

Dust particles come from two major sources: volcanic activity and industrial pollution. The Strahlers explain that dust particles introduced into the upper atmosphere deflect shortwave radiation back to space before it can reach the earth and be converted into longwave radiation. Consequently, less heat is retained (78). The effect of dust particles on the climate can be seen by studying the relationship between fuel consumption, forest denudation,[3] and the global temperature increase that took place between 1880 and 1940, in which the average temperature increased by about 0.6 degrees Celsius. This increase corresponds with that expected, but from the 1940s to the present the earth has experienced a general cooling trend even though the rate of fuel consumption and forest cutting has been increasing. Researchers have also discovered the appearance of an opposite pattern in the Southern Hemisphere from latitude sixty degrees south to the South Pole. From about 1960 this area has experienced a warming trend of approximately 0.6 degrees Celsius. The Strahlers suggest that the cooling trend is restricted to the Northern Hemisphere and go on to speculate that the cooling trend is related to an increase of dust particles in the atmosphere caused by a significant amount of volcanic activity in northern latitudes,

Blocked Quotations

For long quotations, those of more than four lines, a special blocked technique is used. Whereas shorter quotations are integrated by using the normal left and right margins of the paper, a blocked quotation is indented ten spaces from the left margin and then carried to the normal one-inch right margin.

When blocking a single paragraph or a portion of a paragraph, do not indent the first line more than ten spaces. If, however, two or more complete paragraphs are quoted, indent the first line of each paragraph three extra spaces (thirteen spaces from the left margin). Double-space the blocked portion like the rest of the paper, and double-space both before and after the quotation. The lead-in for a blocked quotation is normally punctuated with a colon.

Example

Patricia Kingston describes the procedure:

The reader will know automatically that your indented passage is quoted. Therefore, do not enclose the blocked passage in quotation marks. Quotations within the blocked quote (quotations within quotations), however, should be set off at beginning and end with double quotation marks (see page 199).

A parenthetical citation placed at the end of a blocked quotation is usually placed outside of the sentence end (two spaces to the right of the period).

Note, too, that short passages and lines of verse, fewer than five lines in length, can be blocked to give them special emphasis or to retain their original layout.

Use Good Judgment—Do Not Over-Quote

Train yourself not to quote frequently. Instead, develop the habit of taking the time to skillfully summarize and paraphrase your researched information. When should you quote! Although no definite answer can be given to this question, the general guidelines are (1) select passages for quoting that seem to be especially well written, and (2) consider quoting passages that are very difficult to summarize or paraphrase. Never quote material that is badly written, for example, sentences containing grammatical errors. Remember that almost all material can be reworded if you take the time.

As a general rule, avoid long quotations whenever possible. One or two long quotations in the block format look good and enhance the readability of a paper. But readers resent having to slow down to plow through a long quotation every few paragraphs. They especially resent long quotations when they suspect the writers have quoted without good reason or that writers have padded their papers to make them long enough.

beginning with the eruption of the volcano Hekla in Iceland and continuing to the more recent eruptions of Mount St. Helens in Washington state and El Chichon in Mexico. They also consider the possibility that dust derived from industrial pollution may have contributed to the cooling trend (78-79).

One possible explanation for the temperature rise in the Southern Hemisphere may be sunspot cycles. Sunspots are blemishes on the sun generated, says Robert W. Noyes, by magnetic fields beneath its surface (83). Two separate cycles have been plotted, an 11-year cycle and a 22-year or double cycle (107-09). More recent research on sunspot cycles conducted by John Eddy seems to indicate a correlation between active sunspot production and warmer temperatures (Noyes 219-220). The warmer temperatures could be the result of an increase of solar radiation to the troposphere near sunspot maximum, giving rise to warm air near the equator which travels toward the poles (Noyes 223). Warm air holds more moisture; consequently, the result may be precipitation at the poles (Christopherson).

But as the warmer air reaches the South Pole, could the subsequent increased moisture cause both more snowfall and contribute to the melting of the West Antarctic ice sheet? Experiments conducted by Ian Whillans and John Bolzan, researchers for Ohio University's Institute of Polar Studies, indicate that this chain of events is possible. In their experiments these scientists dug a number of 10-foot-deep pits in an area of East Antarctica called Dome C. They expected to find soft snow on top of hard, firm snow as they dug deeper. But that was not the case. "The top two feet of snow, about six year's worth, are hard and firm," said Whillans. "But below that, it turns soft again" (qtd. in "More Evidence" 3-4). That layer of soft snow, equivalent to about ten years of snowfall during the 1960s, corresponds with a general temperature rise and cycle of intense sunspot activity.

What this could mean is that if, in fact, an increase of carbon dioxide does cause a general upturn in the earth's temperature, an increase in the snowpack of Antarctica

Quotation within a Quotation

Use single quotation marks (' ') to indicate where a quotation within a quotation begins and ends. You will recognize the need to use this punctuation when the passage you want to quote is already enclosed in double quotation marks.

If the quotation within a quotation and the main quotation in your paper both end together at the end of the sentence, the period should be placed inside the single quotation mark, and the double quotation marks should be placed outside the single quotation mark.

Example

"Upon later being asked about his observations of flying saucers, pilot Kenneth Arnold explained, 'By no stretch of the imagination did I observe balloons, mock suns, ice crystals, or clouds, and I certainly would not classify my observations in the categories of illusions, hallucinations, apparitions, temperature inversions, or mirages' " (Reese 6).

is imminent. The eventual breakup and melting of the uniquely structured West

Antarctic ice sheet would follow. East Antarctica, a true continent with a solid bedrock

base, is not likely to have a problem with melting. West Antarctica, however, has

virtually no base above sea level. This characteristic contributes to its instability while

adding to its vulnerability to warmer weather. Although it is true that warmer air

carries more moisture and consequently more snow, unfortunately, any additional snow

is less apt to contribute to the ice pack and more apt to melt and help speed up

Antarctica's overall disintegration process.

While attempting to determine the influence of increased atmospheric carbon

dioxide on the earth's climate, researchers have taken into account other factors. A

group at the National Aeronautics and Space Administration headed by James E.

Hansen used a model which allowed for the effects of heat absorption by oceans along

with the important properties of water vapor and volcanic aerosols. The group found

that a temperature rise of about 0.4 degrees Celsius from the latter 1880s to 1980

related to the increase of atmospheric carbon dioxide of over 43 parts per million during

that same time (Revelle 37-38). Armed with this information, one can surmise that a

warming trend is occurring and will continue, possibly causing the erosion of a large

area of Antarctica. Still, questions remain concerning the length of time it will take and

the resultant effect upon the world.

Roger Revelle shares the belief of some climatologists that if the warming trend

continues along predicted lines, eventually the West Antarctic ice sheet could

disintegrate at a rate of as much as 20 kilometers a year (43). Geologist George Denton

of the University of Maine, interviewed by Newsweek's Begley, Dallas, and Givens, adds

that it would take thousands of years for the warmer climate to directly produce an

effect on Antarctica. "But," summarize the reporters, "it [Antarctica] would be

threatened by rising seas. The melting northern ice would raise sea levels around the

globe, and Antarctica's ice shelves . . . would rise with the water until they were ripped

Ellipsis Marks

An ellipsis denotes an omission. You may shorten quotations by using ellipsis marks to indicate where the omissions occur (see pages 207 and 209). Use three periods—with a space before and after each—for an ellipsis in the middle of a sentence.

> *Example*
>
> Ayensu explains, "All the Earth's . . . great ecological realms . . . have evolved and continue to maintain themselves by the power of the sun" (34).

If you omit the end of a sentence, use three spaced periods before the final period.

> *Example*
>
> Ayensu continues, "Atmospheric water vapor absorbs the infrared rays, and the sun's energy is transformed into long-wave energy. . . ."

If the ellipsis falls at the end of the sentence and the ellipsis is accompanied by a parenthetical reference, type three spaced periods, the quotation marks, then the citation, and finally the fourth period.

> *Example*
>
> "Atmospheric water vapor absorbs the infrared rays, and the sun's energy is transformed into long-wave energy . . ." (Ayensu 34).

When you omit a portion of the quotation after a complete sentence, follow the period at the end of the sentence with three spaced periods.

> *Example*
>
> "Thus, a warming trend may already be under way on Earth, creating a hot, moist atmosphere like the one you experience in a glass-covered greenhouse. . . . Mix this with man's apparent destruction of the Earth's protective ozone layer and you have a recipe for global disaster" (Ayensu 34).

If you omit a line or more of verse or a long portion of prose, for example, a sentence or a paragraph, use four periods.

Use a lead-in to take the place of ellipsis marks when beginning a quotation in the middle of a sentence.

> *Example*
>
> Janet Brown found that "twenty-two of the thirty-five mice had severe birth defects caused by the drug."

Never use ellipsis marks to alter the meaning of a passage, and make sure the ellipsis does not create an awkward or incorrectly punctuated sentence.

from their moorings" (73). To make matters worse, the orphaned ice shelves would no longer restrain the ice streams that flow within Antarctica. "The runaway streams would draw ice down from the interior of the continent until the whole sheet disappeared within 200 years . . ." (73).

With the ice sheet's disintegration, the consequences for the rest of the world would be devastating. At present, approximately 500 cubic kilometers of ice are being deposited into the sea each year; this rate corresponds to a world-wide sea level increase of 1.5 millimeters per year (Revelle 43). Although 1.5 millimeters does not seem like much, it is a significant rise, and it is already causing concern. Kenneth Emery, oceanographer at Woods Hole Oceanographic Institution, has detected a rise of about 1/4 of an inch (6.35 mm) each year along the coastlines of most temperate and tropical regions. Forty years ago the rise was less than 1/32 of an inch (0.79 mm) per year ("Antarctic Meltdown?" 19). Calculations by Orrin Pilkey, Jr., a marine geologist at Duke University, show that for every foot of ocean rise there will be a 100- to 1,000-foot submergence of coastline area. This submergence is due to the land's tendency to warp downward as the ocean's level increases, due to the increased weight of water on the continental shelf. "The beaches along North Carolina, for example, are already retreating an average of four to five feet a year" ("Antarctic Meltdown?" 19).

Researchers are currently at work on a new project to validate the work done by scientists over the past two decades. Ice cores were cut out of the ice in Greenland and Antarctica and transferred to laboratories in the United States where they were analyzed. As Bill Scanlon explains, "The Antarctic core could validate the startling findings from the Greenland core—that climate can change suddenly and dramatically, from glacial to temperate in 10 to 20 years (D11). A reporter recently commented that, "It is hoped the information scientists gather from glacial ice will help explain how global warming from greenhouse gases, such as carbon dioxide from cars and coal-fired power plants, may influence climate conditions" (Roberts). Researchers in the Southern

Subsequent References

Most subsequent references—references to previously cited sources—are simply variations of the lead-in/parenthetical citation combinations used in the initial references. Repeating all of the information in each subsequent reference is not always necessary, however, depending on the situation. If the context of the paragraph makes it quite clear that you are still referring to the same author or article, all that may be needed is a parenthetical reference to the page number(s) of the material. Or, if the subsequent material is in the same paragraph and comes from the same page or pages of the earlier material, a brief reference such as "Jones states further that" or "The study results also show that" may suffice.

Raised Note Numerals (Superscript)

To mark the place where readers should turn to the Notes page for supplemental information or additional references, type or key in the appropriate numeral, raising it one half space above the line (superscript). Although you will probably have very few note numerals, perhaps none, make certain that the numerals are consecutive throughout the paper, 1, 2, 3, and so on. These raised note numerals should not be confused with "footnote numbers," which were formerly used in the place of parenthetical references. (See pages 197 and 201.)

Hemisphere are constantly providing new information about the dangers of global warming and the holes in the ozone layer. A research team reported that "Ultraviolet radiation caused severe deterioration to our tents and tarps" (Howes 60). Information such as this helps illustrate the danger of the expanding Antarctic ozone hole and global warming so we can take steps to avoid a world-wide environmental disaster.

Therefore, on the basis of a review of the literature published thus far, it seems apparent that as atmospheric carbon dioxide increases, so will the earth's temperature; as this phenomenon occurs, the West Antarctic ice sheet will gradually disintegrate. Even if fossil fuel consumption and forest clearing were to cease completely within the next 50 to 60 years, the oceans would not be able to absorb carbon dioxide fast enough. Also, the West Antarctic ice sheet need not melt entirely before the effects would be felt. For example, California's Sacramento-San Joaquin River delta with its rich agricultural land faces the strong possibility of becoming an extension of San Francisco Bay because the land is normally lower than sea level a good part of the year. Although it is protected from flooding by levees, those levees have proven susceptible to breakage. Apparently, though, a significant reduction in atmospheric carbon dioxide is not practical at this time, given the predominant practices of fossil fuel burning for energy. The alternatives are few and not yet practicable. Solar energy is still in its infancy, as are synthetic fuels. Nuclear fusion has not been developed as an energy source and probably will not be for some time. Instead of hoping for an instant alternative to carbon dioxide-emitting energy systems and a miraculous switch to prudent forest conservation, scientists and politicians should begin to consider options to current living patterns and look seriously at new locations for coastal cities, as existing ones may end up under water. As Carl Pope observed, "Acknowledging our addiction to the burning of fossil fuels is difficult. But denying it will, in the long run, be even more painful" (19).

Notes

Supplementary information, additional references, and comments about references can be made on a Notes page. Raised numerals in the text (see page 210) alert readers to turn to the Notes. The general directions for the Notes page are as follows:

1. Place your last name and page number in the upper right corner of the page one-half inch from the top, as in preceding pages.

2. Center the title, **Notes,** one inch from the top of the page.

3. Skip two spaces after the title, and double-space the rest of the page.

4. To begin each entry, indent five spaces, type or key in the appropriate note numeral one-half space above the entry line, return back to the original line, skip one space, and begin the note.

5. Indent only the first line of each entry; for any subsequent lines do not indent.

6. Any references cited in the Notes must be listed in the Works Cited (see page 215).

NOTE: Notes are not mandatory. In fact, they may not be needed. Avoid long explanatory notes that should either be integrated in the text of the paper or be omitted because they are not relevant or relate trivial information. Also avoid the temptation to update your paper at the last minute by adding information or references discovered too late to be included in the first draft. If you want to include this information, revise the entire paper.

Notes

[1] Kerr ("Carbon Dioxide" 1053-54) explores oceanic carbon dioxide in more detail; also see the results of Peter G. Brewer's study reported by Ryan (66-67).

[2] Carbon dioxide-induced temperature changes have not been officially confirmed because of the earth's natural yearly variation of plus or minus two degrees Celsius, as explained by Revelle (38).

[3] Global deforestation is examined extensively by Woodwell et al. (1081-85). The potential extinction of species due to the loss of forests is predicted by Paul Ehrlich and Daniel Simberloff (see Lewin 1168-69).

Works Cited

The Works Cited lists all of the materials referred to in your paper and Notes. The Works Cited is arranged alphabetically so readers can easily locate more information about your sources than is given in the lead-ins and parenthetical references in the paper. Each type of entry—book, magazine, journal, newspaper, pamphlet, recording, computer service, interview, and so on—has a correct format to be used.

Read the general guidelines below, study the Works Cited on the facing page, and for additional directions and a more comprehensive list of sample entries, turn to Appendix A, page 356.

1. Place your last name and the page number in the upper-right corner as on previous pages in the paper.

2. Center the title, **Works Cited,** one inch from the top of the page. Capitalize as shown, and do not underline.

3. Skip two spaces after the title, and double-space the rest of the page. In other words, double space the lines within each entry, and double-space between entries.

4. The first line of each entry begins at the left margin, but any other lines in the same entry are indented five spaces from the left margin.

5. The author's last name is listed first. When more than one author is given for a source, only the first author's name is listed in reverse order.

6. If a source does not have an author listed, alphabetize it by its title, ignoring *A, An, The, La,* and other articles when used as the first word.

7. The prescribed punctuation must be used consistently. Note, for example, that article titles are enclosed in quotation marks whereas magazine and book titles are underlined. Note that periods are used to separate different parts of the entry and that a period is placed at the end of each entry. Notice that no punctuation is used to separate the title of a magazine and the date of issue.

8. The names of publishers should be shortened (e.g., Prentice-Hall to Prentice, Cambridge University Press to Cambridge UP, and Alfred A. Knopf, Inc. to Knopf). Also see "Publisher's Imprint," pages 359-360.

9. Page numbers are not needed when listing a book unless the book is a collection of poems, plays, stories, or essays. In such cases, list the total pages covered by the selection being referred to (e.g., 30-36). Precede the page numbers with a colon but not p. or pp.

10. Note that weekly and monthly magazine entries do not include volume and issue numbers whereas some professional journals do, in front of the year in parentheses.

11. For articles in periodicals, list the pages covered by the article (e.g., 23-27), but when the article begins on one page and skips to other pages, merely signify "and other pages" by placing a + immediately after the first page number (e.g., 17+).

12. Instead of repeating an author's name when more than one work by the author is listed, use three hyphens followed by a period (---.) in place of the author's name for the second and any other entries by that author (see sample Works Cited, page 215).

13. For a list of commonly used abbreviations, see page 365. For instance, use n.d. for "no date" and N. pag. or n. pag. for "no page numbers."

14. See page 379 for further directions regarding capitalization. For example, use capitals for names of most computer and information services (e.g., DIALOG, ERIC, NewsBank ENV).

Works Cited

"Antarctic Meltdown?" Science Digest Jan. 1982: 19.

Ayensu, Edward S. Fire of Life. Smithsonian Exposition Books. 1st ed. New York: Norton, 1981.

Begley, Sharon, Rita Dallas, and Ron Givens. "Is Antarctica Shrinking?" Newsweek 5 Oct. 1981: 72-74.

Christopherson, Robert. Professor of Geology. Personal Interview. 12 Dec. 1994.

David, Leonard. "Slip Sliding Away." Ad Astra May 1991: 15-17.

Feldstein, Dan. "Study Shows Effects Won't Be Disastrous." Houston (Texas) Post 2 Jan. 1994 NewsBank ENV 2: D4-5.

Howes, Deanne. "Our Year in the Tasmanian Wilderness." Australian Geographic Oct/Dec. 1994: 56-71.

Katz, Abram. "Greenhouse Effect Real, But a Long Way Off." New Haven Register 1 Jan. 1984. NewsBank ENV 2: B11.

Kerr, Richard A. "Carbon Dioxide and the Control of Ice Ages." Science 9 Mar. 1984: 1053-54.

---. "CO_2 Climate Models Defended." Science 13 Aug. 1982: 620.

Lewin, Roger. "No Dinosaurs This Time." Science 16 Sept. 1983: 1168-69.

Meredith, Dennis. "Greenhouse Advantage." Science Digest Sept. 1982: 64.

"More Evidence of Antarctic Warming." USA Today Dec. 1980: 3-4.

Noyes, Robert W. The Sun Our Star. Cambridge, MA: Harvard UP, 1982.

Pope, Carl. "Weather Retorts." Sierra. Jan./Feb. 1994: 18-19.

Revelle, Roger. "Carbon Dioxide and World Climate." Scientific American Aug. 1982: 35-43

Roberts, Mark. "Global Warming." All Things Considered. National Public Radio. 20 Nov. 1994.

Ryan, Paul R. "Concerns: High Sea Levels and Temperatures Seen Next Century."

    Oceanus 26.4 (1983/84): 63-67.

Scanlon, Bill. "Clues to Global Warming on Ice." Rocky Mountain News 6 July 1994.

    NewsBank SCI 14: D11.

Strahler, Arthur N., and Alan H. Strahler. Elements of Physical Geography. 1st ed. New

    York: Wiley, 1979.

Woodwell, M., et al. "Global Deforestation: Contributions to Atmospheric Carbon

    Dioxide." Science 9 Dec. 1983: 1081-85.

Electronic Sources

Citing electronic sources presents unique problems, but the same general rules apply: You must give enough information to allow your reader to locate the source. Note that there are a few changes dictated by the computer systems offering the information. As always, begin with the author's name (last name first), the title of the work (article title, poem, song, etc.), the title of the complete work (book, newspaper, magazine, etc.), and then tell where the work can be found (the protocol and address, the path, and the date).

When writing Works Cited entries for electronic sources, remember that every colon, period, slash, space, and abbreviation is critical. If you get something out of place, your reader won't be able to find the source. If you suspect that a source you wish to use will change or not be available at a later date, don't include it in your paper.

Documenting Electronic Sources

The following Works Cited is from a student paper and illustrates how electronic sources should be listed. Notice that some sources are online, others are CD-ROM, others are traditional print sources, and one documents an e-mail communication. You should check with your instructor about how you should document electronic sources if you are unsure.

Works Cited

"Fusion Energy Overview." Online. Internet. http://wwwofe.er.doe.gov. 3 Apr. 1995.

"Fusion and the Environment." Online. Internet. http://wwwofe.er.doe. 29 Mar. 1995.

"Harnessing Fusion for Peaceful Use." Compton's Encyclopedia: CD-ROM. 1994.

Heppenheimer, T. A. The Man-Made Sun Boston: Omni, 1984.

Kerr, J. Alistair. "Deuterium." The New Grolier Multimedia Encyclopedia. Grolier, 1993.
CD-ROM. Funk and Wagnalls. 1994.

---. "Hydrogen." The New Grolier Multimedia Encyclopedia. Grolier, 1993. CD-ROM. Funk
and Wagnalls. 1994.

Lemonick, Michael D. "Blinded by the Light." Time 28 Dec. 1993. America Online Time
Archives. 3 Apr. 1995.

Marshall, Eliot. "Johnston Takes Project Hostage." Science 12 Aug. 1994: 865.

"New Heights in Fusion Power." Science News 11 June 1994: 391.

Ransom, Michael. E-mail to author. 29 Apr. 1995.

Vargas, Dale. "Rancho Seco Described as Model in Search for Fusion Site." Sacramento Bee
6 May 1994: A1.

"What Is Inertial Confinement Fusion?" Online. Internet. http://neutrino.nuc.berke-
ley.edu/fusion/icf/icf.html. 4 Apr. 1995.

Wiley, Walt. "They're Still Hot on Cold Fusion Despite Doubt, Ridicule, Researchers Pursue
Elusive Energy Source." Sacramento Bee 29 Dec. 1994: B1. CD-ROM. NewsBank. Mar.
1995.

EXERCISE 4.8

After reviewing your note cards and thinking about what you want to say in your paper, formulate a thesis statement.

_____

_____

_____

_____

Make a list of the topic sentences you imagine you will need in your paper. Put them in the same order they will appear in the paper, and number them 1, 2, 3, etc. Keep in mind that you may find it necessary to revise your outline as you write the first draft of your paper.

Note: If your instructor prefers that you use a *topic outline*, use the sample on page 286 as a model.

_____

_____

_____

_____

_____

_____

_____

_____

_____

_____

_____

_____

_____

_____

_____

_____

_____

_____

_____

_____

_____

_____

_____

_____

Have your thesis and outline approved.

First Draft

By now you have probably developed an approach to writing preliminary drafts of your papers, either completing an entire draft and then returning to revise and correct it or perfecting it as you proceed from paragraph to paragraph.

Two suggestions will help you write the first and any subsequent preliminary drafts of a library research paper:

1. Work from an outline that has evolved in conjunction with your research notes. Above all, your thesis should be composed along with the outline before you begin writing the first draft of the paper.

2. Integrate your research material as you write the first draft. Be very careful to use appropriate lead-ins (see page 198) and to include parenthetical references wherever needed (see pages 200, 202). Never plan to insert the parenthetical citations and lead-ins later! Always insert your documentation as you proceed through the first draft. Furthermore, you must be aware of whether you are using summaries, paraphrases, or quotations; otherwise, your paper may end up with quoted portions but no quotation marks (see pages 182 and 202).

Following the above advice may save you hours of revision later if your documentation turns out to be faulty or if your citations are mixed up. Always assume that the documentation in your paper will be checked by the instructor for accuracy and correct format. More important, if you are going to be proud of what you write, you want your documentation to be meticulously correct.

Certainly you want to avoid being guilty of having conducted "sloppy" research. Before you begin writing the first draft, arrange your note cards in piles that correspond with the categories in your outline. Evaluate your note cards, selecting those that seem best for inclusion and putting the others aside. Make some preliminary decisions as to which information will be included as quotations and which will be paraphrased or summarized. See if there are any gaps in your research that will require additional trips to the library for more information.

EXERCISE 4.9

Write the first draft of your paper. Work from your note cards, referring frequently to your thesis and outline. Integrate your documentation as you work. You can write your first draft on notebook paper, on a computer, or on a typewriter. Assume that your final draft must be prepared using a computer or typewriter, unless your instructor specifically authorizes you to write out your paper. If you are allowed to write out your paper in longhand, you will be expected to use 8 1/2 x 11-inch paper, write on every other line, write on one side of the paper only, and use black or blue ink.

This is not to be a "rough draft"! When your first draft is completed, you should have a paper that is as close as you can make it to the final version you will submit for grading. Use the same heading, title, and format that you will use for the final copy. Include all documentation, Notes, and Works Cited, observing all format conventions. Edit and proofread your first draft until it represents the best work you can possibly accomplish within the time limits of the assignment. Your instructor will be happy to assist you during the drafting process. (See the

"Research Paper Checklist," below, and do not forget the explanations and directions accompanying the sample research paper; also, refer to Appendix A: "Documentation" and Appendix B: "Stylistic Revision" whenever necessary.)

Research Paper Checklist

1. Have all of the preliminary steps been approved before you begin writing the first draft?
2. Does the introductory paragraph open with an interesting statement and proceed smoothly to the thesis?
3. Does each body paragraph begin with a topic sentence? Is each topic sentence thoroughly supported by a network of primary and secondary support sentences? At least five sentences in each body paragraph? Smooth transitions connecting ideas, sentences, and other paragraphs?
4. Is research material smoothly integrated by using a combination of summary, paraphrase, and quotation? Quotations not used excessively? Quotation marks at the beginning and end of each quotation or long quotations blocked properly? Quotations double-checked for accuracy? Lead-ins and parenthetical references skillfully combined?
5. Does the concluding paragraph begin with a summary statement and end with an appropriate generalization?
6. Check all sentences for clarity, structure, punctuation, grammar, capitalization, and spelling.
7. Title page and outline pages in correct format (if required)? Heading, title, pagination completed correctly?
8. Cross-check each reference in the paper and Notes with the corresponding Works Cited entry. Notes included only when information is really worth adding? Note numerals in paper are raised one-half space? Entire Works Cited checked for alphabetical order, format, punctuation, and spelling?

EXERCISE 4.10

After your first draft has been completed, begin working immediately on the final manuscript. If necessary, confer with your instructor about the improvements and corrections that have been recommended. When you have completed your final manuscript, check it over, using the "Research Paper Checklist," just as you did after completing the first draft. (Your instructor may want you to attach the cover sheet on page 224.)

EXERCISE 4.11

If assigned by your instructor, write a revision of your final draft, being sure to ask when the revised paper is due.

CHAPTER FOUR LIBRARY RESEARCH PAPER

Name _____   Date _____

Class _____   Instructor _____

Meeting Time _____   Day _____   Circle One: Original Paper

                                                                              Revision

Approved

1. Topic _____
2. Working bibliography _____
3. Research notes _____
4. Thesis _____

5. Outline _____
6. First draft _____
7. Notes _____
8. Works Cited _____

IMPORTANT: REVISED PAPER MUST BE ACCOMPANIED BY THE ORIGINAL!!

CHECKLIST

I. Content
  A. Research effort
  B. Logic and ideas
  C. Reader interest

II. Structure
  A. Overall essay plan and structure
  B. Thesis sentence
  C. Opening sentence
  D. Topic sentences
  E. Primary and secondary support sentences
  F. Irrelevant material
  G. Transitions

III. Sentence style and mechanics
  A. Sentence structure
  B. Agreement, pronoun reference, tense, person
  C. Spelling, punctuation, capitalization

IV. Documentation
  A. Plagiarism
  B. Use of quoted, summarized, and paraphrased material
  C. Lead-ins and parenthetical references
  D. Notes
  E. Works Cited

V. Format
  A. Heading and title (or title page)
  B. Outline page (if required)
  C. Pagination and margins
  D. Lead-ins and parenthetical references
  E. Works Cited
  F. Charts, tables, graphs (if included)
  G. Legibility and neatness

Grade for Original Paper _____

Grade for Revision (if required) _____

CHAPTER FIVE

The Critical Review Paper

Objectives

When you have completed this chapter, you will have

1. selected and viewed a film or television program, selected and read a story or poem, or selected and attended an event for a *critical review.*

2. identified, classified, described, and evaluated the topic for critical review.

3. developed a thesis and list of main points for a critical review.

4. compared critical review papers.

5. written a 750-1,000 word critical review.

5

A **critical review paper** introduces and assesses the worth of a subject that is unfamiliar to the reader. Critical reviews are chiefly about something new to the audience for whom reviews are written. They may be about a book, a movie, an event, or a social phenomenon. You might, for example, familiarize your readers with the setting, plot, characters, and theme (thesis) of a novel and let them know whether or not, in your opinion, the book is worth reading. Your basic goal should be to introduce readers to something—not to analyze every detail and every shade of meaning. In reviewing a movie, for instance, you cannot reveal how the story ends because you will be destroying the potential viewers' chance to experience that ending. But you can explain where the story takes place, who the main characters are, their situation, some of the challenges they face as they attempt to improve their situation or solve a problem, and the message you think the writer or director is attempting to communicate. And you can venture your opinion as to whether or not the movie is successful and the rationale for your conclusions. The idea is to review your subject in order to help your readers decide whether or not they want to read the book, see the movie, or investigate the social phenomenon—or to give readers enough guidance so they will have some perspective if they do explore further.

For you as the writer, reviews offer additional benefits that can enhance your critical perspectives. Obviously, writing reviews can inspire you to learn about a subject that is new to you as well as to your readers. But further, you are afforded the opportunity to consider points of view different from your own, thereby expanding your intellectual horizons. Also, the review may provide you the opportunity to trace the evolution of an artist or author through changes in style, theme, or developmental phase. Moreover, considering and writing reviews are perfect opportunities for expressing your personal values and engaging in holistic thinking. Further, writing reviews offer you an occasion for integrating and using your knowledge from other sources, such as other classses or outside interests. All in all, writing reviews can be a refreshing change of pace from the other types of compositions that you are learning to write in *Survival*.

With all the opportunities inherent in writing reviews, you do need to be careful not to confuse critical review with critical analysis. If you are assigned to write a **critical analysis,** your main task will be to provide your readers with insights into works of art, the uses of language, or political or social issues with which they are familiar. Critical analysis is the subject of Chapter Six. While the critical analysis is usually a more difficult undertaking than the critical review, both types of critical papers are frequently assigned in school and college courses. By understanding the essential differences between the critical review and the critical analysis, you will be prepared to write either type.

LESSON ONE: *Planning to Write a Critical Review*

Most critical reviews deal with books, movies, plays, television programs, concerts, recordings, or art exhibits. When the critical paper is written as a review, the writer is usually referred to as a critic. You must be careful, however, that you do not begin to share the popular misconception of the critic as primarily preoccupied with only the negative. The critic's obligation is to be as free as possible from bias in his or her writing, for the task is to *"re" - view,* to look again, to evaluate.

A critical review must accomplish the following tasks: first, report what the work (book, movie, play, etc.) does; second, judge how well it does it; third, cite evidence from the work that supports or illustrates your conclusions; finally, be fair.

A critical review that fails to accomplish each of these four objectives is incomplete. If your paper fails to "report what the work does," for example, readers who are unfamiliar with the subject will not be able to follow you to your conclusions. If the paper reports only what a work does and not "how well it does it," then the paper is merely a summary, not a critical review at all. Most important, if your paper contains no supporting evidence from the work itself, readers will be unable to appreciate your conclusions. Finally, you can never assume that your unsupported opinion will be accepted; in fact, unsupported opinion is as unfair to your subject as is allowing your prejudice to influence your judgments.

Since a critical review is typically a **description** and **evaluation** of something that is new to your readers, it is especially appropriate for many school subjects and courses in which your instructor assigns you to assess a fresh topic; you can write about the topic, expressing the opinions that you formed from firsthand observation. Furthermore, the critical review paper is not one that is especially difficult to write because the essential points contained in reviews have become fairly standardized.

The steps for writing a critical review:
1. Read or view the work to be reviewed.
2. Consider the work.
   a. Identify it.
   b. Classify it.
   c. Describe what it does.
3. Evaluate the work's worth.
   a. Is it a success?
   b. Is it a failure?
   c. Is it somewhere in between?
4. Develop a thesis or a point that you wish to illuminate.
5. Cite the evidence to support your judgment.
6. Make an outline.
7. Write the review.

EXERCISE 5.1

Review the sections on "Assignment Analysis" and "Work Schedule" in Chapter Two (pages 60-61). Now prepare your schedule for completing your critical review on time.

Work Schedule

Project Title: Critical Review   **Due Date** _____

Exercise	Project Assignment	Sample Allotment	Your Time Allotment	Date Due
Ex. 5.2	Subject	(1/2 day)	_____	_____
Ex. 5.3	Review	(1/2 day)	_____	_____
Ex. 5.4	Thesis	(1/2 day)	_____	_____
Ex. 5.5	Main Points	(1 day)	_____	_____
Ex. 5.6	Topic Sentences	(1/2 day)	_____	_____
Ex. 5.7	Sample Reviews	(1 day)	_____	_____
Ex. 5.8	First Draft	(1 day)	_____	_____
Ex. 5.9	Final Manuscript	(1 day)	_____	_____

EXERCISE 5.2

Select a movie, story, poem, television program, or other event unfamiliar to your intended audience as the subject for your critical review.

Your choice (be specific):

_____

_____

_____

_____

Have your choice approved.

LESSON TWO: *Planning the First Draft*

Before writing a critical review, you must thoroughly read or closely view your chosen and approved work. Then you must *identify the subject* so that your readers may, after reading your paper, find it and experience it themselves (unless, of course, it is a one-time occurrence, such as a concert). This means that for a book, a short story, or a poem, you will need to cite the title, the author, the publisher, and the date of publication. For movies and plays, you need to cite the title, the author, the producer and director, leading members of the cast, and the theater where it is playing. For concerts and other events, you will need to cite the time and place, the performers, and the sponsoring organization. The information needed for identification is usually stated in a sentence or two near the beginning of the paper, although publications that regularly print reviews frequently set aside a place at the beginning for this information where it is presented in a standardized format. You should integrate your identification for any review you write; the standardized heading is optional.

While the *classification* of your subject can frequently be written in a phrase or two, it is an important part of any critical paper; by classifying a movie, for example, as a musical, a comedy, a western, a drama, science fiction, a documentary, or some combination of classifications, you will give readers an immediate understanding of what your subject is; furthermore, the classification will give them a reference for comparison by suggesting a category into which it might best fit. Other facts for classification, while seemingly incidental, may help readers to form a frame of reference by relating your subject to other, similar subjects. You should, then, work into your text such classifying details as "the writer's second novel," "the director's first western," "the poet's third collection of poems," "Bonnie Raitt's tenth appearance of her current tour," or "first in a new series of Public Television Specials."

The longest part of a critical review will probably be your *description*, which contains specific details about the subject. These details may be presented either in a single block of description or throughout the paper as evidence for your observations. All that is required of you in gathering this descriptive material is *attentive observation* while reading the book, story, or poem; while viewing the movie or play; or while hearing and viewing the concert or other event. A worthwhile paper can result from your careful attention to details. While a description summarizes for readers the content, the writer of a critical review must be careful not to spoil the reader's experience of the story by revealing the outcome. Professional reviewers are usually quite good at summarizing the story without giving too much away. Frequently, they summarize only sample incidents that are representative of what the reviewer considers either successful or unsuccessful. You must always be careful, however, not to write description that is without purpose; all of your description must support your thesis. A real temptation, especially with books and movies, is to write only a plot summary; however, your fundamental task in the critical review is to describe for the purpose of judgment.

Evaluation and Evidence

The most important part of your critical review is the *evaluation:* your opinion. Your evaluation may not be the longest portion of your paper, and it may vary from a rather informal discussion of your reaction to the subject to a structured argumentative judgment based upon considerable reflection and experience. Nonetheless, the evaluation is the most important portion of your paper, the part your reader will be most interested in reading. To support your opinion, you must *give your reasons* and then *cite evidence* that makes your evaluation persuasive and believable. Avoid the temptation to hide your opinion behind general, sweeping pronouncements and such unsupported phrases as "It is the best . . . ," "It is the worst . . . ," or "This reviewer likes it." An easy way to avoid this problem is to cite particular aspects of your subject that you feel are especially successful or especially weak.

Using Comparisons

One technique that is popular with reviewers is to compare or contrast a more familiar subject with one that is unfamiliar to your intended readers. This technique is particularly worthwhile in comparing (or contrasting) subjects that are similar. Comparison and contrast offer the opportunity for considerable insight. For example, you might choose to compare (or contrast) books by the same writer, poems with similar form, or movies with similar themes. Some specific examples of subjects that might be reviewed in this fashion are as follows:

1. A critical review of a film—Contrast John Badham's *Point of No Return* (1993) with Luc Besson's *La Femme Nikita* (1990) to assess the different techniques employed by American and French filmmakers.

2. A critical review of an emerging celebrity—Compare or contrast Asia's top movie star, Jackie Chan, with the previous top martial arts star, Bruce Lee.

3. A critical review of computer software programs—Compare or contrast Word for Windows 6.0 with WordPerfect for Windows 6.1.

4. A critical review of a new book—Compare the theme of Salman Rushdie's book *Midnight's Children* with the theme of his novel *The Satanic Verses*.

5. A critical review of an event—Contrast the new art show (boat show, auto show, concert, street fair, or restaurant) opening with a previous, similar event.

As you can see from these suggestions, this technique can offer the writer opportunities to identify, classify, and describe by using comparison or contrast. Once these steps are complete, the evaluation follows naturally. Does it stand up well against the comparison? Is the work better than the more familiar work or not? Is it worth the expense and time required to experience it? Whether you like or dislike something you are reviewing, you need a good strong thesis that indicates your position; do not leave your readers wondering about your position.

EXERCISE 5.3

Take the topic you chose in Exercise 5.2 and briefly carry it through the review steps.

I. Consider the work.

A. Identify it.

_____

_____

_____

_____

_____

B. Classify it.

_____

_____

_____

_____

_____

_____

C. Describe it.

_____

_____

_____

_____

_____

_____

II. Evaluate the work

Is it a success, failure, or somewhere in between? Why?

_____

_____

_____

_____

_____

_____

Have your work checked.

Your Thesis and Outline

Carefully read the following thesis-topic sentence outline for an assigned review.

(The student chose a special event, the televised production of an opera).

Devoured by Myths

Thesis: Viewing and hearing the work so well presented on television rather than in a theater better allows the audience to evaluate it as a drama, a tragedy comparable to the Greek original by Sophocles.

1. As was evident in the production, *Elektra* is brief as an opera can be in its one act, yet is bristling with the musical challenges it poses for its large cast, chorus, and orchestra.

2. The Strauss-Hofmannsthal collaboration is strikingly divergent from Sophocles' *Electra* in some ways, and indicates just how different two versions of the same myth can be.

3. In an ordinary reshaping of ancient tragedy, the result of so much omission would be to impair the opera's truthfulness and force, but the fact is that both *Electra* (Sophocles) and *Elektra* (Hofmannsthal) convey the desired message: revenge is ultimately futile, however noble the cause, however satisfying for the moment.

4. As portrayed by Wagnerian soprano Hildegard Behrens, Strauss's *Elektra* invoked pity and terror about equally, and the camera accentuated her peculiar strengths, most of them theatrical.

5. Most of the time, Behrens's voice was equal to the heavy demands placed upon it.

6. From the announcement of Orestes' death through the end of the opera, Strauss's music is perfectly suited to the arousal and subsequent cleansing of one's murderous instincts.

7. The quality of the performance leaves one free to concentrate on the mythic meaning deep within *Elektra*.

EXERCISE 5.4

Take the topic you chose in Exercise 5.2 and began developing in Exercise 5.3 and create the thesis, or main idea, that you wish to pursue for your reader.

_____

_____

_____

_____

_____

_____

EXERCISE 5.5

Cite the main points of evidence that demonstrate the truth of your thesis.

1. _____

_____

_____

_____

2. _____

_____

_____

_____

3. _____

_____

_____

_____

EXERCISE 5.6

Using the main points of evidence that you identified in Exercise 5.5, compose a topic sentence for each.

1. _____

_____

_____

_____

_____

2. _____

_____

_____

_____

_____

3. _____

_____

_____

_____

_____

Have Exercises 5.5 and 5.6 checked before you proceed further.

Sample Reviews

Often critical reviews contain matters of interest designed to illuminate the subject: information on how the subject was created, something about the subject's background, and, perhaps, generalizations about the reviewer's view on the subject's place in society or its proper function. But always keep in mind that whatever else may be included in a critical review, your chief concern will be with description and evaluation. Additionally, remember that by writing a critical review you are doing more than expressing an opinion on a subject: You are furnishing your readers with information on something that is new to them. By offering this service to readers, you assist them in deciding whether it might be worthwhile to pursue the subject for themselves or whether, based upon your opinion, to ignore it. One good example of this process at work is the student who was assigned to write a 1,000-word paper reviewing some literary work of merit. After considering several possible topics, the student-author chose to write about an opera that he planned to see on public television. After viewing, (and probably making a VCR copy for future personal use so that parts of the performance could be reviewed) the student wrote a thesis-topic sentence outline of the assignment. (See page 233.)

EXERCISE 5.7

Read the critical reviews that follow. (Note that those written by professional critics for national publications may not exactly follow the style suggested in this chapter because the conventions differ for journalism and academic writing, but they are well worth examining.)

The first review, "Plants, People, and Healing Powers," employs the comparison and contrast technique for its evaluation and evidence by examining two books. Through freelance writer David Schneider's restrained use of examples and apt quotations, readers can see clearly that he admired both books, but he obviously prefers one over the other.

The second review, "Infobahn Warning Flags," is far more strident in tone than "Plants, People, and Healing Powers." Geoff Lewis's style makes the review one that sparks ideas for other kinds of papers, such as argumentative or investigative. (See the pro-con article on computers in Chapter Three.)

The third review, "No More," is student-written about the film, *I Will Fight No More Forever*. Following the lessons in this chapter, Barbara James's review is much like what your instructor expects your review to be.

Plants, People and Healing Powers

Reviews of *Sacred Trees* by Nathaniel Altman, Sierra Club Books, and Sastun, *My Apprenticeship with a Maya Healer,* by Rosita Arvigo, with Nadine Epstein, Harper, San Francisco

Relationships between people and plants have been the focus of much interest recently, partly in recognition of the practices of indigenous cultures, and partly in recognition of the rapid disappearance of those cultures and the plants they depend upon. This field of study—ethnobotany—has produced two new books, both excellent, although very different from one another.

In *Sacred Trees,* Nathaniel Altman trawls modern and ancient history for stories about peoples who worshiped trees and he lands a rich catch.

In a chapter called "Trees of Fertility" for instance, Altman explains the origins of familiar practices—burning a log at Christmas or dancing around a maypole in the spring. But he reveals unusual customs as well. Tree marriage, he says, is a widespread practice in modern times as well as in old, and on several continents. A young girl or a widow first marries a tree, and only then a human. The rationale is based on trees' power to draw away, or ground, inauspicious luck.

Altman writes with grace and great affection for his subject, but the book's main weakness is its episodic quality, arising from the author's attempt to scan all of history and to fit his vast findings into the tidy chapters of a paperback. Intriguing as it is, the book leaves us wanting, if not more information, then more sustained contemplation.

While Altman deals mostly with plants, Rosita Arvigo and Nadine Epstein focus on the human side of ethnobotanical lore. *Sastun* recounts Arvigo's first five years of apprenticeship with Don Elijio Panti, a respected (and somewhat feared) 90-year-old Mayan healer in the rain forests of Belize.

Trained as a natural healer in the United States but longing for a more primal life, Arvigo moved with her husband and their young daughter to a river-front jungle plot in Belize in 1981 and tried to make a living working out of a small clinic in the nearest town (six miles away by dugout canoe).

Life in their jungle paradise was tough; she writes about the heat, bugs, snakes, encroaching plants, the lack of modern conveniences and constant poverty. On the verge of giving up, Arvigo met Panti.

She quickly realized that the old man was a repository of healing wisdom and that he had no formal teaching methods and no disciples. "'I have been healing this way for 40 years now,' he told us, moving his arms about to punctuate each sentence. 'I cure diabetes, high blood pressure, even cancer. I never went to school cannot even sign my name but up here, it's full.' He tapped his forehead with a plant-stained fingertip."

Arvigo undertook an apprenticeship with Panti, at first informally and later, in a fully recognized way. Her early days were given to plant'collecting expeditions with her teacher and to preparing the materials for use as medicine. The book proceeds in a series of well-constructed and cleanly written chapters detailing Arvigo's deepening knowledge of healing plants. Gradually, Panti introduces her to his arts of diagnosis and prescription.

Arvigo's tale bears little resemblance to an account of medical school. Panti's universe is utterly alive, says Arvigo, not only with plants and animals, but also with a complex pantheon of Mayan spirits who, together with the Christian God, *control* everything. Before picking any leaves from a plant, Panti instructs, a prayer must be said. He is also explicit about healing power: "Faith. That is what cures. I chop the medicine, I look for it in the jungle, I make the fires, roast the herbs, and apply them, but it is the faith that heals."

None of the characters in *Sastun* is drawn simply. Panti—a widower at 90—is lonely and openly sexually desirous. He gets involved with bad women, is robbed, suffers heartbreaks and jealousies. For her part, Arvigo finds it difficult to balance apprenticeship with married life on her little farm. To obtain full power as a healer, Arvigo must summon enormous courage and confidence.

As she moves beyond simple illness of the body to mental derangement and possession by malevolent spirits, Arvigo must contact the Mayan spirits, and most particularly, she needs a ritual jewel—a sastun. Her quest for these things is gripping, and all the more poignant for being carried out within the disappearing rain forest and a pervasive loss of faith in the mystic world of spirits.

Reviewed by David Schneider.
Davis, California writer David Schneider is the author of *Street Zen* (Shambhala).

Reprinted by author's permission.

INFOBAHN WARNING FLAGS

Review of *SILICON SNAKE OIL, Second Thoughts on the Information Highway,* by Clifford Stoll

Clifford Stoll helped make the Internet hip. In recounting his pursuit of a fiendish gang of German hackers who had stolen information from his computers and sold it to the KGB, Stoll's first book, *The Cuckoo's Egg,* made the I-way seem like John Le Carrè territory—even though this true-life adventure was set in the dreary world of operating systems, network nodes, and communications protocols. Published in 1989, *Cuckoo's Egg* sold well and did a lot to bring the then not-widely-used Internet into public view.

Now when you can't seem to get away from the Internet, Stoll is back. But this time, the astronomer-turned-computer-security-expert is waving a yellow caution flag. Before we vault into the online future, Stoll warns in *Silicon Snake Oil,* we should pay careful attention to bogus claims and hidden costs.

The Net, boosters maintain, can help with everything from educating the kids to restoring participatory democracy. It will slash health-care costs with tele-medicine and turn businesses into super-efficient virtual corporations. Disembodied cybercitzens will overcome the boundaries of poverty, inadequate schools, and race. "The key ingredient in their silicon snake oil is a technocratic belief that computers and networks will make a better society" and cure social problems, writes Stoll.

It's not so, and the price of falling for this hype, he says, is staggering. At risk are vital institutions such as the neighborhood library and our entire education system. Rather than fixing our schools, Stoll asserts, we're diverting money from things that could make a difference, such as more books and better teachers. "Edutainment" software, he says, is nothing more than eye candy that actually makes the job of learning harder because, once exposed to it, kids won't sit still for the real thing.

Online libraries also rank high among Stoll's bêtes noires. As libraries race to replace card catalogs with databases and push aside reference books and periodicals to make room for computer terminals, they are courting disaster. Increasingly, only the material that's available online will survive. From your library or home, you'll be able to surf from one end of the World Wide Web to the other, but what you'll get is a jumble of contextless data. In their relentless pursuit of discrete factoids, computers deconstruct conventional forms of information—books—into bytes. "Data isn't information any more than fifty tons of cement is a skyscraper," Stoll insists. You would learn more about a topic by leafing through a card catalog or by asking a librarian. But, Stoll fears, by the time we figure that out, libraries will have been undermined.

And what of the online communities that come alive in the chat rooms of cyberspace? Intelligent online discourse, he says, is drowned out by drivel and extremist bullies. If cyberspace is a neighborhood, it's not a nice one.

It would be easy to dismiss Stoll as a Luddite, a curmudgeon, or a spoil-sport—the kind of kid who, now that everybody has discovered his playground, wants to take his ball and go home. But Stoll is none of the above. Through highly conversational prose that includes tales of spelunking in Arizona and studying in China, Stoll reveals himself to be a thoughtful, witty observer. He's the type of person you'd like to meet in an online chat room but never do. He admits he's not the first to warn about Information Age perils. But his is a unique point of view: that of a quilt-making, cookie-baking Berkeley dweeb—who also happens to be a serious scientist.

It's his scientific experience that informs Stoll's most fundamental criticism: Our faith in computers and in "information" is built on shaky foundations. He describes his own two-year effort to analyze the composition of Jupiter's clouds using satellite data. It's a thrilling breakthrough when the computer model "reveals" that the atmosphere is composed of particles of ammonia topped by ice crystals. "Yes, but do I believe it today?" asks

Stoll. "The question makes me squirm." His computer model, like every other, is founded on the programmer's assumptions, choice of data, and understanding of the material—none of which is infallible.

Yet government, businesses, investors, and ordinary citizens increasingly look to the computer for the definitive answer. "Simply by turning to a computer when confronted with a problem, you limit your ability to recognize other solutions," he warns. What makes a business excel are good ideas and smart, hard-working people. The Net can't do anything to make up for a lack of those.

Stoll hasn't turned his back on the Net. While pointing out what a waste of time Net-surfing can be, he still spends hours a day in the glow of his monitor. And in the end, he allows that he's hopeful. "For all my kvetching, I'm all grins to see people pressing limits and finding new ways to express themselves." Indeed, in the months since Stoll's manuscript was completed, there has been an explosion of innovation on the Net. Some of this work—such as new indexing systems—will address some of Stoll's concerns. Meantime, Net enthusiasts would do well to heed his advice: Proceed with caution and keep an eye on the rear-view mirror.

By *Geoff Lewis*
Senior Editor Lewis heads up *Business Week*'s coverage of information technology.

Reprinted from April 3, 1995, issue of *Business Week* by special permission, copyright ©1995 by The McGraw-Hill Companies.

Barbara D. James

English 1-A MWF 10

Dr. Frew

15 May 1995

(Critical Review)

                            No More

     Until recently, Hollywood has portrayed Native Americans as

vicious savages. <u>I Will Fight No More Forever</u>, a video originally made

as a movie for television, has effectively changed that image in the

minds of many people. It is a dramatization of the story of the last

stand of the Nez Perce Tribe. The story centers around Chief Joseph, a

man of peace, and General Howard, who sympathizes with the Nez Perce.

Chief Joseph is the spokesman for the tribe and tries to maintain peace,

but many of the other chiefs and warriors want to fight. General Howard

makes an effort to help the Nez Perce keep their land; however, he makes

it very clear that he is a soldier and will follow orders. <u>I Will Fight</u>

<u>No More Forever</u>, about the injustices perpetrated against the Nez Perce

Tribe, is very moving, compassionate, and truthful.

     The story begins with the events leading to the war. The Nez Perce

are the victims of many injustices but try to remain at peace. Many

conflicts break out between them and the white migrants who are invading

their territory. Finally, one of the migrants kills a Nez Perce elder

and steals several horses. The white authorities arrest the man to

placate Chief Joseph, who keeps insisting on justice; however, the

killer is quickly acquitted and released. The brother of the slain man

and two warriors seek revenge and kill the migrant. Consequently,

soldiers and a civilian posse are dispatched to arrest the young

warriors. The Nez Perce are holding peace flags, but the members of the civilian posse begin shooting at them anyway. Although the tribe successfully fights the soldiers with only a hundred warriors, they realize they will be defeated eventually and decide to flee to Canada. So begins the long journey to freedom with the cavalry, led by General Howard, pursuing them over 1,500 miles.

Chief Joseph is a wise man who frequently manages to keep the others from going to war. He takes grievances to the Native American agents and tries to secure justice for his people. Chief Joseph is the leader of only one band, but because he is wise and a great leader, the other chiefs respect him and follow his advice. At one point he tells General Howard,

> If we ever owned the land we own it still, for we never sold it. In the treaty councils the commissioners have claimed that our country had been sold to the government. Suppose a white man should come to me and say, "Joseph, I like your horses, and I want to buy them." I say to him, "No, my horses suit me. I will not sell them." Then he goes to my neighbor and says to him, "Joseph has some good horses. I want to buy them, but he refuses to sell." My neighbor answers, "Pay me the money, and I will sell you Joseph's horses." The white man returns to me and says, "Joseph, I have bought your horses, and you must let me have them." If we sold our land to the government, this is the way they [sic] were bought.

However, Joseph reluctantly decides to leave the land of his fathers rather than have blood on his hands. When war becomes inevitable, he leads his people and outwits and eludes General Howard many times. During their flight, the Nez Perce come upon a stage coach and terrorize the passengers. Joseph makes the passengers believe he is sparing their lives because they tell him the best trail to take. Actually, he lets them go to misinform General Howard, and he takes the opposite trail. This ploy enables the tribe to enlarge the distance between themselves and the cavalry.

Realizing that the Nez Perce are being mistreated by the government, General Howard feels compassion for them and decides to help. He writes a letter on their behalf stating that it would be a mistake to take the Wallowa Valley from the peaceful Nez Perce. In one scene he presents Chief Joseph and his wife with a doll his wife made for their unborn child. General Howard wants to avoid war with the Nez Perce if at all possible. He has fought many battles and lost an arm during one of them. However, when he receives orders to move the tribe to the reservation by force if necessary, he immediately begins to comply. Because General Howard's superiors know he is sympathetic toward the plight of the Nez Perce, he is accused of not really trying to capture them.

The film is characterized by considerable realism and credibility. One of the realistic aspects that stands out most is that the Nez Perce roles are played by Native American actors. This casting is unusual because for many decades Native Americans were portrayed by white actors in make-up. Nez Perce characteristics and the sound of their speech lend believability to the film. Although they speak limited English in this movie, their meanings come through quite clearly. In addition, the film shows the concern the Nez Perce have for one another. On the long and arduous journey, the young children and old people are looked after and made as comfortable as possible; any food is shared by all.

The scene in which Chief Joseph surrenders and speaks against war

is very touching and memorable, and evokes feelings of sympathy for the
Nez Perce. He tearfully speaks of the chiefs who were killed and the old
men who are dead. He tells about the people who ran away with no
blankets or food and the children who are freezing to death. He asks for
time to gather up as many of his people as he can find. He says, "Hear
me, my chiefs, my heart is sick and sad. From where the sun now stands,
I will fight no more forever."

This film is very good and quite unusual. Hollywood has finally
begun to produce more accurate portrayals of Native Americans. I Will
Fight No More Forever is realistic and believable while providing a
deeper understanding of the Nez Perces' side. The film is of
high-quality, capable of holding the viewer's full attention from the
beginning until the end; it is well worth seeing.

LESSON THREE: *Writing the Critical Review*

One of the conventions of usage in writing critical papers that some students find troubling at first is the use of the **present tense.** Most of the papers that you have written in the past (and most of the essays that you have written or will write for this book) are written in past tense. That is not the case, however, for most of the critical papers (whether they are reviews for this chapter or analysis in Chapter Six). This convention rests upon the fact that a story, whether read or viewed, is considered a living entity that may be read or seen time and again. While it is true that you personally may have read someting in the past, you may still read it again, and others may read it in the future. In any case, it is still happening, the story is still unfolding, and the plot is still developing, offering suspense and enjoyment at each reading. For example, Captain Ahab is in mortal conflict with the great white whale in *Moby Dick,* and the children are desperately fleeing the rampaging Velociraptors in *Jurassic Park* in the present of whoever is reading or viewing these works. To see how this works, examine the sample reviews in this chapter.

Avoid	Past Tense:	In the opening scene of the movie, an accident claimed the life of one of the gamekeepers.
Correct	Present Tense:	In the opening scene of the movie, an accident claims the life of one of the gamekeepers.

You have now arrived at the point where you must make some decisions about how to organize your review. Remember, you need to integrate the four essentials—*identification, classification, description,* and *evaluation*—into a review that will have an introduction, a body, and a conclusion. How, for example, can you write the introduction without including some description in addition to the identification and classification? Will you include your description as a block in the body and your evaluation in another block in the conclusion, or will you integrate your evaluation and description? Ideally, these decisions should be made as you organize your review and before you begin your first draft. There is not a single right way to integrate each of a review's elements; a successful paper should result as long as each of the elements is included.

EXERCISE 5.8

Using the material you have assembled in the preceding exercises, write a first draft 750-1,000 word critical review.

EXERCISE 5.9

After receiving feedback on your first draft, prepare the final manuscript of your critical review.

CHAPTER FIVE CRITICAL REVIEW PAPER

Name _____ Date _____

Class _____ Instructor _____

Meeting Time _____ Day _____ Circle One: Original Paper
                                                                Revision

IMPORTANT: REVISED PAPER MUST BE ACCOMPANIED BY THE ORIGINAL!!

CHECKLIST

I. Content
    A. Research effort
    B. Logic and ideas
    C. Reader interest
    D. Evidence
    E. Evaluation

II. Structure
    A. Overall essay plan and structure
    B. Thesis sentence
    C. Opening sentence
    D. Topic sentences
    E. Primary and secondary support sentences
    F. Irrelevant material
    G. Transitions
    H. Identification, Classification, and Description

III. Sentence style and mechanics
    A. Sentence structure
    B. Agreement, pronoun reference, tense, person
    C. Spelling, punctuation, capitalization

IV. Documentation
    A. Plagiarism
    B. Use of quoted, summarized, and paraphrased material
    C. Internal documentation
    D. Works Cited

V. Format
    A. Heading
    B. Pagination and margins
    C. Documentation
    D. Works Cited
    E. Legibility and neatness

Grade for Original Paper _____

Grade for Revision (if required) _____

CHAPTER SIX

The Critical Analysis Paper

Objectives

When you have completed this chapter, you will have

1. selected, had approved, and read a literary work for critical analysis.

2. chosen a topic for critical analysis.

3. narrowed (and if necessary) divided the topic for critical analysis.

4. compared critical analysis papers.

5. written a thesis and topic sentences for a critical analysis.

6. written a 1,000-word analysis.

6

A **critical analysis paper** explains and interprets. Instructors of literature, history, art, and music often assign this kind of paper. A typical assignment might ask you to write 1,000 words analyzing a poem, play, novel, short story, film, painting, statue, symphony, or other creative work.

Your instructors will ask you to write many critical analysis papers. Critical, analytical thinking and writing skills are fundamental to a good education. In order to write good critical analysis papers, you must fully understand the subject matter of the class and understand how to structure your writing. Certainly, then, the sooner you become proficient in the writing of critical analysis the more quickly you can expect to improve your classroom performance.

LESSON ONE: *What Is a Critical Analysis Paper?*

To begin with, a critical analysis, like many research papers, is expository; that is, it explains. As a matter of fact, the more meticulously the paper clarifies what is being written about, the more successful it becomes. As you might guess, if you were writing a critical analysis paper of a novel such as *Moby Dick; or, The Whale*, it could become an extremely long paper if you attempted to interpret the work fully. Even if you were writing about a book with fewer than the nearly 500 pages in Herman Melville's novel, your paper might become much too long. To control the paper's length when you write a thorough critical analysis, you must deal with only a small aspect of the work being analyzed. For instance, if you were to write a paper on Herman Melville's epic novel, you would be able to think of many appropriate topics. Here are some examples of narrowed topics:

1. The author's perspective on the whaling industry in the mid-19th century.
2. The author's illumination of his theme through allusions to the Bible.
3. The author's technique of increasing suspense through the description of gams, the meeting of two ships at sea.
4. The author's use of symbols for good and evil to illustrate his theme.

Any one of these topics could be the subject of a critical analysis of *Moby Dick; or, The Whale*, but you could not write a paper on anything without first focusing on a small aspect, unless you were planning a paper of unlimited length.

To say a critical analysis paper is expository also means more, however. Perhaps most important, it means that your paper will interpret rather than retell. This is a particularly difficult concept for some students to grasp because they were previously required to retell a story when they wrote book reports. The typical book report consisted of a plot summary with a few critical comments added at the end. Remember that a critical analysis paper does not merely summarize a story, a play, or a poem—or end after only *describing* a painting or other art work.

Another common error that some students make is to confuse **critical review** and **critical analysis.** As a result, they try to evaluate the work being discussed. While critical review papers evaluate a work, critical analysis papers strive to illuminate. A critical review is an attempt to demonstrate that a work is worth reading or reviewing. A review, for example, of a new novel or film, is aimed at readers who are unfamiliar with the work. Furthermore, reviews are often loosely structured, commenting on everything related to the appearance of the work in public; they are often written with an informal, conversational style (see Chapter Five). The critical analysis, by contrast, is an in-depth look at a work aimed at readers who have read or viewed the work. In other words, they are familiar with the subject and are not reading for evaluation but rather for deeper understanding.

A critical analysis paper is written in formal English and follows a tightly controlled structure. It includes a clearly stated thesis and topic sentences. Before writing critical analysis papers, most students prepare a thesis-topic sentence outline, and as they write, they follow the outline carefully. The following outline was taken from a paper written by a student. The assignment was to write a 1,000-word paper analyzing some aspect of the novel *Moby Dick*. After considering several topics, the student-author chose to write about the technique Melville used to create suspense.

THE GAMS IN *MOBY DICK*: The Creation of Suspense

Thesis: In *Moby Dick*, Herman Melville uses gams, the meeting of two ships at sea, to demonstrate Captain Ahab's obsession, intensify his malignant excitement, and develop suspense for the novel's readers.

1. The first few gams establish the white whale's purported destructiveness and the power the legend of the white whale has upon the crew.
2. The early gams suggest that Moby Dick directs his vengeance at only the one who is directly responsible for inflicting injury upon him.
3. The middle gams are both satirical, and function as foils for Captain Ahab and the *Pequod*.
4. The last two gams clearly foreshadow the imminent and catastrophic conclusion of the tale.

Notice that you can tell exactly what the student's points are, even without being able to read the entire paper. Any well-written analysis should have this obvious structure.

Contrary to what you might at first think, a critical analysis paper is not negative in tone. Writing a critical paper does not mean that you concentrate on the alleged flaws or perceived shortcomings of a work. In terms of common usage, that may indeed be true, but the critical analysis paper never attempts to pick anything apart to reveal its weaknesses. The purpose of an analysis paper is to illuminate, in depth, one or both of the following:

1. The author's meaning or theme, an idea, a point of view, a perception, or an underlying artistic representation in a work of art
2. The author's technique in achieving the above

If you choose the first purpose, your paper will explain what the author's point is. The theme is very much like the thesis of a paper, except that a theme is not neatly stated at the end of the introduction. Examine the thesis in the outline on page 250 for an example. Also, earlier in this chapter you read four narrowed topics for a critical analysis paper on *Moby Dick*. One was related to the author's theme and three to the author's techniques. You should now be able to distinguish between them. (Look back at page 249).

Regardless of what aspect of a work you choose to write about, the all-important consideration is that you clearly support whatever position you take in your thesis. Body paragraphs must clearly explain some part of what your thesis states. Use key words or concepts to make the relationship between the thesis and the topic sentences evident at a glance. The student author of the *Moby Dick* outline, for example, uses the key word *gam* in each sentence to establish an obvious relationship between the thesis and the topic sentences.

EXERCISE 6.1

Develop a work schedule for your paper.

Work Schedule

Project Title: Critical Analysis   **Due Date** _____

Exercise	Project Assignment	Sample Allotment	Your Time Allotment	Date Due
Ex. 6.2	Select Literary Work	(1/2 day)	_____	_____
Ex. 6.3	Study Sample	(1 day)	_____	_____
Ex. 6.4	Read and Compare	(1 day)	_____	_____
Ex. 6.5	Read Literary Work	(2 days)	_____	_____
Ex. 6.6	Select Topic	(1/2 day)	_____	_____
Ex. 6.7	Divide Topic	(1/2 day)	_____	_____
Ex. 6.8	Develop Thesis	(1/2 day)	_____	_____
Ex. 6.9	Outline	(1 day)	_____	_____
Ex. 6.10	Draft and Proofread	(2 days)	_____	_____

Have your work schedule approved.

The critical analysis paper explains one possible interpretation of the topic you are writing on, not the only one. That is, you must understand that one-and-only explanations do not exist. Not even the person who wrote, painted, or sculpted the work in question can say exactly what it means; everyone's opinion is merely an educated speculation based on a close reading of the work. If you have read the work carefully and honestly considered the possibilities, your opinion is as good as anyone else's.

The key to analysis is to support your observations with specific details and examples from the work in question. Your analysis must seem plausible in terms of the detailed explanation you have composed. Although the main purpose of a critical analysis is not to persuade, you do have the responsibility of organizing a discussion that convinces readers that your analysis is astute.

EXERCISE 6.2

Select a literary work—a short story, a novel, a poem, or a play—that you will read in preparation for writing a critical analysis.

Title of Work: _____

Author: _____

Have your selection approved.

LESSON TWO: *How to Read a Literary Work for Analysis*

Before you can plan a critical analysis, you must completely understand the work about which you wish to write. Far too many students think that simply reading a poem, play, novel, or short story once thoroughly is enough, but once through will develop only a superficial understanding. Follow these steps as you plan your critical analysis paper:

1. Examine the title carefully. The title is often a clue to what is considered important in the work.

2. Consult a dictionary or other source for every word or reference you do not understand. Sometimes a single word, often a unique word, will give a clue to the meaning of the story. The following quote from a short story contains a word that is pivotal to the meaning of the story in which it appears.

   > A sawmill was nearby. Its pyramidal sawdust pile smouldered. It is a year before one completely burns. Meanwhile, the smoke curls up and hangs in odd wraiths about the trees, curls up, and spreads itself out over the valley . . . . Jean Toomer, "Karintha," *Cane*

   The student who reads this short story and fails to look up the word *wraith* will invariably misinterpret the author's meaning. In fact, a "wraith" is a ghost or visible spirit. In this case, the wraith refers to the ghost of a baby who is buried and burning in that sawdust pile.

3. After you have read through the first time, ask yourself about the obvious structure of the work. For instance, is there a geographical, historical, or social aspect to the work? If so, what is it, and how do the characters fit into this setting? Who tells the story? How does that influence the work? Is there a central character, and if so, what conflicts does he or she encounter? How are the different characters related, and what motivates them to do what they do?

4. Think about how the work is organized. Does it have a beginning, a middle, and an end? Are there parts or sections? Can you trace the development and resolution of the conflict? Is the conclusion the logical outcome of the events and actions of the characters? If you are reading a poem, can you paraphrase what the poem is saying?

5. As you read the work the second time, search for deeper meanings. Your understanding of words and images will help you perceive a deeper meaning. You should make notes in the margin or on separate paper during this reading as you speculate about the work. For example, what is the author's purpose in writing this work? Is it to present a slice of life, to make social commentary, or to reveal the complexities of human character? Is the author attempting a combination of purposes? After all is considered, what is the main underlying message of this work? Can you summarize the author's meaning in a paragraph? Can you state the theme of the work in a single sentence? If you are contemplating symbolism in the work, what are the symbols and what do they mean? What other aspects of the work interest you? Is it possible that the work means different things on different levels, for instance, in terms of pure action and outcome, in terms of social or historical commentary, and on a deeper symbolic level?

6. Ask yourself the significance of all repeated numbers, colors, or images. For example, when an author of one short story uses the number three five times in two pages, the reader should begin to look for a significant relationship among the items described.

You may want to discuss the work with someone else. Just talking about the work will help, but asking questions will promote even more understanding. Always keep asking yourself, what is the author trying to say? What is the point?

If you are unable to decide what the author is saying, you may be wise to do some research. Even though not expected by instructors who assign critical analysis papers, research will sometimes suggest possible meanings of a work. For instance, if you are reading a short story by the British writer Saki (H. H. Munro), it would probably help you to know that he frequently makes fun of boring adults in his writing. The fact that he was raised by aunts who pretended to care for him (but really did not) might also help you decide what he was thinking as he wrote the story.

If a writer has written about the same type of people or problems in earlier works, you may be able to use them to decide what is important. You might also find it helpful to read about the events that took place at the time the work was written. If you were doing an analysis of John Steinbeck's *Grapes of Wrath*, it might help you to interpret the work if you knew what life was actually like for the farmers who were forced from their lands during the Depression. Often material from other courses, such as anthropology, history, or sociology, may establish a context for a given work. It should take little research to discover such additional information. Ask your librarian for assistance in finding what has been written about the literary work or about the context of the literary work you are studying.

Documenting Your Sources

Any researched information that you include in a critical analysis paper must be documented. Keep a record of your research on working bibliography and note cards. Use lead-ins and parenthetical references to integrate researched material, just as you did in your library research paper. Any time you use researched information (secondary sources), be sure to include a Works Cited page at the end of the paper (see Chapter Four and Appendix A).

EXERCISE 6.3

For practice in critical reading, study the following short story carefully. Use a dictionary whenever necessary. As you read the story, look also at the questions on the left. These are questions and comments you should be asking yourself as you read. Normally, when you are reading a literary work for analysis, you should be writing out questions and comments like these.

Paragraph
Number

1. The author describes the railroad car as a "great Pullman" with a "dignity of motion." Could this be a symbol? Note that the plains are compared to a river pouring eastward toward a waterfall.

2. The man's face and hands reflect a man of the outdoors; this contrasts sharply with his "new black clothes." He appears out of place. Is this why his glances at other passengers are "furtive and shy"?

3. Why is the bride embarrassed by her clothes? Is she, too, out of place in the pullman car? Other passengers have noticed something odd and have stared. Is she an average working woman dressed as a lady? Why else is she embarrassed?

The Bride Comes to Yellow Sky
By Stephen Crane

1.   The great Pullman was whirling onward with such dignity of motion that a glance from the window seemed simply to prove that the plains of Texas were pouring eastward. Vast flats of green grass, dull-hued spaces of mesquite and cactus, little groups of frame houses, woods of light and tender trees, all were sweeping into the east, sweeping over the horizon, a precipice.

2.   A newly married pair had boarded this coach at San Antonio. The man's face was reddened from many days in the wind and sun, and a direct result of his new black clothes was that his brick-coloured hands were constantly performing in a most conscious fashion. From time to time he looked down respectfully at his attire. He sat with a hand on each knee, like a man waiting in a barber's shop. The glances he devoted to other passengers were furtive and shy.

3.   The bride was not pretty, nor was she very young. She wore a dress of blue cashmere, with small reservations of velvet here and there, and with steel buttons abounding. She continually twisted her head to regard her puff sleeves, very stiff, straight, and high. They embarrassed her. It was quite

4. The groom does not seem to know much
about his bride.

5-8. The bride has never been on a train before. What does she mean by the word fine?
What is Jack's attitude toward the expense
of eating in the diner?

9. The groom, Jack, has apparently been on
trains before. What does the comment "He
had the pride of an owner" mean? Is he
showing off for his new bride?

10. Why does Jack's happiness make him appear
ridiculous to the porter? Why does the porter bully the newly married pair? And why
are other travelers laughing at them? Are
the bride and groom such obvious "country
cousins"?

apparent that she had cooked, and that she
expected to cook, dutifully. The blushes
caused by the careless scrutiny of some passengers as she had entered the car were
strange to see upon this plain, under-class
countenance, which was drawn in placid,
almost emotionless lines.

4. They were evidently very happy. "Ever
been in a parlour-car before?" he asked,
smiling with delight.

5. "No," she answered; "I never was. It's fine,
ain't it?"

6. "Great! And then after a while we'll go
forward to the diner, and get a big lay-out.
Finest meal in the world. Charge a dollar."

7. "Oh, do they?" cried the bride. "Charge a
dollar? Why that's too much—for us—ain't
it, Jack?"

8. "Not this trip, anyhow," he answered
bravely. "We're going to go the whole
thing."

9. Later he explained to her about the
trains. "You see, it's a thousand miles from
one end of Texas to the other; and this train
runs right across it, and never stops but four
times." He had the pride of an owner. He
pointed out to her the dazzling fittings of the
coach; and in truth her eyes opened wider as
she contemplated the sea-green figured velvet, the shining brass, silver, and glass, the
wood that gleamed as darkly brilliant as the
surface of a pool of oil. At one end a bronze
figure sturdily held a support for a separated
chamber, and at convenient places on the
ceiling were frescos in olive and silver.

10. To the minds of the pair, their surroundings reflected the glory of their marriage
that morning in San Antonio; this was the
environment of their new estate; and the
man's face in particular beamed with an ela-
tion that made him appear ridiculous to the
Negro porter. This individual at times surveyed them from afar with an amused and
superior grin. On other occasions he bullied
them with skill in ways that did not make it
exactly plain to them that they were being
bullied. He subtly used all the manners of
the most unconquerable kind of snobbery.

He oppressed them; but of this oppression they had small knowledge, and they speedily forgot that infrequently a number of travelers covered them with stares of derisive enjoyment. Historically there was supposed to be something infinitely humorous in their situation .

11-14. Time is the subject in these paragraphs. Both have watches—could they be symbols? Since it is the arrival time in Yellow Sky that seems crucial, this is an interlude before whatever will happen when they arrive. With more than three hours before their arrival, Jack seems happy.

11. "We are due in Yellow Sky at 3:42," he said, looking tenderly into her eyes.

12. "Oh, are we?" she said, as if she had not been aware of it. To evince surprise at her husband's statement was part of her wifely amiability. She took from a pocket a little silver watch; and as she held it before her, and stared at it with a frown of attention, the new husband's face shone.

13. "I bought it in San Anton' from a friend of mine," he told her gleefully.

14. "It's seventeen minutes past twelve," she said, looking up at him with a kind of shy and clumsy coquetry. A passenger, noting this play, grew excessively sardonic, and winked at himself in one of the numerous mirrors.

15. Their waiter in the dining car, although friendly and kind, "patronizes" the couple, but they do not even notice. Or do they choose to ignore the waiter's behavior to avoid looking foolish?

15. At last they went to the dining-car. Two rows of Negro waiters, in glowing white suits, surveyed their entrance with the interest, and also the equanimity, of men who had been forewarned. The pair fell to the lot of a waiter who happened to feel pleasure in steering them through their meal. He viewed them with the manner of a fatherly pilot, his countenance radiant with benevolence. The patronage, entwined with the ordinary deference, was not plain to them. And yet, as they returned to their coach, they showed in their faces a sense of escape.

16. Jack becomes increasingly nervous as the train draws nearer his home town of Yellow Sky. Why?

16. To the left, miles down a long purple slope, was a little ribbon of mist where moved the keening Rio Grande. The train was approaching it at an angle, and the apex was Yellow Sky. Presently it was apparent that, as the distance from Yellow Sky grew shorter, the husband became commensurately restless. His brick-red hands were more insistent in their prominence. Occasionally he was even rather absent-minded and far-away when the bride leaned forward and addressed him.

17. Jack Potter feels guilt about marrying without talking it over with the citizens of Yellow Sky. Why should a town marshal who is a well-respected member of the community ask permission?

18. Apparently, Jack's guilt is due to his own sense of duty. Why is his marriage an "extraordinary crime"? What do the lines "At San Antonio he was like a man . . . in that remote city" mean?

19. How could his marriage be so important to the town? What kind of reception does he expect? What kind of reception do married couples usually receive?

20-22. He is going to sneak from the station to his house to avoid friends and the brass band. In paragraph 19, Jack thinks his friends will not forgive him; yet here he thinks that the citizens will be happy about his marriage and offer congratulations—explain the apparent contradiction.

17. As a matter of truth, Jack Potter was beginning to find the shadow of a deed weigh upon him like a leaden slab. He, the town marshal of Yellow Sky, a man known, liked, and feared in his corner, a prominent person, had gone to San Antonio to meet a girl he believed he loved, and there, after the usual prayers, had actually induced her to marry him, without consulting Yellow Sky for any part of the transaction. He was now bringing his bride before an innocent and unsuspecting community.

18. Of course people in Yellow Sky married as it pleased them, in accordance with a general custom; but such was Potter's thought of his duty to his friends, or of their idea of his duty, or of an unspoken form which does not control men in these matters, that he felt he was heinous. He had committed an extraordinary crime. Face to face with this girl in San Antonio, and spurred by his sharp impulse, he had gone headlong over all the social hedges. At San Antonio he was like a man hidden in the dark. A knife to sever any friendly duty, any form, was easy to his hand in that remote city. But the hour of Yellow Sky—the hour of daylight—was approaching.

19. He knew full well that his marriage was an important thing to his town. It could only be exceeded by the burning of the new hotel. His friends could not forgive him. Frequently he had reflected on the advisability of telling them by telegraph, but a new cowardice had been upon him. He feared to do it. And now the train was hurrying him toward a scene of amazement, glee, and reproach. He glanced out of the window at the line of haze swinging slowly in toward the train.

20. Yellow Sky had a kind of brass band, which played painfully, to the delight of the populace. He laughed without heart as he thought of it. If the citizens could dream of his prospective arrival with his bride, they would parade the band at the station and escort them, amid cheers and laughing congratulations, to his adobe home.

21. He resolved that he would use all the devices of speed and plainscraft in making the journey from the station to his house. Once within that safe citadel, he could issue some sort of vocal bulletin, and then not go among the citizens until they had time to wear off a little of their enthusiasm.

22. The bride looked anxiously at him. "What's worrying you, Jack?"

23-25. Both feel guilty about the marriage. Do they seem to understand one another without discussion?

23. He laughed again. "I'm not worrying, girl; I'm only thinking of Yellow Sky."

24. She flushed in comprehension.

25. A sense of mutual guilt invaded their minds and developed a finer tenderness. They looked at each other with eyes softly aglow. But Potter often laughed the same nervous laugh; the flush upon the bride's face seemed quite permanent.

26. The word "traitor" drives home the idea that Jack is not loyal to the townspeople. Pause here to note the point of view from which the story is told. The narrator tells the story and seems to know everything about what will happen and what the people are thinking and feeling. How would the story be different if it were told from the limited point of view of one of the characters?

26. The traitor to the feelings of Yellow Sky narrowly watched the speeding landscape. "We're nearly there," he said.

27-28. Why does the porter treat the couple differently now?

27. Presently the porter came and announced the proximity of Potter's home. He held a brush in his hand, and, with all his airy superiority gone, he brushed Potter's new clothes as the latter slowly turned this way and that way. Potter fumbled out a coin and gave it to the porter, as he had seen others do. It was a heavy and muscle-bound business, as that of a man shoeing his first horse.

28. The porter took their bag, and as the train began to slow they moved forward to the hooded platform of the car. Presently the two engines and their long string of coaches rushed into the station of Yellow Sky.

29. Potter is like a man going to his death. Is that what is about to happen?

29. "They have to take water here," said Potter, from a constricted throat and in mournful cadence, as one announcing death. Before the train stopped his eye had swept

the length of the platform, and he was glad and astonished to see there was none upon it but the station agent, who, with a slightly hurried and anxious air, was walking toward the water-tanks. When the train had halted, the porter alighted first, and placed in position a little temporary step.

30. The station-agent sees the couple leaving. Does he react as Jack feared he would?

30.   "Come on, girl," said Potter, hoarsely. As he helped her down they each laughed on a false note. He took the bag from the Negro, and bade his wife cling to his arm. As they slunk rapidly away, his hang-dog glance perceived that they were unloading the two trunks, and also that the station-agent, far ahead near the baggage car, had turned and was running toward him, making gestures. He laughed, and groaned as he laughed, when he noted the first effect of his marital bliss upon Yellow Sky. He gripped his wife's arm firmly to his side, and they fled. Behind them the porter stood, chuckling fatuously.

II

31-33. The scene shifts abruptly to the Weary Gentleman Saloon "twenty-one minutes" before the train arrives. Who all is there? What is a "drummer"? Could this be the "lull before the storm"? This abrupt shift in time and in scene tells you something about how the story is organized. What does it tell?

31.   The California Express on the Southern Railway was due at Yellow Sky in twenty-one minutes. There were six men at the bar of the Weary Gentleman saloon. One was a drummer who talked a great deal and rapidly; three were Texans who did not care to talk at that time; and two were Mexican sheep-herders, who did not talk as a general practice in the Weary Gentleman saloon. The barkeeper's dog lay on the board walk that crossed in front of the door. His head was on his paws, and he glanced drowsily here and there with the constant vigilance of a dog that is kicked on occasion. Across the sandy street were some vivid green grass plots, so wonderful in appearance, amid the sands that burned near them in a blazing sun, that they caused a doubt in the mind. They exactly resembled the grass mats used to represent lawns on the stage. At the cooler end of the railway station, a man without a coat sat in a tilted chair and smoked his pipe. The fresh-cut bank of the Rio Grande circled near the town, and there could be seen beyond it a great plum-coloured plain of mesquite.

32.   Save for the busy drummer and his companions in the saloon, Yellow Sky was dozing. The new-comer leaned gracefully upon

the bar, and recited many tales with the confidence of a bard who has come upon a new field.

33. "—and at the moment that the old man fell downstairs with the bureau in his arms, the old woman was coming up with two scuttles of coal, and of course—"

34-37. Scratchy Wilson is apparently a much-feared person. Although the drummer is oblivious, how do the others react?

34. The drummer's tale was interrupted by a young man who suddenly appeared in the open door. He cried: "Scratchy Wilson's drunk, and has turned loose with both hands." The two Mexicans at once set down their glasses and faded out of the rear entrance of the saloon.

35. The drummer, innocent and jocular, answered: "All right, old man. S'pose he has? Come in and have a drink anyhow."

36. But the information had made such an obvious cleft in every skull in the room that the drummer was obliged to see its importance. All had become instantly solemn. "Say," said he, mystified, "what is this?" His three companions made the introductory gesture of eloquent speech; but the young man at the door forestalled them.

37. "It means, my friend," he answered, as he came into the saloon, "that for the next two hours this town won't be a health resort."

38. The barkeeper's actions leave no doubt that all take the danger from Wilson as a very real threat. Why is the bar compared to a chapel?

38. The barkeeper went to the door, and locked and barred it; reaching out of the window, he pulled in heavy wooden shutters, and barred them. Immediately a solemn, chapel-like gloom was upon the place. The drummer was looking from one to another.

39. "But say," he cried, "what is this, anyhow? You don't mean there is going to be a gunfight?"

39-50. The author uses the drummer to relate essential background information to the reader. What can Scratchy Wilson be expected to do?

40. "Don't know whether there'll be a fight or not," answered one man, grimly; "but there'll be some shootin'—some good shootin'."

41. The young man who had warned them waved his hand. "Oh, there'll be a fight fast enough, if any one wants it. Anybody can get a fight out there in the street. There's a fight just waiting."

42. The drummer seemed to be swayed between the interest of a foreigner and a perception of personal danger.

43. "What did you say his name was?" he asked.

44. "Scratchy Wilson," they answered in chorus.

45. "And will he kill anybody? What are you going to do? Does this happen often? Does he rampage around like this once a week or so? Can he break in that door?"

46. "No; he can't break down that door," replied the barkeeper. "He's tried it three times. But when he comes you'd better lay down on the floor, stranger. He's dead sure to shoot at it, and a bullet may come through."

47. Thereafter the drummer kept a strict eye upon the door. The time had not yet been called for him to hug the floor, but, as a minor precaution, he sidled near to the wall. "Will he kill anybody?" he said again.

48. The men laughed low and scornfully at the question.

49. "He's out to shoot, and he's out for trouble. Don't see any good in experimentin' with him."

50. "But what do you do in a case like this? What do you do?"

51. Jack Potter is connected to the action in town. Obviously, the townspeople think Potter is the only one who can stand up to Wilson. At this point, who do you think Potter's antagonist is, the townspeople or Wilson?

51. A man responded: "Why, he and Jack Potter—"

52-59. The marshal role Jack has taken on earns respect but obvious danger, too. Do the townspeople seem to take it for granted that Potter should fight Scratchy on a regular basis?

52. "But," in chorus the other men interrupted, "Jack Potter's in San Anton'."

53. "Well, who is he? What's he got to do with it?"

54. "Oh, he's the town marshal. He goes out and fights Scratchy when he gets on one of these tears."

55. "Wow!" said the drummer, mopping his brow. "Nice job he's got."

56.   The voices had toned away to mere whisperings. The drummer wished to ask further questions, which were born of an increasing anxiety and bewilderment; but when he attempted them, the men merely looked at him in irritation and motioned him to remain silent. A tense waiting hush was upon them. In the deep shadows of the room their eyes shone as they listened for sounds from the street. One man made three gestures at the barkeeper; and the latter, moving like a ghost, handed him a glass and a bottle. The man poured a full glass of whisky, and set down the bottle noiselessly. He gulped the whisky in a swallow, and turned again toward the door in immovable silence. The drummer saw the barkeeper, without a sound, had taken a Winchester from beneath the bar. Later he saw this individual beckoning to him, so he tiptoed across the room.

57.   "You better come with me back of the bar."

58.   "No, thanks," said the drummer, perspiring; "I'd rather be where I can make a break for the back door."

59.   Whereupon the man of bottles made a kindly but peremptory gesture. The drummer obeyed it, and, finding himself seated on a box with his head below the level of the bar, balm was laid upon his soul at sight of various zinc and copper fittings that bore a resemblance to armourplate. The barkeeper took a seat comfortably upon an adjacent box.

60. Scratchy Wilson is "a wonder with a gun—a perfect wonder." What evidence is there that he is a character left from an older, wilder West?

60.   "You see," he whispered, "this here Scratchy Wilson is a wonder with a gun—a perfect wonder; and when he goes on the war trail, we hunt our holes—naturally. He's about the last one of the old gang that used to hang out along the river here. He's a terror when he's drunk. When he's sober he's all right—kind of simple—wouldn't hurt a fly—nicest fellow in town. But when he's drunk—whoo!"

61. As the trouble starts, the men in the bar wish Potter was back. How do you know Potter is a skillful gunfighter and that there have been previous fights?

61.   There were periods of stillness. "I wish Jack Potter was back from San Anton'," said the barkeeper. "He shot Wilson up once—in the leg—and he would sail in and pull out the kinks in this thing."

62. What effect does Scratchy's rampage have on the men in the bar?

63-65. Which articles of Scratchy's clothng seem incongruous? Why does the author go out of his way to make Wilson appear a misfit? Note that Section Three of the story begins here.

66. Wilson is unable to find any human to shoot, so he picks on the dog. Note the foreshadowing in paragraph 31.

62. Presently they heard from a distance the sound of a shot, followed by three wild yowls. It instantly removed a bond from the men in the darkened saloon. There was a shuffling of feet. They looked at each other. "Here he comes," they said.

III

63. A man in a maroon-coloured flannel shirt, which had been purchased for purpose of decoration, and made principally by some Jewish women on the East Side of New York, rounded a corner and walked into the middle of the main street of Yellow Sky. In either hand the man held a long, heavy, blue-black revolver. Often he yelled, and these cries rang through a semblance of a deserted village, shrilly flying over the roofs in a volume that seemed to have no relation to the ordinary vocal strength of a man. It was as if the surrounding stillness formed the arch of a tomb over him. These cries of ferocious challenge rang against walls of silence. And his boots had red tops with gilded imprints, of the kind beloved in winter by little sledding boys on the hillsides of New England.

64. The man's face flamed in a rage begot of whisky. His eyes, rolling, and yet keen for ambush, hunted the still doorways and windows. He walked with the creeping movement of the midnight cat. As it occurred to him, he roared menacing information. The long revolvers in his hands were as easy as straws; they were moved with an electric swiftness. The little fingers of each hand played sometimes in a musician's way. Plain from the low collar of the shirt, the cords of his neck straightened and sank, straightened and sank, as passion moved him. The only sounds were his terrible invitations. The calm adobes preserved their demeanour at the passing of this small thing in the middle of the street.

65. There was no offer of fight—no offer of fight. The man called to the sky. There were no attractions. He bellowed and fumed and swayed his revolvers here and everywhere.

66. The dog of the barkeeper of the Weary Gentleman saloon had not appreciated the advance of events. He yet lay dozing in front

67-68. He cannot enter to buy another drink, and no one will even yell back to him. Are you surprised that he leaves the saloon so quickly?

69. Jack Potter is called Wilson's "ancient antagonist." Is this referring to the marshal's age and ability? Or is it focusing the reader's attention of the fact that only Potter is capable of stopping Wilson? How does his chanting reveal again that he is a character from the vanishing old West?

70. Although Scratchy is working himself into a rage, his confrontation with the house seems part of a ritual. Explain (remember the chanting).

71. How much time has probably elapsed since paragraph 31? How has the author skillfully and dramatically set the scene for a climax?

of his master's door. At sight of the dog, the man paused and raised his revolver humourously. At sight of the man, the dog sprang up and walked diagonally away, with a sullen head, and growling. The man yelled and the dog broke into a gallop. As it was about to enter an alley, there was a loud noise, a whistling, and something spat the ground directly before it. The dog screamed, and, wheeling in terror, galloped headlong in a new direction. Again there was a noise, a whistling, and sand was kicked viciously before it. Fear-stricken, the dog turned and flurried like an animal in a pen. The man stood laughing, his weapons at his hips.

67. Ultimately the man was attracted by the closed door of the Weary Gentleman saloon. He went to it and, hammering with a revolver, demanded drink.

68. The door remaining imperturbable, he picked a bit of paper from the walk, and nailed it to the framework with a knife. He then turned his back contemptuously upon this popular resort and, walking to the opposite side of the street and spinning there on his heel quickly and lithely, fired at the bit of paper. He missed it by a half-inch. He swore at himself, and went away. Later he comfortably fusilladed the windows of his most intimate friend. The man was playing with this town; it was a toy for him.

69. But still there was no offer of fight. The name of Jack Potter, his ancient antagonist, entered his mind, and he concluded that it would be a glad thing if he should go to Potter's house, and by bombardment induce him to come out and fight. He moved in the direction of his desire, chanting Apache scalp music.

70. When he arrived at it, Potter's house presented the same still front as had the other adobes. Taking up a strategic position, the man howled a challenge. But this house regarded him as might a great stone god. It gave no sign. After a decent wait, the man howled further challenges, mingling with them wonderful epithets.

71. Presently there came the spectacle of a man churning himself into deepest rage over the immobility of a house. He fumed at it as

the winter wind attacks a prairie cabin in the North. To the distance there should have gone the sound of a tumult like the fighting of two hundred Mexicans. As necessity bade him, he paused for breath or to reload his revolvers.

IV

72-73. Where do you expect Scratchy Wilson to be?

74. Wilson could shoot Potter easily. Why does he wait?

75-77. The story has been building to this point since the beginning. Do you expect violence and death?

78. Did you expect Potter to be armed? Is a gun a symbol here of more than one idea?

72. Potter and his bride walked sheepishly and with speed. Sometimes they laughed together shamefacedly and low.

73. "Next corner, dear," he said finally.

74. They put forth the efforts of a pair walking bowed against a strong wind. Potter was about to raise a finger to point the first appearance of the new home when, as they circled the corner, they came face to face with a man in a maroon-coloured shirt, who was feverishly pushing cartridges into a large revolver. Upon the instant the man dropped his revolver to the ground and, like lightning, whipped another from its holster. The second weapon was aimed at the bridegroom's chest.

75. There was a silence. Potter's mouth seemed to be merely a grave for his tongue. He exhibited an instinct to at once loosen his arm from the woman's grip, and he dropped the bag to the sand. As for the bride, her face had gone as yellow as old cloth. She was a slave to hideous rites, gazing at the apparitional snake.

76. The two men faced each other at a distance of three paces. He of the revolver smiled with a new and quiet ferocity.

77. "Tried to sneak up on me," he said. "Tried to sneak up on me!" His eyes grew more baleful. As Potter made a slight movement, the man thrust his revolver venomously forward. "No; don't you do it, Jack Potter. Don't you move a finger toward a gun just yet. Don't you move an eyelash. The time has come for me to settle with you, and I'm goin' to do it my own way, and loaf along with no interferin'. So if you don't want a gun bent on you, just mind what I tell you."

78. Potter looked at his enemy. "I ain't got a gun on me Scratchy," he said. "Honest, I ain't." He was stiffening and steadying, but yet somewhere at the back of his mind a

vision of the Pullman floated: the sea-green figured velvet, the shining brass, silver, and glass, the wood that gleamed as darkly brilliant as the surface of a pool of oil—all the glory of the marriage, the environment of the new estate. "You know I fight when it comes to fighting, Scratchy Wilson; but I ain't got a gun on me. You'll have to do all the shootin' yourself."

79-80. Why does Wilson's face go "livid" when he finds Potter is unarmed? Is he playing a game with the marshal or does he believe Potter is lying?

79. His enemy's face went livid. He stepped forward, and lashed his weapon to and fro before Potter's chest. "Don't you tell me you ain't got no gun on you, you whelp! Don't tell me no lie like that. There ain't a man in Texas ever seen you without no gun. Don't take me for no kid." His eyes blazed with light, and his throat worked like a pump.

80. "I ain't takin' you for no kid," answered Potter. His heels had not moved an inch backward. "I'm takin' you for a damn fool. I tell you I ain't got a gun, and I ain't. If you're goin' to shoot me up, you better begin now; you'll never get a chance like this again."

81. Wilson tries to humiliate the marshal. Why?

81. So much enforced reasoning had told on Wilson's rage; he was calmer. "If you ain't got a gun, why ain't you got a gun?" he sneered. "Been to Sunday-school?"

82-87. Why is Wilson overwhelmed by news that Potter is married? Why is he "like a creature allowed a glimpse of another world?"

82. "I ain't got a gun because I've just come from San Anton' with my wife. I'm married," said Potter. "And if I'd thought there was going to be any galoots like you prowling around when I brought my wife home, I'd had a gun and don't you forget it."

83. "Married!" said Scratchy, not at all comprehending.

84. "Yes, married. I'm married," said Potter, distinctly.

85. "Married?" said Scratchy. Seemingly for the first time, he saw the drooping, drowning woman at the other man's side. "No!" he said. He was like a creature allowed a glimpse of another world. He moved a pace backward, and his arm, with the revolver, dropped to his side. "Is this the lady?" he asked.

86. "Yes; this is the lady," answered Potter.

87. There was another period of silence.

88-89. What does Wilson mean when he says, "I s'pose it's all off now"? What is all off!

88. "Well," said Wilson at last, slowly, "I s'pose it's all off now."

89. "It's all off if you say so, Scratchy. You know I didn't make the trouble." Potter lifted his valise.

90. Why is marriage a "foreign condition" to Scratchy?

90. "Well, I'low it's off, Jack," said Wilson. He was looking at the ground. "Married!" He was not a student of chivalry; it was merely that in the presence of this foreign condition he was a simple child of the earlier plains. He picked up his starboard revolver, and, placing both weapons in their holsters, he went away. His feet made funnel-shaped tracks in the heavy sand.

After the first reading of *The Bride Comes to Yellow Sky*, you may have more questions than answers. If so, it is time to reread and think carefully about the story. When you finally have answers to all your questions, you are ready to study a paper about the story.

LESSON THREE: *The Structure of a Critical Analysis Paper*

At this point you may be asking yourself what the paper you are expected to write should look like. Examine the student-written critical analysis paper on the following pages. As you read the paper on the right-hand pages, consider the accompanying explanations on the left-hand pages.

Heading

The heading is standard. It should look just like the one on your argumentative paper. On the upper left corner of the first page, place the following:

1. Your name
2. Course title and meeting time
3. Instructor's name
4. Date paper is to be submitted
5. Type of paper submitted

Title of Paper

The title of the paper is centered at the top.

Page Numbers and Headers

Begin numbering your paper on the first page with your last name and the number 1 in the upper right-hand corner. Subsequent page numbers follow your last name: e.g., Bronson 2. (If you are required to have a title page do not number it; if you include an outline page it should be Roman-numbered following your name: e.g., Bronson i.)

Present Tense

Analysis papers on literary works are written in present tense because if you were to reread the work, the characters would still be doing the same things. The present tense is the way readers think about what is happening; consequently, that is the tense you should use in writing about those actions. Thus, you would say:

"Jack Potter *is* the marshal in the story."

NOT

"Jack Potter *was* the marshal in the story."

Title Page

If your instructor requires a traditional title page instead of a heading on the first page of the paper, it should look just like the sample title page for the research paper (see page 188 for detailed directions).

Outline Page

If your instructor requires an outline page, see pages 190-193 for instructions and a sample outline.

Purpose of Paper

The purpose of any critical analysis paper is to explain the work's meaning or the author's technique. In this paper the student does both: She explains the theme of changes and she interprets the symbols that Crane uses to elaborate on his theme.

Sandra L. Ewers

English 1A TTH 10:30

Mr. Mehaffy

21 April 1995

(Critical Analysis)

A Historic Day in Yellow Sky

Stephen Crane's short story "The Bride Comes to Yellow Sky" is an illustrative tale of history's inevitable course. On the surface, Crane relates the journey of Marshal Potter and his bride to the small Texas town of Yellow Sky. In a larger sense, however, Crane contrasts a story of the passage of the old West with its simple values and way of life to the arrival of the more complex life and ideas of the civilization from the East, a story of greater historical significance. The characters are not extensively developed; instead, they are simply presented, even understated. Crane's intent is not to draw vivid characterizations but to present objects and characters as symbols with larger meanings.

The pullman car is the first symbol of the East presented in the story. With its elaborate interior, the parlor-car expresses the greater sophistication of Eastern culture, for the velvet, brass, and finely-polished wood furnishings found in the coach would not be useful or practical in an adobe house or a Texas saloon. Rather, the harshness of the frontier demands sturdy, functional furniture and equipment requiring little care. The superior attitude of the porter and the scornful conduct of the other passengers, all Easterners, towards the weather-worn marshal implies the culture of the West is primitive and unrefined. The westward movement of the train, a powerful machine of steel run by steam, signifies that the advancement of Eastern culture into the Western frontier is an accelerating force which cannot be

Transitions

The relationship between the thesis and the topic sentences must be clearly established. Here the writer uses **repetition of a key word** to remind the reader of the relationship. (The key word is "symbol".)

AND

The paragraphs are joined by transitions to make sure the paper flows smoothly. The first body paragraph is read immediately after the thesis, so a smooth transition is achieved by the words "first symbol." The second body paragraph, however, is farther from the thesis and requires a more obvious transition. Here the writer uses "In addition to objects, . . . " to contrast this paragraph with the preceding paragraph and "Crane" and "symbols" to connect this paragraph to the thesis. The third body paragraph is connected back to the second by the character Scratchy Wilson; he is mentioned in both the topic sentence of body paragraph three and the third from the last sentence of body paragraph two.

checked. It is almost as though the West rushes to meet the East. As the train moves westward, "the plains of Texas were pouring eastward. . . . all were sweeping into the east, sweeping over the horizon, a precipice"

In addition to objects, characters are used as symbols. The marshal's bride, for instance, is a sexual metaphor for the ideals and principles of Eastern society. First, women traditionally represent complexity over men in literature because women are viewed as biologically more complex. Beyond this simple representation, women are not only bearers of the children of the next generation, but they protect the customs valued by the culture for posterity. Second, the arrival of the bride in Yellow Sky portends feminine values supplanting the current masculine values of the town. Women, for instance, culturally value peace over conflict. As a result, Yellow Sky can no longer permit Scratchy Wilson his binges of drunken shooting. Furthermore, the bride's new status as the marshal's wife will change the caliber of the entire town since the marriage anticipates a more complex life approaching all the town's residents. The appearance of other women, children, churches, schools, and libraries in the town will closely follow the bride's, permanently changing the lives of all the men in Yellow Sky.

Described by the town bartender as "kind of simple," Scratchy Wilson represents what remains in the town of the life and values of the old frontier. Requiring sturdy men and offering only simple food, simple clothing and simple shelter, the life of the early West was severe and arduous. Scratchy's clothes symbolically convey that the encroachment of the East upon the West has been gradual. Entirely unsuitable in the wilderness, the flannel shirt he now wears was sewn in a New York ghetto. Furthermore, Scratchy sports a pair of red-topped boots with

Sentence Variety

Paragraphs should contain different sentence types. Too many of any particular type of sentence will create boring writing. However, do not worry about writing a variety of different sentence types when you write the first draft. Those are inserted during the revision process.

Conclusion

The concluding paragraph summarizes the observations made in the paper.

gilded imprints that would have made him the object of contemptuous humor in previous times. However modern Scratchy may dress, he is not truly able to fit into the transitional progress of town life. Rather, he is tolerated because among the men the old skills remain respected, and Scratchy is "a wonder with a gun."

While Scratchy and the bride represent the opposing forces of old and new, the marshal and the other town residents exemplify the groups intermediate to the vanishing frontier and the approaching civilization. These are the ordinary, hard-working men who brought the law and established order to the wild lands subdued by men like Scratchy. Specifically, the marshal symbolizes change. Because the marshal did not consult the town about his intent to marry, town residents are neither aware nor prepared for the changes in the marshal and, therefore, for the town that lie ahead. In this manner, Crane suggests that the course of history is neither determined nor prevented by any one person or group.

The simple frontier life giving way to a more advanced and complex civilization is symbolized by Scratchy's acquiescence to the marshal's bride. To Scratchy, Jack Potter seems less masculine with the bride. Even though, according to the code of the West, Scratchy can challenge and fight the marshal, man to man, gun to gun, Scratchy is defenseless against the power of progress. Even Scratchy's primitive code will not permit gunning down an unarmed man in front of his bride. Guns cannot prevent the inexorable course of history. With the arrival of the bride, Yellow Sky, the West, is maturing, and Scratchy, still a child, has no role to play. As Scratchy turns and dejectedly trudges away from the newlyweds, his boot heels leave deep imprints in the sand, illustrating that the old West will soon become only memories. Before long, gusts of

wind blowing in from the hot prairie will shift the grains of sand; the

frontiersmen, along with their ideals, their values, and their code will

have vanished.

The paper on *The Bride Comes to Yellow Sky* is limited by a carefully written thesis because the assignment was to write a 1,000-word paper. Had the student been writing a longer paper, she would have composed a much broader thesis. Notice, also, that she does not use a divided thesis, demonstrating that a divided thesis is an option, not a requirement. Both are equally correct; either one can result in a successful critical analysis.

EXERCISE 6.4

Read the following critical analysis paper and compare it with *A Historic Day in Yellow Sky* (page 269). Observe how each student writer seeks to explain the author's technique in communicating differing literary themes.

Also observe how the student writer Micki Blankenfield creates transitions in *Ruby Turpin's Revelation* so that her words flow smoothly from point to point, paragraph to paragraph throughout her paper. These transitions, like the ones in Sandra Ewers's essay, *A Historic Day in Yellow Sky*, assist readers in following the paper's points.

As you write your paper, use these two compositions as models for the effective use of transitions, as well as thoughtful papers of critical analysis.

Micki Blankenfield

English 1A TTH 2:30

Mr. Mehaffy

10 January 1995

(Critical Analysis)

Ruby Turpin's Revelation

Flannery O'Connor's short story "Revelation" is a study of personalities and what happens when undue pressure is brought to bear on two of the people who come into conflict with one another. The main character, Ruby Turpin, is under the assumption that she is of a superior class and a special person who has been given the divine right to judge the rest of society by virtue of her righteousness. Opposing Ruby is an extremely bright and well educated young woman who unfortunately does not have the maturity or depth of character to know how to combat a powerful personality such as Ruby's in a socially acceptable manner. Furthermore, this hapless young woman, overweight and blighted with acne, is in conflict with her upbringing and her family, particularly her mother. As Ruby and her husband Claude enter the town doctor's waiting room, the situation is ordinary enough, but it is one that will soon explode because of the elements in the personalities of those in the room. To create this conflict and give deeper and more complex meaning to the characters and the story, Flannery O'Connor uses many symbols throughout "Revelation" to underscore and illustrate her theme by evoking images in the reader's mind.

One of the dominant symbols in "Revelation" is Ruby's physical attributes, which are reminiscent of an old sow. In the very first paragraph, O'Connor describes her lead character as "large" with "little

black eyes," a very porcine picture, and the analogy is further
compounded when Ruby, using her weight advantage, shoves her husband
into the only vacant chair. Even when Ruby settles into a chair, she is
reminiscent of a pig; as the chair squeezes around her and she laughs,
her flesh shakes. The animal imagery is also strongly present when,
after the incident with the young woman, the doctor pats Ruby as though
she is a pet and she, in turn, growls. Furthermore, by her use of the
wart hog symbol, an emblem of evil, O'Connor slams home the message that
Ruby's attitude concerning her superiority and racism is evil. For Ruby
Turpin to believe that the very Jesus to whom she was so grateful for
her advantaged position before the "revelation" would send her the
message that she, who has always considered herself so much better than
almost everyone else, is the lowest of the low-classed animals is an
almost fatal blow to her psyche.

A second way the author uses symbols is perhaps more subtle but
just as effective. Ruby notices that the fabric of the old woman's
dress is the same as the "three sacks of chicken feed" which she and
Claude have in their pump house; this shows her snobbery, and of course,
her intimate appraisal of everyone's shoes is a mark of her bias and
unjust judgment of other people. In addition, the bucket of ice water,
which Ruby so generously supplies to the field hands, is a small but
effective symbol used by the author to deliver her message about
inequality and bigotry of the class system in the South. Furthermore,
the thick book entitled Human Development, which hits Ruby not only in
the head but directly over her eye is irony of the purest form, the book
being a symbol of judgment. The gospel music playing in the background
is representative of Ruby's smug, self-satisfied mindset about her place
in the life and her righteous behavior. She feels that she is blessed

by a rather vindictive Christ-figure who metes out people's class and place in the world according to His whims.

"Revelation" is, above all, an example of extreme class distinction through racism and intolerance; moreover, it is a story of color. O'Connor uses over 60 references to colors, perhaps making color the prevailing symbol. Color is an effective device masterfully employed by the author to convey symbolic meanings, from the Christian name of the lead character to the powerful color imagery of the evening sky. The double meaning of color, used not only as a method of description but as a way to ensure class subjugation, is expertly and ironically woven into the story. For example, the photographic negative effect of black and white, which is often thought to be the absence of color, presents the most potent symbolism of the entire account. The picture evoked by the vision in which Ruby sees hosts of souls traveling upward into Heaven, African Americans in "white robes" and white trash "clean for the first time in their lives," is a powerful one indeed, and the meaning of such an image is not lost on Ruby. Furthermore, O'Connor cleverly integrates the term "white face" into the conversation in the doctor's waiting room, knowing that the reader will understand the phrase refers to a certain type of cattle.

In addition to the black and white aspects of color, the author uses ancient meanings of color to create images, such as blue, the color of the book that plays such an important role in the plot. Personifying the intellect and the rarefied atmosphere of the heavens, blue is also the color of the girl's eyes, which so completely captivate Ruby's attention. Noticing the blue of the young woman's eyes which seem to burn and smolder in turns, Ruby compares them unfavorably to the sparkling blue of the girl's mother's eyes. After venting her fury on

Ruby, the young woman's eyes appear to be "a much lighter blue...as if a door that had been tightly closed behind them was now open to admit light and air." Moreover, red, the color of the two Lincolns owned by the rich African-American dentist in town, who so thoroughly destroys Ruby's classification of people, is used to show that the dentist is flaunting his wealth by driving such flashy cars, labeling red as a color of poor taste not only in cars, but in high heeled shoes as well. Perhaps red is only suitable as a color for a plastic bucket for field hands to drink from. In addition, the color yellow plays a significant part in the plot. Separating the people inside the waiting room from the outside world, the yellow curtains symbolize a sudden light or illumination, or in this case a revelation. Outside of the curtains, shapes are distorted and blurred, but inside the room a sharp clarification is taking place. Even the green sun hats worn by the cotton pickers are symbolic of the fertility of the fields, just as the lavender weeds of the Turpin's pasture are meant to represent the nostalgia and sentiment of Ruby and Claude's homecoming after the tumultuous events at the doctor's office.

The symbols used throughout "Revelation" are effective in communicating Flannery O'Connor's theme, and they leave a lasting impression in the reader's mind. Unfortunately, the Ruby Turpins of this world are seldom forced to confront their sins quite as effectively as O'Connnor's heroine is in this short story. When the young woman hurls the book into Ruby's face and then follows the assault with a venomous indictment of Ruby's character, the revelation that will change Ruby Turpin forever has begun. The scene as Ruby receives the true but painful insight into herself is a dramatic and powerful conclusion to the story. Laden with representative meanings from the people involved to the colors of the evening sky, the account is an examination of

racism and injustice, and the story exposes these qualities for the

evils they truly are.

EXERCISE 6.5

Read the literary work approved in Exercise 6.2.

Work Selected: _____

LESSON FOUR: *Writing the Critical Analysis Paper*

After studying the samples, you should now be ready to write your own critical analysis. As with all other essays you write, following a deliberate step-by-step procedure will produce a well-written paper with a minimum of frustration. The following approach is suggested:

After selecting and reading a literary work:

1. Identify some aspect of the work you wish to examine. (This is your topic.)
2. Divide the topic into its various parts.
3. Conduct any necessary research.
4. Develop a thesis that will limit your paper.
5. Compose an outline.
6. Write your paper, documenting any research material.
7. Revise, revise, and revise until your paper represents your best efforts.

Identify a Topic for Examination

The first step in developing any paper, of course, is to identify the topic about which you plan to write. As always, be certain your topic is one that you can make into a paper that is worthy of your effort. Whatever you do, do not choose a topic merely because it sounds easy or because you think your instructor is interested in it. Logically, the topic you choose should be one that developed out of the questions you asked, like those above. The following are topics you might consider if you were preparing to write a paper on *The Bride Comes to Yellow Sky*.

Possible topics:

1. Jack Potter's extraordinary crime
2. Why Potter and his bride appear ridiculous to others on the train
3. Crane's use of color in the story
4. How Crane uses Scratchy Wilson to make a point
5. Crane's use of minor characters to develop Potter's character
6. The role of time in the story
7. The significance of setting in the story

8. Crane's use of characters and objects as symbols (This topic is the one used by the author of the paper "A Historic Day in Yellow Sky.")

EXERCISE 6.6

Select a topic from the literary work approved in Exercise 6.2.

Topic Chosen: _____

Dividing the Topic into Parts

Dividing your topic into parts is important because unless every aspect is examined an unbalanced analysis may result. This danger can be demonstrated through an analogy. An analysis of a pencil should divide it into its parts:

eraser

metal band

wood body

paint

printing on the wood

lead

Obviously, any analysis of a pencil would be incomplete if a part were omitted. Suppose, for instance, that the writer neglected to discuss the metal band. When a final draft was submitted, the paper would not include any explanations about the connection device used to attach the eraser to the wooden pencil. Certainly, the omission would be noticed.

Although Crane's use of people and objects as symbols cannot be listed as easily as the parts of a pencil, a breakdown can be made. The following list, for example, was perhaps used by the writer of the "Yellow Sky" paper presented earlier.

Crane's use of people as symbols:

1. The train represents East
2. The marshal represents forces of change
3. The bride represents civilization
4. The townspeople represent an intermediate society
5. Scratchy represents frontier
6. The showdown represents frontier giving way to civilized life

Ordering these parts is the next step. Here you may use either **chronological** (time) ordering or ordering by **importance.** Chronological ordering begins with the event which occurs earliest in the work being analyzed and progresses event by event to the last. By contrast, importance ordering begins with the **least** important part and progresses to the **most** important. The type of ordering you choose depends upon your preference and upon the story. Some analysis papers can be approached either way without making any discernible differences. Other papers, however, will be more effective if approached in a particular way.

EXERCISE 6.7

Divide the topic that you selected in Exercise 6.6 into its various parts. You may have to narrow the topic before you begin dividing it.

Topic: _____

Parts: _____

1. _____

2. _____

3. _____

4. _____

5. _____

6. _____

Conduct Research—Optional

The critical analysis paper is not a literary research project; therefore, you should not need to use secondary sources. However, if you are unsure of yourself and do not feel that you understand the work after discussing it with classmates or others, you may wish to search for the information you need. One place to begin searching is in critical studies of the author's work. In libraries or online databases, such as America Online or CompuServe, using your author's name, check offerings that examine criticism; that is, selections that discuss and offer evaluation of your author's writing. Begin by checking for references to the work you are analyzing or the subject you are researching. For example, if you were searching for information on Stephen Crane's use of symbolism in *The Bride Comes to Yellow Sky*, you would examine critical studies on Crane under the headings of "The Bride Comes to Yellow Sky," and "symbolism." You would then review the information listed under both headings.

If you need more information to help gain a complete understanding, you would proceed into journals and magazines or their database equivalents. Providing you were researching a modern work, you would search for references to the author in the indexes

(*Readers' Guide, New York Times Index, InfoTrac, Magazine Article Summaries* [MAS], *Humanities Index, MLA International Bibliography,* and *Social Sciences Index*). Another source that is frequently helpful is the *Abstracts of English Studies.*

If you find helpful sources which you use in your paper, in either direct quotes or just ideas that you summarize, you must be certain to give credit to your sources by documenting them so that you cannot be charged with plagiarism. A Works Cited page should then be included at the paper's end if you have included references.

Developing a Thesis Statement

As in every paper you write, the proper development of the thesis statement is crucial in a critical analysis. (If you need to review thesis development, turn back to Chapter Two.) For this paper, simply convert the topic that you chose in Exercise 6.6 into a thesis. The best approach is to begin by asking a "thesis question" similar to the following:

Topic:	Crane's use of characters and objects as symbols
Question:	What is Stephen Crane's point in using characters and objects as symbols?
Rough thesis:	Crane's intent is to present characters as symbols with larger meanings.
Thesis:	Crane's intent is not to draw vivid characterizations but to present characters and objects as symbols with larger meanings.

This is only speculation about how the author of the paper on "Yellow Sky" developed her thesis, but it is, perhaps, close. You should approach the writing of your thesis in a similar fashion.

EXERCISE 6.8

Develop the topic you wrote in Exercise 6.6 into a thesis.

Developing an Outline

After developing the thesis, write an outline for your paper. An outline should become as normal a part of your writing procedure as choosing a topic and writing a thesis. A basic thesis-topic sentence outline may be adequate for you, but you can also use an elaborate outline format such as the one used by the author of the paper on "Yellow Sky" (see next page). The advantage of the more elaborate outline is that it makes it easier to develop the outline into a paper.

1. Repeat the title of your paper at the top of the page.
2. Double-space and write your thesis. Precede your thesis sentence with the word **Thesis,** followed by a colon.

3. Skip three spaces after the thesis and write your topic sentence outline: a consecutively numbered list of all the topic sentences that appear in the body of your paper. (Double-space.)

OR

You may use a more elaborate outline that shows the major ideas used in each paragraph to support the topic sentence. Many students find that the more complete outline, such as the one below, makes the paper easier to write. (Double-space before each new topic sentence.)

A Historic Day in Yellow Sky

Thesis: Crane's intent is not to draw vivid characterizations but to present objects and characters as symbols with larger meanings.

I.   The train is the first symbol of the East presented in the story.
 A. The elaborate interior of the parlor car expresses the greater complexity of the advancing culture.
 B. The superior attitude of the porter and other passengers implies the simplicity of Western ways.
 C. The westward movement of the train symbolizes the accelerating force of the advancing culture.

II. The bride is a sexual metaphor for the ideals and principles of Eastern society.
 A. Women are viewed as more complex.
 B. Feminine values will replace masculine values.
  1. Women value peace.
  2. Women do not value conflict.
 C. The marriage depicts the complex future of the town.
  1. Children will soon appear.
  2. Schools, churches, and libraries will follow.
 D. The lives of all the men will change.

III. Scratchy Wilson represents the simple life and values of the frontier life.
 A. The frontier was severe; the men were tough.
 B. Scratchy's clothes say the encroachment of the East upon the West has been gradual.
  1. The flannel shirt would have been impractical in wilderness.
  2. The red-topped boots would have been ridiculed.
 C. Scratchy does not fit into the transitional progress of town life.
  1. He is tolerated because old ways are still valued.
  2. His skill with a gun is respected.

IV. The marshal represents the groups intermediate to the frontier and the approaching Eastern societies.
 A. These men tamed the land conquered by men like Scratchy.
 B. The marshal is the symbol of change to Yellow Sky.
 C. The marshal did not advise the town of his intent to marry; therefore, they are unaware and cannot be prepared for the changes.
 D. The course of life and the sweep of history is fate.

V. Simple frontier life giving way to a more advanced culture is symbolized by Scratchy acquiescing to the bride.
    A. Scratchy cannot fight against the power of progress.
    B. Yellow Sky is becoming a grown-up town.
    C. The boot tracks in the sand symbolize the fading away of the old West.

EXERCISE 6.9

Write an outline for the thesis you wrote in Exercise 6.8.

_____

_____

_____

_____

_____

_____

_____

_____

_____

_____

_____

_____

_____

_____

_____

_____

_____

_____

_____

Writing the Paper

Once you have completed the other steps, writing the critical analysis paper is easy. In fact, at this point little more than an expansion of your outline is required. One final note of caution should be sounded, however; do not expect to go from outline to final draft in one swift step. Begin by writing a preliminary draft. Writing the first draft gives you an opportunity to revise extensively. Also, if you have used information from other sources, you must insert documentation in the first draft, using lead-ins and parenthetical references, and compile your Works Cited. Then, when your preliminary draft is written, corrected, and revised, you are ready to write the final manuscript.

Reminders:

1. While the occasional use of first person is acceptable, the use of third person is preferable.
2. With literary subjects, you should use the present tense.

Use the sample student papers from this chapter for a model of what your completed paper should look like.

EXERCISE 6.10

After you write the final draft of your critical analysis, proofread it one more time to discover and correct any errors. Submit your critical analysis for evaluation.

CHAPTER SIX CRITICAL ANALYSIS PAPER

Name _____   Date _____

Class _____   Instructor _____

Meeting Time _____   Day _____   Circle One: Original Paper

Revision

IMPORTANT: REVISED PAPER MUST BE ACCOMPANIED BY THE ORIGINAL!!

CHECKLIST

I. Content
   A. Research effort
   B. Logic and ideas
   C. Reader interest

II. Structure
   A. Overall essay plan and structure
   B. Thesis sentence
   C. Opening sentence
   D. Topic sentences
   E. Primary and secondary support sentences
   F. Irrelevant material
   G. Transitions

III. Sentence style and mechanics
   A. Sentence structure
   B. Agreement, pronoun reference, tense, person
   C. Spelling, punctuation, capitalization

IV. Documentation
   A. Plagiarism
   B. Use of quoted, summarized, and paraphrased material
   C. Internal documentation
   D. Works Cited

V. Format
   A. Heading
   B. Pagination, headers, and margins
   C. Documentation
   D. Works Cited
   E. Legibility and neatness

Grade for Original Paper   _____

Grade for Revision (if required)   _____

CHAPTER SEVEN

The Investigative Paper

Objectives

When you have completed this chapter, you will have

1. selected a problem to investigate.

2. conducted secondary research.

3. engaged in primary research, including interviews.

4. written a thesis and outline.

5. drafted a 1,250-1,500 word investigative paper.

6. received feedback and revised the paper.

7. produced the final manuscript in the required format.

7

An investigative paper explores a problem in depth and provides plausible solutions. At first glance the investigative paper may appear similar to the library research paper because it requires research and includes documentation and a Works Cited page. But the two papers are dissimilar in some important ways. As you proceed through this chapter, these differences will become quite apparent.

One of the advantages of writing this popular kind of paper is the open-ended nature of the investigative assignment. It gives you the freedom to do something different that may include a personal involvement in a subject that matters to you. In addition to developing your own topic, the investigative paper assignment provides you with the opportunity to gather information without spending nearly as much time in the library as you would with research papers. You will substitute primary research for some of the secondary research you would do for a research paper. The depth of your investigative research probe determines the success of your paper. And this means **primary research**. Primary research is the kind you do personally: for example, experiments you perform in science and psychology laboratories, surveys, on-the-scene reporting, or reading original documents, such as letters and memos. **Secondary research**, by contrast, refers to such things as library investigation; reading reports, books, periodicals, newspapers, and pamphlets; and viewing documentary films. Both primary and secondary sources are valid; however, for papers on local, current topics, primary sources are more powerful persuaders than secondary sources. However, as a general rule, if both primary and secondary sources are available, you should include both in the preparation of your investigative paper.

The culminating step after researching a problem is to write a paper or a report. For example, in your sociology class you might be assigned to write a term paper discussing the problems of single parenting. At work you might be assigned to a team that will write a report recommending a solution to a product quality problem. In either situation you should be able to write a report that defines a particular problem, presents several solutions, discusses and evaluates them, promotes the best one, and makes recommendations for implementing it. Furthermore, you should be able to write by yourself, with a co-writer, or on a writing team.

EXERCISE 7.1

Develop a work schedule that will help you finish your paper on time.

Work Schedule

Project Title: Investigative Paper   **Due Date** _____

Exercises	Project Assignment	Sample Allotment	Your Time Allotment	Due Date
7.2	Problem Identification	(1 day)	_____	_____
7.3-7.4	Secondary Research	(3 days)	_____	_____
7.5-7.8	Primary Research	(5 days)	_____	_____
7.9	Thesis	(1/2 day)	_____	_____
7.10	Outline	(1/2 day)	_____	_____
7.11	First Draft	(1 day)	_____	_____
7.12	Feedback	(1 day)	_____	_____
7.13	Final Manuscript	(1 day)	_____	_____

Have your work schedule approved.

LESSON ONE: *Identify a Problem*

Choosing a good topic for the investigative paper is a challenge; however, it is easier than you might at first imagine. Your regional newspaper is full of local problems begging for solutions. Generally speaking, newspaper articles focus on problems rather than solutions. Once you discover a topic you wish to investigate, read the article closely to identify the problem.

You may discover a problem that is sufficiently narrowed right from the beginning. More likely, though, you will first decide upon a general subject area and then discover within it the topic for your investigation. To work your way from a problem area to the specific problem you will investigate, use one of the techniques you have learned for narrowing subjects:

> Brainstorming
> Freewriting
> Clustering
> Analytical Questioning
> Pyramiding

Begin by locating a problem area that interests you, for example, crime. Then divide that problem area into more specific topics.

Example

Brainstorming List

auto theft	illegal immigration
white-collar crime	drug dealing
mugging	arms trade
shoplifting	terrorism
computer crime	smuggling
robbery	auto theft
home invasions	rape
rustling	child molesting
cable piracy	spousal abuse
gang violence	drunk driving
prostitution	vandalism

Next, carefully consider whether the problem is sufficiently narrowed to be suitable for a 1,250-1,500 word paper. Again, employ one of the prewriting discovery techniques.

Example

Crime

White-collar crime

Fraud

Insurance fraud

Worker's compensation fraud

Organized worker's compensation fraud

Pyramiding

Considerations When You Are Identifying a Problem

1. Select a problem that really interests you.
2. Choose a problem that will also be of interest to whoever will be reading your paper.
3. Select a controversial topic or one with several possible solutions.
4. As an alternative, think about the possibility of investigating a problem in your workplace.
5. Identify a problem that will allow you to conduct both primary and secondary research.
6. Make certain that it is feasible to conduct whatever primary research will be needed.
7. Select a problem that can be investigated within the time frame available.
8. If you will be working with a co-writer or on a project team, make certain that you are all in agreement on the choice of topics.

EXERCISE 7.2

Using the prewriting techniques that work for you, identify a problem area that interests you, and within it identify the problem that you will investigate for your paper. (Your instructor may want to see your prewriting exercises.) Write your final topic in the space below.

Problem Identified: _____

_____

Have your topic approved.

LESSON TWO: *Secondary Research*

After identifying a problem, the next step in the planning phase is to conduct **secondary research.** To gather background information during your secondary research, you should use your library just as you would for any research project. Begin by searching a variety of sources: magazines, newspapers, books, professional journals, reference books, pamphlet file materials, recordings and video cassettes, CD-ROMs, electronic information services and databases. If your library has electronic indexes, begin with those before exploring other sources such as the pamphlet file and reference books. If the technology for electronic searching is available, instruct the computer to search for and print a list of references on your narrowed topic. Then highlight the references listed that look worthwhile and fill out a working bibliography card for each reference that you intend to locate and read.

On the other hand, if a manual search is necessary, you might begin by consulting the *Readers' Guide to Periodical Research, NewsBank,* and the *New York Times Index* for references on your topic. Begin with the most recent issue of the index and search back in time until you have examined the five most recent years. Fill out a working bibliography card for each reference that looks promising. After you have completed your work with the indexes, including other indexes such as the *Art Index, Education Index,* and *Humanities Index,* move on to the card catalog. Once you have located books that look relevant to your investigation and recorded them on bibliography cards, search through the pamphlet file (vertical file). For background information on a local topic, the pamphlet file is one of your most valuable sources. Articles clipped from local newspapers and pamphlets gathered by industrious librarians are filed in folders labeled by subject. Then consider other library sources, too—bibliographies compiled by the librarians, reference books, recordings, CD-ROMs, and special library collections. The reference librarians can be of enormous assistance at this stage of your investigation.

When you have located at least fifteen references and written a working bibliography card for each, begin reading your sources and taking notes. Unlike in a research paper, you do not need to take notes on a large number of sources. In fact, you may need only half as many. At this point, you should be certain that you have a sufficient number of sources; that is, do you have enough sources to be assured of a well-documented paper? The investigative paper, like the research paper, should contain a minimum of *ten sources* of information. However, the investigative paper may need only *five secondary sources*. The other five sources will come from your primary research.

EXERCISE 7.3

Prepare at least fifteen working bibliography cards for the most promising secondary sources for your investigative paper. (Have your working bibliography cards approved.)

EXERCISE 7.4

Using your working bibliography cards, find and read enough sources to develop an understanding of the topic. Take notes (one idea per card) on the problem and the possible solutions you discover in your reading.

LESSON THREE: *Primary Research—Planning*

When you have finished taking notes on your secondary sources, you should understand the subject thoroughly enough to become involved personally. You should have a general understanding of the problem and any solutions that have been proposed by others. If you are working on a local problem, your secondary research should have enabled you to put the problem into perspective.

Primary research, the investigation of an issue firsthand, can be conducted in a number of ways. You may choose to distribute a survey, examine original documents, view picture evidence, conduct a site visit, or record an event on video.

Interviews

The most commonly used method of conducting primary research is to talk to people individually, interviewing them about the problem you have identified. To be an effective interviewer, you will need to plan ahead, discovering whom you might interview, setting up appointments, and deciding what to ask them. This will require you to select carefully those who can give you the most information about your topic.

Choosing People to Interview

Deciding whom to interview is your first step. Who might be willing to talk to you, who can help you better understand the nature of the problem, its possible consequences, and ways of solving the problem? Your first feeling, understandably, might be that you don't know anyone who can help you. The best thing to do is to start asking people you know if they know anyone who could speak knowledgeably about the problem you are investigating. Ask your instructors, relatives, classmates, friends, relatives, and co-workers. Study local news articles on your topic carefully, looking for the names of people you might interview, including the reporter who wrote the article. Often, too, someone you interview will refer you to someone else, even giving that person a call to help set up an appointment. As one lead follows another, you will find more and more potential sources. Look for those people who would be most likely to be involved with the problem you are investigating. Use good judgment, looking for people to interview who can speak with authority on the topic either because of the work they do or because of relevant personal experience. Suppose you were investigating teenage marriage as a problem. The following mix of people would provide you with information from different viewpoints:

1. a school counselor
2. a psychology instructor
3. an employee at a local family planning center
4. a parent of a married teenager
5. married teenagers
6. an author on the subject
7. a member of the clergy
8. an anthropologist
9. a social historian

EXERCISE 7.5

List five or six people you would like to interview as primary sources for your paper. (Add names to your list as new leads develop.)

Name	Role/ Position	Telephone Number
1. _____	_____	_____
2. _____	_____	_____
3. _____	_____	_____
4. _____	_____	_____
5. _____	_____	_____
6. _____	_____	_____

Have your list reviewed.

Writing the Questions

After deciding who can give you the information you need, you are ready to begin developing your questions. You need to investigate the seriousness of the problem locally and determine what is being done—or what could be done—to resolve it. Before you interview anyone, you should have six to ten carefully developed questions.

Your questions must elicit thoughtful responses. That is, make certain the person you interview cannot answer your questions with a "yes" or "no," or your interview will be over very quickly. If you were preparing a paper on the problems of teenage marriage and you asked someone the following questions, you would find that the first version of each is inadequate.

Examples

(weak) Are many teenagers marrying?
(revised) Why are so many teenagers choosing to marry?

(weak) Is enough being done to counsel teenagers who wish to marry?
(revised) What do you think should be done to discourage teenage marriage?

The basic problem with the two "weak" questions above is that they fail to require the interviewee to express any more than a one-word opinion. Remember, the person you interview is a valuable source with information you want; treat the person accordingly. Many interviewers ask the people they speak with to explain how they would do things differently if they had the authority.

Besides reducing your nervousness during an interview, possibly the most significant advantage of writing out your questions in advance is that you are forced to think about your topic in depth. Until you have thought seriously about the topic and its possible solutions, you will never truly understand the topic. Putting the questions on paper will require this thoughtfulness.

EXERCISE 7.6

Write six to ten questions to ask the people you identified in Exercise 7.5.

1. _____

_____

2. _____

_____

3. _____

_____

4. _____

_____

5. _____

_____

6. _____

_____

7. _____

_____

8. _____

_____

9. _____

_____

10. _____

_____

Have your questions approved.

Scheduling Your Interviews

Now you are ready to begin contacting people to schedule interviews. Persuading people to agree to an interview is remarkably easy, provided you approach them with respect and confidence. When you call for an interview appointment, you should identify yourself and explain the topic you are investigating. Explain exactly why you want the interview. Do not attempt to flatter your way into an appointment; just explain why you think the person's experience or connections would be helpful to you. One final point to emphasize as you request an interview is that you will keep the interview as brief as possible. This approach should reward you with an interview, but if not, simply move on to the next person on your list. No successful investigative paper depends on a single source.

Conducting the Interview

If you are prepared, your interview will be productive. Before your interview appointment, review the notes of your secondary research. If others have suggested solutions to the problem you are investigating, be certain to be familiar with them. Mentioning proposed solutions in your interview will clearly establish your interest in and knowledge of the topic. If your interviewees discover you are informed, they will be more willing to assist you.

Part of being prepared for your interview is being certain that you take sufficient paper and several pens. It is also a good practice to take 3-by-5-inch note cards with your questions neatly typed on them. It would be very distracting to forget your questions or to search through pages of loose notes looking for them.

Be on time for your interview. Arrive early enough to catch your breath and organize your interview materials. If an emergency arises so that you are unable to keep your appointment, telephone as soon as possible, suggesting that the interview be rescheduled.

Further hints for conducting successful interviews:

- Maintain eye contact as much as possible.
- Request permission to use a tape recorder if you wish to use one.
- Take notes (even if you are taping—the machine might not clearly record everything you need).
- Transcribe your tape or rewrite your notes immediately after the interview (while all the information is fresh in your mind).

Note! Telephone interviews are sometimes acceptable; they can involve less time for both you and the person interviewed. However, you must be no less prepared with intelligent questions than if you interview in person. Also, the answers to your questions may not be as complete during telephone interviews as during personal interviews.

EXERCISE 7.7

Conduct the interviews you have scheduled. Prepare for each one carefully following the advice given in this lesson. Follow through immediately after each interview, rewriting your notes or listening to your tape and making notes. Send a thank-you letter to each person interviewed. (Have your interview work approved.)

Focus Group Option

Originally used for marketing research in business, **focus groups** are frequently used by researchers investigating a problem. With a little planning you can conduct a focus group right at school. Simply assemble a cross section of students in a place where they can talk, for example, at a table in the cafeteria. Then ask them a short series of open-ended questions that solicit their opinions or feelings about a particular problem, for instance, cheating on campus. Then listen carefully, taking notes on the conversation. If possible, have a classmate or friend take notes or tape-record the discussion. Then later, review your notes, analyzing the comments of the focus group participants.

Other Kinds of Primary Research

If you are conducting other kinds of primary research, organize your task carefully, keeping in mind the time frame within which you must operate. One student, for example, made a trip to the Farallon Islands—twenty-five miles from San Francisco by boat—to investigate, first hand, environmental problems on the islands. To do this the student had to write to two government agencies for permission to visit the islands (a wilderness area and bird refuge). Twice, storms forced postponement of the trip to the rugged islands. All of these preparations were made in addition to interviews with environmentalists, government officials, and instructors at a local university.

EXERCISE 7.8

Conduct other research that you have planned. (Have your record of that research approved, for example, journal, survey tallies, video record of site visit.)

LESSON FOUR: *Organizing the Paper—Writing the Thesis*

When your primary research has been completed and the notes have been written, you should have all the information needed to write the paper. But be cautious, for it is here that you may feel a tremendous temptation to simply begin writing. Nevertheless, one important step remains: the deliberate, concentrated plan for organizing your paper. A well thought-out plan not only results in a better paper but makes the paper much easier to write. Rather than false starts at writing, you should begin by creating an outline. The organization of your notes and thoughts into an outline should begin with your working thesis.

Creating a thesis can be accomplished only after deciding which type of organization is most appropriate for your paper. One type of investigative paper attempts to convince the reader that a problem exists or is sufficiently serious to warrant public concern (see diagram for Type I, page 312). This kind of paper seeks to raise reader consciousness, and it is related to the exposé. Examples of this type abound, particularly on the editorial pages of the popular press. A thesis for this kind of paper dwells upon the problem rather than any proposed solution. In fact, the point of the paper is to convince the reader that there is a problem that needs to be solved. The solution, except for a brief summary of the possibilities, is saved for some future analysis. Consequently, the thesis is straightforward; it states what it is that the writer wants the reader to believe by the end of the paper.

The other style of investigative paper, rather than only analyzing a problem, analyzes the problem and proposes solutions. A clearly organized thesis for this kind of investigative paper must identify a problem and suggest a solution. The paper's introduction should briefly introduce the problem and culminate with a thesis covering both the problem and the solution—or at the very least hinting to the reader that a solution will be suggested. In general, a simple or complex sentence stating the thesis may be clearer than a compound sentence. This rhetorical principle can be demonstrated by studying four versions of the thesis developed by a student who investigated environmental problems on the Farallon Islands west of San Francisco.

Version One—Compound Sentence

> Ignorance, carelessness, and economic exploitation have resulted in tremendous suffering by the wildlife on the Farallon Islands; consequently, coordinated action by Congress, the Fish and Wildlife Service, and concerned citizens is imperative to repair the damage and reverse the trend.

Version One of the thesis summarizes the problem well and also suggests a solution. However, because it is a compound sentence, this thesis may mislead readers by making them think that the problem and the solution will receive equal coverage. In fact, although the solution is covered adequately in a single, long paragraph at the end of the body of the paper (see the diagram for Type IIA, page 313), the problem is covered in much more detail in a series of paragraphs preceding the solution paragraph. Independent clauses in a compound sentence demand equal coverage. Thus, just as an investigative paper without an introduction and conclusion would be "broken-backed," a compound thesis sentence could be termed "broken-backed," too (see diagram on page 312).

Version Two—Simple Sentence

The tremendous suffering caused by human ignorance, carelessness, and economic exploitation on the Farallon Islands can only be stopped by the coordinated action of Congress, the Fish and Wildlife Service, and concerned citizens.

This version allows the writer to emphasize either the problem or the solution and clearly shows the relationship between the two without blatantly breaking into two parts as does the first version.

Version Three—Complex Sentence Emphasizing Problem

Decades of ignorance, carelessness, and economic exploitation have resulted in tremendous suffering by the wildlife on the Farallon Islands, although coordinated action by Congress, the Fish and Wildlife Service, and concerned citizens can repair the damage and reverse the trend.

By using a complex sentence for the thesis, a writer can emphasize either the problem or the solution. Normally, students' investigative papers devote more space to the problem than to the solution (see the diagram for Type IIA). In that case the sample thesis could be stated as above. In this version the problem is summarized in the independent clause while the solution is summarized in the dependent clause. In a complex sentence the main idea is stated in the independent clause, and related but less important ideas are stated in one or more dependent clauses.

Version Four—Complex Sentence Emphasizing Solution

Because decades of ignorance, carelessness, and economic exploitation have resulted in tremendous suffering by the wildlife on the Farallon Islands, coordinated action by Congress, the Fish and Wildlife Service, and concerned citizens is imperative to repair the damage and reverse the trend.

This version clearly indicates that the writer's emphasis is on the solution because it is summarized in the independent clause. The problem is subordinated because it is in the dependent clause.

Read the first sample student paper, "Daycare." Its organization is Type IIA, although the solution section is almost as long as the problem section. Four paragraphs are devoted to the problem and three to the solution. The paper is interesting because it compares daycare in the United States with that in other industrialized countries and because it includes the personal anecdotes of the student who had previously been a professional daycare operator. The writer focuses on government solutions to the problems of inadequate training of daycare personnel and the high cost of daycare. The paper's basic premise is that daycare is not just the working mother's problem—it's a family and social issue.

Kimberly Brokaw

English 1-A MW 11:30

Mr. Mehaffy

19 April 1995

(Investigative Paper)

Daycare

Every day millions of parents must rely on strangers to care for their children. The issues of daycare, including who provides it and how much it should cost, are a major source of problems for working parents. Oftentimes this care is inadequate. Of the Western industrialized nations, only the United States, Britain, and Canada do not have family daycare policies (Foreman, "How East" F4). While many countries have very successful programs, the United States has an outdated view on daycare. According to one author, there are three main reasons why America has such a poor childcare system: an ambivalence towards working mothers, a lack of a coordinated system, and a resistance toward government involvement in childcare (Foreman, "Working Parents" n.pag). Although our current daycare system is not effective for working parents, solutions exist for the many problems these parents face.

Daycare, according to parents, is expensive. However, when people ask daycare providers if they think daycare is too expensive, they get a different reply. According to the pamphlet Women, Work and Childcare, childcare is the fourth largest expense of working parents. The cost of childcare ranges from $2,400 to $9,000 annually per child, with low-income households spending approximately 25 percent of their incomes on childcare alone (National Commission

n.pag). Because many families cannot afford this kind of expend-
iture, they are forced to leave their children alone or in a
childcare situation that may be cheaper but not safe. While parents
complain of the rising costs of daycare, those who provide childcare
complain of long hours and low wages. Lily Monem, a family daycare
provider, works from 7:30 a.m. until 6:30 p.m. She charges $20 to
$25 a day. Her hourly wage is much less than most people make today
in the working force. The discrepancy between parents and providers
is a major problem with our current daycare system. Parents are
turning away from typical daycare situations because they simply
cannot afford the cost, especially if they have more than one child.

One concern parents have with daycare is the fear that the
provider could intentionally or unintentionally hurt a child. Every
parent's worst nightmare is that someone will hurt his or her child.
A student who is the mother of a young child said, "I feel like he
comes home with more cuts and bruises than when I am with him"
(Heverly). In the media in recent years, we have seen cases of
daycare providers who have become so frustrated with children in
their care that they have actually shaken the children to death.
Stories like these only promote the feelings of anxiety that parents
experience every day when they leave their children in the care of
someone else. Most daycare providers don't intentionally hurt the
children in their care, but often they have too many children in
their care to give them adequate supervision and to prevent all of
the minor spills and tumbles that are bound to occur. As a retired
daycare operator, I know from first-hand experience that with five or
six children in my care, youngsters were sometimes falling or hitting

each other, and I just didn't have enough hands or eyes to stop them all before there were minor cuts or bumps.

Availability is another big issue for working parents. While our society has shifted from working 9-to-5 shifts Monday through Friday to working around the clock, daycare providers have not adjusted to this demand for longer hours. Parents today are working day and/or night and need childcare at all hours of the day/night. Oftentimes parents who work late (or early) shifts cannot find adequate care for their children. As one working father put it, "My shifts vary sometimes from week to week. It is very hard to keep daycare providers because they get frustrated with my changing hours, and a lot of times I work nights, and they [daycare providers] don't want to watch kids late at night" (Ginocchio). Situations like this are a great source of frustration for many working parents.

Currently, daycare providers receive little scrutiny or training. The licensing process is simple. All prospective providers must do is go to a meeting and sign some papers, and as long as they don't have a felony on their records, they can become daycare providers. Ten to fifteen years ago, these guidelines were not even enforced, according to a retired daycare provider. She says the system was extremely lax in past years (Perrine). It is almost more difficult to obtain a driver's license than it is to get a daycare license. Parents entrust the care of their children to the licensed professionals for 8 to 10 hours a day. It is frightening to think that daycare providers are required to have little training or knowledge about children and how to handle them. Having once owned a daycare myself, I know that I was required to have only a C.P.R.

certification and an additional eight hours of training per year;
anything else I did was by my own choice. The lack of good training
programs for daycare providers causes many parents to fear for the
safety of their children.

The first step in reforming or building a daycare system is for
parents to demand better training for daycare providers. Parents are
most often the best advocates for their own children (Goffin and
Lombardi 32). A set training program should be implemented with
requirements that all daycare providers must meet in order to be
licensed. As a former daycare owner, I know the importance of
learning how to deal with different children who have conflicting
attitudes, needs, wants, and ways of expressing themselves in order
to be prepared to handle potentially frustrating situations. A good
screening process needs to be developed. One type of screening that
should be implemented is personal interviews for all prospective
daycare owners. A working mother said, "How do I know the person
caring for my son has the patience to deal with six kids and still
treat my son with love and respect?" (Vasquez). Requiring potential
caregivers to undergo personal interviews and screening would help
weed out the people who cannot handle the pressure.

A second step that we need to take is to implement subsidized
daycare programs. It doesn't matter how well prepared caregivers are
if working parents can't afford to pay for childcare. An example of
a daycare system that wasn't expensive was the former East Germany's.
The state paid all daycare fees ($8 a day). The infant and toddler
centers were run by the state, and almost 100 percent of their 3- to
6-year-olds were in a kindergarten-type program (Foreman, "How East"

F4). In the United States, on the average, parents pay more for daycare than anywhere else (Williams B6). Companies must become more aware of employee needs and offer childcare programs, such as providing flexible benefits and voucher programs (both of which are programs that help working parents pay for daycare). Some government programs are available to parents, such as federal income tax credits (for working parents) and subsidized childcare (for low-income parents). Parents need to be informed about these programs so they may take advantage of them (Miller and Weissman 27). Making daycare affordable is not easy, but it is possible. Some programs exist already that parents just need to know about.

Another solution to the daycare dilemma working parents face is for them to use alternatives to typical paid childcare. Some parents already are choosing these options. Oftentimes parents overlook the best person or people to care for their child--a family member. In a growing trend, more parents are leaving their children with spouses or even the children's grandparents. A 1984 survey revealed that approximately 29 percent of parents were leaving their children with a relative (Rubin 24). If relatives aren't available, another popular idea is to trade babysitting with someone. There are many options out there; sometimes it just takes a little creativity. Parents need to ask around and find other people in similar situations. Many of the alternatives to regular daycare cost much less money than the typical family daycare situation.

Daycare is a topic of major concern for millions of people. Every day it affects families all over the country. Unfortunately, it has been a neglected subject by the government because it has been

viewed as a problem of working parents, not the government. For
leadership in making daycare policies, the government should look to
the former East Germany, a small country that lead the world in
childcare policy. The national policy in the former East Germany was
that the task of raising children is not one which parents should or
would want to bear alone (Foreman, "How East" F4). We live in a very
advanced society, and we need to bring daycare out of the Stone Ages
and into the here and now. Daycare would greatly benefit from better
training programs and assistance from the federal government.
Parents also need to be more informed of programs that already exist
and to become more creative in finding daycare for their children.

Works Cited

Foreman, Judy. "How East Germany Provides Total Childcare."

 <u>Sacramento Bee</u> 25 Dec. 1980: F4. Pamphlet file.

---. "Working Parents Around the World." <u>Boston Globe</u> n.d.:

 n.pag.

Ginocchio, Guy. Private Interview. 4 Apr. 1995.

Goffin, Stacie, and Joan Lombardi. <u>Speaking Out: Early Childhood</u>

 <u>Advocacy</u>. Washington, D.C.: NAEYC, 1988-89.

Heverly, Melissa. Private Interview. 4 Apr. 1995.

Miller, JoAnn, and Susan Weissman. <u>The Parents Guide to Daycare</u>.

 New York: Bantam Books, 1986.

Monem, Lily. Private Interview. 2 Apr. 1995.

National Commission on Working Women of Wider Opportunities for

 Women. <u>Women, Work and Childcare</u>. 1988: n.pag. Pamphlet

 file.

Perrine, Vickie. Private Interview. 3 Apr. 1995.

Rubin, Sylvia. "The Best Place." <u>San Francisco Chronicle</u>.

 4 May 1984: 24.

Select Committee on Children, Youth, and Families. <u>U.S. Children</u>

 <u>and Their Families: Current Conditions and Recent Trends,</u>

 1989. Washington, D.C.: U.S. Government Printing Office,

 1989.

Vasquez, Stacie. Private Interview. 1 Apr. 1995.

Williams, Norman. "Sacramentans May Pay More for Childcare."

 <u>Sacramento Bee</u> 16 Sept. 1992: B6. Pamphlet File.

BROKEN-BACKED PAPER

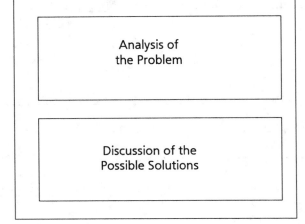

No
Introduction

Analysis of
the Problem

Discussion of the
Possible Solutions

Without an introduction and
conclusion to give the investigative paper a three-part
organization, the result is
what professional writers
call a "broken-backed"
paper.

INVESTIGATIVE PAPER
Type I (Problem Only)

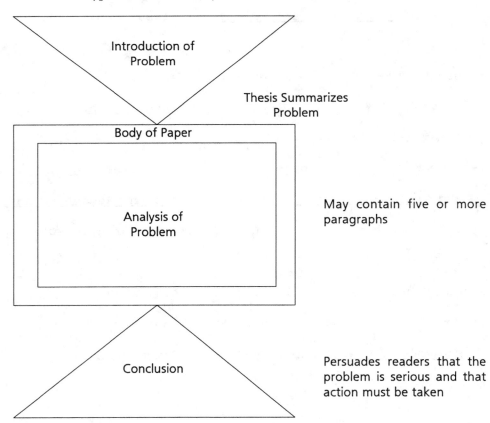

Introduction of
Problem

Thesis Summarizes
Problem

Body of Paper

Analysis of
Problem

May contain five or more
paragraphs

Conclusion

Persuades readers that the
problem is serious and that
action must be taken

INVESTIGATIVE PAPER
Type IIA (Emphasis upon Problem)

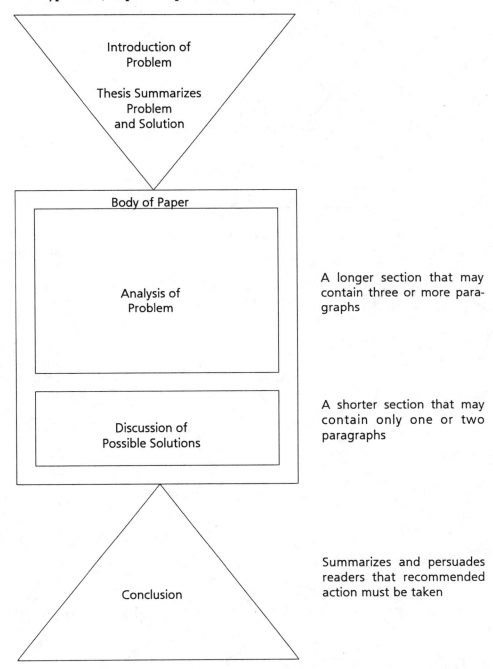

Introduction of
Problem

Thesis Summarizes
Problem
and Solution

Body of Paper

Analysis of
Problem

A longer section that may
contain three or more paragraphs

Discussion of
Possible Solutions

A shorter section that may
contain only one or two
paragraphs

Conclusion

Summarizes and persuades
readers that recommended
action must be taken

INVESTIGATIVE PAPER
Type IIB (Emphasis upon Solution)

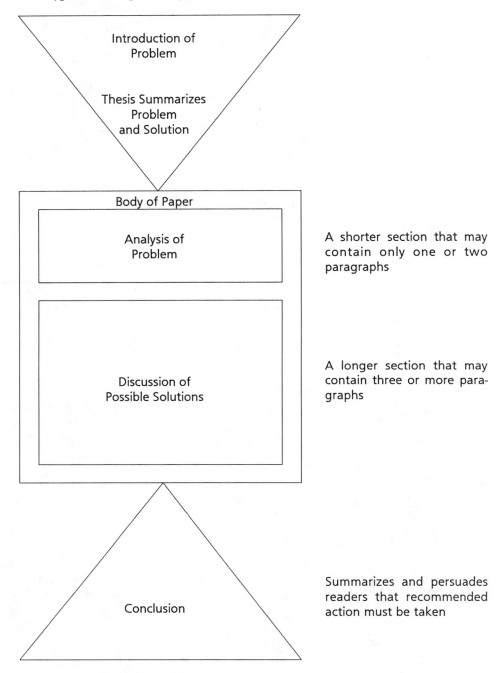

Introduction of
Problem

Thesis Summarizes
Problem
and Solution

Body of Paper

Analysis of
Problem

A shorter section that may contain only one or two paragraphs

Discussion of
Possible Solutions

A longer section that may contain three or more paragraphs

Conclusion

Summarizes and persuades readers that recommended action must be taken

EXERCISE 7.9

In the space below write a thesis sentence appropriate for the organizational plan you will use.

_____

_____

_____

EXERCISE 7.10

When you have written and planned your strategy, write a thesis-topic sentence outline for the paper.

LESSON FIVE: *Writing and Editing the Paper*

Now you are ready for the culminating phases of your investigation: writing and editing a paper that will effectively communicate the results of your investigation. Concentrate on blocking in your outline and integrating the mass of information you have accumulated. The actual writing techniques are the same as with the library research paper, so if you need to review, refer again to Chapter Four.

If possible, have someone who can provide constructive feedback read the first draft of your paper —a peer editing group, your instructor, a classmate, tutor, friend, co-worker, or relative. If time permits, let your first draft "cool" a day or two. Then when you read it again, you will probably see improvements that can be made that would not have occurred to you otherwise. Furthermore, the cooling-off period may allow you to accept some of the revision suggestions that your readers made that seemed unacceptable when they were first made. It is quite natural to resent criticism no matter how constructive and well-meaning it is. All experienced writers will tell you that every writer needs an editor, with no exceptions. Learning to keep an open mind when receiving feedback about your writing is an important part of becoming a competent writer.

Before you write your paper, also read "The Burden of Love," another student paper included as an example of an investigative paper. Its organization is closest to Type IIB because the entire body of the paper, which begins with the fourth paragraph, is devoted to strategies caregivers can employ to cope with the disease. The problem is the nature of Alzheimer's disease and how it incapacitates its victims. Since there is no cure, the solutions presented are the steps needed to provide proper care for the patient; they are as close as one can get to solutions. The writer relies heavily on secondary research, skillfully weaving in her information, but she does include two interviews. Note, too, that the writer includes three paragraphs in her introduction, placing her thesis at the end of the third paragraph.

Geep S. Butner

English 1A TTh 7:30

Mr. Mehaffy

9 November 1994

(Investigative Essay)

                          The Burden of Love

      Alzheimer's disease knows no social or racial lines: the rich and

the poor, the wise and the simple alike become victims. Sometimes the

brain does not work the way it should. Many names have been given to the

symptoms of memory loss, loss of thinking and reasoning capacity in

adults. According to one authority, Alzheimer's disease was first

described by Dr. Alois Alzheimer, a German physician, in the early 1900s

when he identified a presenile disease in a deceased patient who was in

her fifties (Henig 122). By 1985, Alzheimer's disease had become the

most frequent cause of irreversible dementia in adults. As reported in

the Columbus Dispatch, it is now the fourth leading cause of death

("Chasing" C6).

      During the past 20 years, research by the National Institute of

Health has found that Alzheimer's disease is not caused by

arteriosclerosis, emotional stress or strain, and that it is definitely

not contagious (Alzheimer Disease 4). However, in 1984 a study conducted

by Minneapolis University found other possible causes, such as a hormone

disorder, a genetic factor, a faulty immunological system, a viral

disease, and the presence of high levels of aluminum ("Study" 13:1).

Researchers do not know yet why certain people develop Alzheimer's

disease while many others do not, but the National Institute of Health

has reported the disease has modified the brain and nerve cells of approximately one million adults, leaving the cells a tangled network of filaments (Alzheimer Disease 1). Further, it causes mental confusion, memory loss, disorientation, intellectual impairment, drowsiness, and restlessness. Even worse, the intellectual impairment gradually progresses from forgetfulness to total disability (Alzheimer Disease 1-2).

As with any disease, proper diagnosis is essential, but with Alzheimer's, it is extremely difficult. Just as fever, coughing, vomiting, and dizziness are symptoms of several different conditions, memory loss, confusion, and personality change are also symptoms of several maladies. Again, the National Institute of Health advises that all other causes of memory loss must be ruled out. A diagnosis of Alzheimer's disease can be made on the basis of the type of symptoms, the way symptoms progress over time, the absence of any other cause for the condition, and a comparable CAT (computerized axial tomogram) scan (Alzheimer Disease 3). When the cause of the memory impairment is organic, as with Alzheimer's disease, early diagnosis can lead to treatment that will give patients and their families a better opportunity to deal with their problems and prepare to manage their care successfully. As the disease progresses, steady mental and physical deterioration occurs slowly over time; however, in some cases the progression occurs rapidly. Although as yet no cure exists for Alzheimer's disease, it is important to recognize that much can be done to ease the lives for both patients and their families.

In order to provide care for their loved ones, families must come to terms with their own embarrassment, anger, confusion, and fear. Sadly, they will watch the slow disappearance of those characteristics that made up the unique personality of their afflicted relatives. They often feel guilty about not being able to do enough and, indeed, feel guilt when they welcome some respite from the burden of loving. Alzheimer's authority Robin Henig suggests patience as the best prescription of caring for Alzheimer's patients, but it should also be prescribed for their families (116). To be sure, nothing in the past could possibly prepare families for an experience of this magnitude. The best course of action is to acknowledge the illness, and to accept the fact that nothing can be done to reverse the condition; hence, the goal must be to make each patient as comfortable as possible and take one day at a time.

Alzheimer's disease is a family affliction because the patient requires continuous care, constant attention, and emotional support from the family. One published account indicates that families are now caring for somewhere between six hundred thousand and one million family members at home (Geyelin E8). When patients are only mildly to moderately impaired, they can take part in managing their problem; however, as the disease progresses, they can no longer perform simple tasks or evaluate consequences. They lose the ability to distinguish among different patterns or pieces of clothing, even though they may have been very clothes-conscious all their lives, and eventually they become unable to even dress themselves. According to a Life magazine report, regardless of the degree of deterioration, their stubbornness remains; therefore, adaptation is the key to success (Hollister 36). If patients want to eat with their fingers, if they want to go home and they are home, if they insist on sleeping with their hats on, then care givers should go along with them. Families should maintain a sense of humor; it just may be the gift that helps them sustain sanity in the face of despair.

Communication, both verbal and nonverbal, is essential in treating patients like the unique individuals they are. They will have trouble expressing themselves to others and will not understand what is being expressed to them. In the early stages of Alzheimer's disease, they will have difficulty finding words. They will have trouble remembering the names of familiar objects or people, and they may substitute a word that sounds similar. Furthermore, they may substitute a word with a similar meaning. As one doctor emphasized, the limited ability to communicate becomes very frustrating for patients and families (Trenton). In order to reduce the frustration level of the patient, the care giver can keep the communication open by using short words, asking only one question at a time, speaking slowly, lowering the voice when speaking, using short, simple sentences, and making sure the patient hears the verbal communication. These patients will lose their ability to communicate verbally; therefore, nonverbal communication will become necessary. Pointing, gesturing, touching, using body language, and hugging help mitigate tension and anger.

A structured environment and routines that do not change offer patients the necessary feeling of comfort, security, and safety from physical hazards. Dr. John Morrison, neuroscientist of the Scripps Clinic and Research Foundation in La Jolla, proclaims, "An Alzheimer's patient isn't blind, but he can't make sense of what he is seeing" (Froelich F1). In as much as structured environments make life more comfortable for patients and families, orderliness is often difficult to maintain. As a result of the illness, the forgetful person is likely to disorder things as quickly as they are organized. It is imperative to establish a schedule and abide by that schedule as much as possible. A person with mental confusion, certainly, does not need a confusing, changing environment. One must pay special attention to the patient's nutritional and mealtime needs, simple exercises, and incontinence. People with dementing illnesses are especially sensitive to incorrect dosages of medication; therefore, it is imperative they be given their medication in the amounts and times as specified by their doctors. Some patients may not understand why they must take a medication and they may refuse to accept it, but care givers should not argue with them. There are several ways medicine can be disguised or hidden in foods that make this routine easy to handle. Memory impaired people are unable to protect themselves from household hazards simply because they have forgotten how. According to one nurse who cares for Alzheimer patients, many things can be done to reduce safety hazards for dementia patients (Reddich). They need bright lighting, conveniently placed handrails, and furniture with round edges. The kitchen and bathroom are perhaps the most dangerous rooms in the house. There should be support bars within easy reach of the bathtub and commode and a skid-proof mat in the tub. All sharp knives and other dangerous kitchen implements should be out of sight and out of reach; in addition, all knobs should be removed from the stove to avoid a serious fire hazard. To prevent them from wandering away from home, locks on exterior doors should be placed either at the top or at the bottom, out of reach of the impaired person.

Finding a physician who is gentle, who understands the patient's condition, and who will take care of general medical problems is an important consideration. No doctor should dismiss patients because they are "senile" or "old." Families must insist that infection be treated and pains diagnosed and relieved. Because of the demented person's vulnerability to delirium, it is wise to check with the doctor about even minor conditions such as colds. Most general practitioners today are not well-informed about Alzheimer's disease; therefore, it may be necessary to pursue more specialized help. Furthermore, the patient's senses such as seeing, hearing, and tasting are not impaired; therefore, special attention should be given to their eyes, ears, and teeth. They may require new glasses, hearing aids, or new teeth in order to reduce their frustration level.

The burden of love is living with the helpless, trying to spare them the pain of losing themselves, yet there are many situations in which placing a confused relative in an outside facility eases not only the patient's circumstances, but the pressures on other family members as well. Taking care of people with Alzheimer's disease is a twenty-four-hour-a-day job and requires skills of professionally trained individuals. At some point families may be unable to continue providing all the care that is needed. Placing the family member in a custodial facility becomes a difficult decision for the family; furthermore, they may again experience a sense of guilt and at the same time a sense of relief. Family members will have mixed emotions. In fact, the term "nursing home" brings negative images to many people's minds, but today there are alternatives for Alzheimer patients. In 1985, the Hillhaven Convalescent Center and Nursing Home in Mobile, Alabama, opened the first specialized wing for Alzheimer patients (Hart A12). Facilities such as this are becoming increasingly well-known for their outstanding care of people with dementing illnesses; unfortunately, they are quite expensive.

Providing care also includes the financial and legal issues of the person with the dementing illness. The cost of care varies from state to state, city to city, county to county, and institution to institution; for instance, Medicaid will absorb the cost after an individual's funds are exhausted. The cost of a chronic major illness can seriously threaten the assets of an individual or a family, and has, indeed, completely wiped out many people's assets. The Life article notes that couples are being forced to divorce to protect their assets, and in California they must spend all their money, except for $1,700, before Medicaid will assist them (Hollister 38). At the present time twenty-five states have legislation pending that would provide funds for family and care givers support, expand the Medicaid and Medicare programs, aid in research, fund diagnosis and evaluation, and fund education and training. An article in the New York Times reported that the government has spent approximately 76 million dollars on Alzheimer's disease research in the past two years ("Five Schools" 2:3).

Despite the best of care that can be given, patients are still dying from a disease for which no cure has been found. Dr. Charles Marotta, one of the principal researchers of the Harvard Medical School in Boston, has started to unravel some of the unanswered questions about Alzheimer's disease; however, research is greatly hindered by the fact that no animal models or living brains can be used for research (Altman, "Pinpointed" 8:2). Surgically implanted experimental drugs are now being tested, and the government is providing grants to medical schools for study of this incurable brain disease, but patients are still dying some

eighty years after the first case was described by Dr. Alois Alzheimer.
Deterioration usually takes eight to twelve years, but there have been
deaths in as little as nine months. This disease of the century is still
a medical mystery, puzzling researchers around the world. Dr. Antonio R.
Damasio heads a team of researchers at the University of Iowa and feels
there is a link between a viral disease or an immunological disorder and
Alzheimer's disease. He recently stated: "Now we have to find out why
these cells are particularly affected by disease. It's like a tornado
that cuts a very narrow path, destroying buildings in a strip 100 yards
wide but leaving everything else standing" (Altman, "New Brain" 1:5).

Works Cited

Altman, Lawrence K. "Pinpointed Damaged Areas." New York Times 7 Sept.

    1984, 1.8:2,

--- "New Brain Study Technique Reveals an Alzheimer Defect." New York

    Times 24 Aug. 1984, 1.1:5.

Alzheimer Disease. U.S. Department of Health and Human Services. NIH

    rpt. 1982.

"Chasing a Relentless Killer." Columbus Dispatch 20 Jan. 1985. NewsBank

    HEA4: C6-8.

"Five Schools Named Alzheimer Centers." New York Times 2 Oct. 1984, III.

    2:3.

Froelich, Warren. "New Hypothesis: Brain Suffers Bad Connections," Union

    23 Jun. 1986. NewsBank HEA59: F1-2.

Geyelin, Mile. "Caring for Alzheimer's Victim Can Be Devastating for

    Family." St. Petersburg Times 3 Jun. 1985, NewsBank HEA62: E8.

Hart, Sylvia. "Special Unit Opens in Mobile for Alzheimer's Patients."

    Mobile Press Register 3 Feb. 1985. NewsBank HEA14: A12.

Henig, Robin. The Myth of Senility. New York: Anchor, 1981.

Hollister, Anne. "The Fading Mind." Life Feb. 1986: 30-38.

Reddich, Tina, RN. Private Interview at Baywood Hospital. 24 Oct. 1984.

    13:1.

"Study by Minneapolis University." New York Times 10 Oct. 1984, 1. 13:1

Trenton, Paul, M.D. Private Interview, 26 Oct. 1994.

EXERCISE 7.11

Write the first draft of your investigative paper.

EXERCISE 7.12

Have at least one person read your first draft and make suggestions for improving its content, organization, and sentence structure. (Your instructor may make this a peer-editing exercise in class.)

EXERCISE 7.13

After you write your first draft and receive feedback on it, revise the paper and prepare the final manuscript. Use the required format and proofread it carefully, correcting any errors you find. Then submit your investigative paper for evaluation.

CHAPTER SEVEN INVESTIGATIVE PAPER

Name _____   Date _____

Class _____   Instructor _____

Meeting Time _____   Day _____   Circle One: Original Paper

Revision

IMPORTANT: REVISED PAPER MUST BE ACCOMPANIED BY THE ORIGINAL!!

CHECKLIST

I. Content
    A. Research effort
    B. Logic and ideas
    C. Reader interest

II. Structure
    A. Overall essay plan and structure
    B. Thesis sentence
    C. Opening sentence
    D. Topic sentences
    E. Primary and secondary support sentences
    F. Irrelevant material
    G. Transitions

III. Sentence style and mechanics
    A. Sentence structure
    B. Agreement, pronoun reference, tense, person
    C. Spelling, punctuation, capitalization

IV. Documentation
    A. Plagiarism
    B. Use of quoted, summarized, and paraphrased material
    C. Internal documentation
    D. Works Cited

V. Format
    A. Heading
    B. Pagination and margins
    C. Documentation
    D. Works Cited
    E. Legibility and neatness

Grade for Original Paper _____

Grade for Revision (if required) _____

CHAPTER EIGHT

Essay Exams

Objectives

When you have completed this chapter, you will have written or studied each of the following:

1. adapted writing processes for essay exams
2. short essay answers
3. longer in-class essays
4. open-book exams
5. take-home exams
6. proficiency exams

8

To complete your development from an inexperienced writer to an accomplished one, you must learn to write different kinds of essay examinations. This task has been left for last to make certain you have the writing experience necessary to perform well under the pressures of essay testing. By adapting the organizational strategies covered in the previous chapters of this book, you can confidently answer almost any kind of essay question assigned. Confidence is a big factor in writing successful exams, and knowing beforehand how to organize different types of essay examinations will help tremendously in building the self-confidence you need. In this chapter you will learn strategies for writing short essay answers, longer in-class essays, open-book exams, and take-home exams.

LESSON ONE: *Short Essay Answers*

When assigned short essay questions, write answers that are condensed paragraphs. Each answer should contain a topic sentence and several supporting sentences. Begin each answer with a topic sentence that clearly states the essential generalization. Suppose, for example, the following question were asked:

> What was the significance of *Brown v. Board of Education* to the African-American community?

Your topic sentence might read:

> In *Brown v. Board of Education* the Supreme Court declared unconstitutional the "separate but equal" doctrine that was used by whites to force African-Americans to use separate public schools.

This **topic sentence** gets right down to business, directly answering the question:

In *Brown v. Board of Education* . . .   Repeats name of case to let reader know that the answer is written on required subject (introductory phrase)

. . . the Supreme Court declared unconstitutional the "separate but equal" doctrine . . .	States the crucial generalization that must be made about the case (main clause of sentence)
. . . that was used by whites to force African-Americans to use separate public schools.	Completes topic sentence by relating answer to the portion of the question, "What was the significance . . . to the African-American community?" (dependent clause following the main clause)

Follow the topic sentence with two or three sentences, each of which serves as a combined primary and secondary support sentence. Making each support sentence perform double duty allows you to condense your paragraph without sacrificing the details necessary to convince your instructor that you really know what you are talking about. The trick is to write support sentences that obviously support the topic sentence with key generalizations and to intersperse these generalizations with facts. To accomplish this task, you will have to use complex sentences, devoting independent clauses to your primary generalizations and dependent clauses and phrases to your secondary supporting details. Study the following support sentences for the previous sample topic sentence:

Support Sentence #1

Questioning the validity of racial segregation in public schools, Chief Justice Warren delivered the unanimous opinion of the court that segregation of children in public schools solely on the basis of race, even though the schools may be equally well equipped and staffed, denies minority children equal educational opportunities.

Support Sentence #2

Citing results of psychological experiments, Warren stated that to separate children from others of the same age and educational qualifications solely because of their race creates a feeling of inferiority as to their community status "that may affect their hearts and minds in a way unlikely to ever be undone."

Notice the tremendous concentration of generalization and fact achieved in these support sentences. If the second sentence were converted to conventional primary and secondary support sentences, they might look like this:

Chief Justice Warren cited the results of scientific experiments by psychologists to support the court's opinion. He stated that researchers had found that separating children from others of the same age and educational qualifications solely because of their race creates a feeling of inferiority. The children feel that their status in the community is lower. This feeling "may affect their hearts and minds in a way unlikely to ever be undone."

Comparing the two versions of support sentence #2, you will see that the recommended version is a single complex sentence whereas the longer version is made up of four complete sentences. Study the following breakdown:

Condensed Version	**Expanded Version**
1. Citing results of psychological experiments, . . .	1. Chief Justice Warren cited the results of scientific experiments by psychologists.
2. . . . Warren stated that to separate children from others of the same age and educational qualifications solely because of their race creates a feeling of inferiority . . .	2. He stated that researchers had found that separating children from others of the same age and educational qualifications solely because of their race creates a feeling of inferiority.
3. . . . as to their community status . . .	3. The children feel that their status in the community is lower.
4. . . . that "may affect their hearts and minds in a way unlikely to ever be undone."	4. This feeling "may affect their hearts and minds in a way unlikely to ever be undone."
_____	_____
1 sentence—50 words	4 sentences—71 words

EXERCISE 8.1

Write a short essay answer—no more than three sentences—answering one of the following questions:

1. How does the structure of an introductory paragraph differ from the structure of a body paragraph?

2. How do Plan #2 and Plan #3 of the argumentative paper differ?

_____

_____

_____

_____

_____

_____

_____

_____

_____

_____

_____

_____

_____

_____

_____

_____

_____

_____

Have your answer checked for accuracy and completeness.

EXERCISE 8.2

For practice, answer this three-part short essay question:

What is a thesis, where is it located, and how should it be written?

Use the following paragraphs as a source of information. Write a topic sentence, and support it with two sentences that combine primary and secondary support. Compress as much information as possible in your support sentences.

Logically, most writers write the introductory paragraph of their essays first. This is as it should be. It does not follow, however, that you should begin by writing the first sentence of it; indeed, it would be more accurate to say you should write the last sentence of your introductory paragraph first. This statement may sound absurd, but it makes far more sense than it would first appear. Since the thesis sentence is the most important sentence of the entire essay, it should be given your complete attention before you begin writing the first line. Frequently, the thesis is called the central idea because it is the idea around which your entire paper is built. If the introduction of your essay has no central idea to hold it together, the paper will fail. Without the thesis statement, the essay may wander aimlessly and be ineffective.

The introductory section of every essay must have a thesis sentence for two distinct reasons. First, a thesis sentence will present the main idea you intend to stress in the rest of the paper. In a single sentence the thesis will preview the explanation or argument to follow in the body and conclusion of the essay; that is, it will assert an idea to be elaborated upon or an argumentative statement to be supported. Second, the thesis sentence will control your writing. By asserting the specific idea you want to elaborate upon, your thesis will narrow your topic and limit the discussion that follows.

Both the presentation of your main idea and the limitation of the paper's scope are important; however, both must be worked out before you begin writing your paper. If you do not have a thesis sentence written out before you write the paper, you will often forget your point long enough to cause yourself problems. Forgetting your point, however briefly, may result in statements being included that are not directly related to the idea you are trying to communicate. Statements of this nature are irrelevant, and every instructor will note such statements as errors because they weaken your essay.

Topic Sentence: _____

_____

_____

_____

_____

Support Sentence #1: _____

_____

_____

_____

Support Sentence #2: _____

_____

_____

_____

Have your sentences checked.

LESSON TWO: *Writing Longer Essay Exams in Class*

While an objective test determines a student's ability to recognize correct information, the in-class essay exam enables an instructor to ascertain student ability to interpret and use information. Furthermore, the essay exam practically eliminates guessing while it encourages thoughtfulness and organization. As a result of the emphasis on these qualities in evaluation, you should expect to demonstrate your competence by writing many essay exams. They will be the source of a major portion of course grades.

PREPARING TO WRITE ESSAY EXAMS

The three-phase writing process can be adapted for use in essay exams. As with all other writing assignments in *Survival*, you must begin with the planning and drafting stages. You will, of course, be under pressure to write essay exams in a limited amount of time; consequently, you will need to shorten the process to have more time to write. But you must not allow yourself to omit the process completely because students who do their planning and drafting consistently earn better grades on their written work. You will find that your essay exam grades will improve if you follow the strategies you have learned and practiced in the first seven chapters of *Survival*.

Consider the following abbreviated version of the writing process outline you have been working with throughout the text. By following this procedure, you could develop an organized approach to writing in-class assignments. The suggested time allotments given in parentheses are for a two-hour exam.

Planning
> Reading before coming to class

Assignment Analysis (10 minutes)
> Analyze the question or assignment carefully.

Time Budget
> Planning (20 minutes)
> Writing (50 minutes)
> Editing—final copy (40 minutes)

These suggested time allotments can be varied to suit individual writing styles, but assignment analysis and time budgeting are essential to avoid confusion and running out of time before the writing project is complete.

You usually won't be allowed to bring research notes or books to class when you are to write an in-class essay exam. The ideas you present in your essay will, therefore, have to be based on the information stored in your memory. In such a situation, your information gathering will consist of doing your prewriting exercises: brainstorming, freewriting, clustering, analytical questioning, and pyramiding. If you don't write out your information before you begin your in-class essay, you will almost certainly forget some of the ideas and facts you had intended to offer as proof of your assertions. This step takes little time; however, you may wish to limit yourself to ten or fifteen minutes for prewriting exercises, definitely to no more than twenty minutes.

Your instructors will expect you to write a 500-word essay or at least two 250-word essays in a one-hour examination period. Writing 500 words or more in one hour may sound impossible to you now, but you can do it if you are properly prepared and know how to approach such an assignment.

To do well on an in-class exam, know the subject matter thoroughly. But in addition to the knowledge of subject matter, you must have the resourcefulness to apply your knowledge when faced with unexpected questions. Systematically studying the material covered by the text and thoughtfully anticipating the questions that might be asked are the best ways of acquiring the knowledge needed for essay exams. But you already know that. What you may not know is that it is possible to arm yourself with an organizational strategy that will be useful in almost any essay exam situation. Being prepared, you will be much freer to concentrate on the writing assignment than if you have to worry about how to organize the essay. This strategy is an adaptation of the basic three-part organizational plan presented in earlier chapters of this text. To employ this strategy, follow these eight easy steps:

1. **Clarify the Assignment.** Make certain that you analyze the required examination question carefully before you begin to write. Essay-exam topics can be quite complicated, and you should never begin writing until you have read and reread the question several times. Students who are overconfident about their preparation sometimes make the mistake of not studying the question and after giving the topic only superficial consideration begin to write and write and write. Then, too late, they discover they have incorrectly anticipated the topic and written the wrong answer even though they were more than adequately prepared to answer the question actually asked. Often students who are poorly prepared for exams make the mistake of beginning to write too soon. Panic-stricken because they think they do not know anything, they conclude that their only chance is to fill several pages with any ideas even remotely connected with the exam topic. Instead, they should take a calmer approach, refraining from writing until they have carefully studied the required topic and surveyed their knowledge.

   Look for key direction words in the exam question. Overlooking these words may result in your misunderstanding what you are to write. If you are asked to analyze how the space shuttles can be used to benefit American business in the future, do not write an exam in which you contrast the shuttles to the older space capsules. You simply would not be writing the paper your instructor wanted. Many key direction words are commonly used by instructors, but the following fifteen are most frequently encountered. Study this list of words and definitions carefully.

   a. **Analyze**—to examine closely, separating the basic parts, steps, or essential features. You may write a critical analysis.
   b. **Attack or defend**—to be for or against, taking a position. Write an argument, pro-con if possible.
   c. **Compare**—to explain similarities, parallels. An instructor may actually want you to compare and contrast: to stress likenesses and differences. Before you write, make a list of your bases of comparison and contrast.
   d. **Contrast**—to stress differences.
   e. **Define**—to explain what something means, or what something is. Begin with a basic definition and use examples to make it clear.
   f. **Discuss**—to explain, to analyze, to elaborate, possibly to debate. This is a vague term, so carefully ponder what direction to take.
   g. **Elaborate**—to explain further, to develop a detailed explanation of something. Take care to use enough primary and secondary support: go into details.
   h. **Evaluate**—to judge, or to analyze critically, discussing the pros and cons. Write a pro-con argument or a critical analysis.

    i. **Examine**—to analyze.
    j. **Explain**—to clarify, to recite, to interpret, to explicate, to summarize. The term "explain" covers all expository writing strategies. Do not write an argument.
    k. **Illustrate**—to clarify through the use of an extended example or several short examples. Do not forget to begin with your basic generalization.
    l. **List**—to write down a series of points. Use a 1, 2, 3, or first, second, third approach.
    m. **Outline**—to discuss briefly, a skeletal discussion, the relationship of major and minor parts. Skip the details.
    n. **Summarize**—to review briefly, omitting details. A review.
    o. **Survey**—to briefly review all of the parts of something in order to gain perspective.

2. **Develop a Thesis.** As rapidly as possible, formulate a thesis statement. You can use an umbrella or a divided thesis, but be careful to avoid writing a thesis that is too broad. Your thesis must control the scope of your essay. You might, for instance, focus your paper by writing, "Congress must take immediate steps to balance the budget." A divided thesis such as "Congress must eliminate all farm subsidies, cut all oil subsidies, eliminate pork barrel projects, and remove welfare fraud to balance the budget" would also focus your essay effectively.

3. **Write an Outline.** Make a list of four or five points or ideas you hope to have time to cover—a simple outline. If you can, number them in order of importance or interest to your instructor. Because you are writing an essay exam, you should begin with the most important or interesting point and proceed down the list, discussing the least important idea last.

4. **Use Short-Cuts Where Possible.** Do **not** write a full introductory paragraph when you are writing an essay exam unless your instructor specifically requires one. Make your thesis statement the first sentence of your first paragraph, or isolate it, making it the first paragraph even though it is just one sentence long. Time will be limited, and your instructor will be more interested in your knowledge of the facts than a formal beginning. Examine the student-written essay exam on page 337; the writer effectively uses an isolated thesis. Compare it to the essay on page 338 to see how the thesis can be incorporated into the first body paragraph on a short exam.

5. **Explain Ideas Fully.** Write a paragraph for each point discussed. Begin each paragraph with a clear topic sentence. If possible, add at least four sentences of support for each topic sentence. Use both primary and secondary support sentences. Include plenty of specific details, and above all, use examples whenever they will demonstrate to your instructor that you know what you are talking about.

6. **Eliminate Traditional Concluding Paragraph.** Do **not** write a concluding paragraph that summarizes your essay and asserts the importance of what has been written as you would in a normal essay. Instead, write a single concluding sentence and place it at the end of the last paragraph; or simply stop writing when you have completed your last point. Your last sentence must not give your reader the idea that you were too rushed to finish—even if you were. Create the impression that you have said everything you wanted to say and that you had ample time to finish.

7. **Make Corrections Quickly as You Write.** Do **not** plan to recopy your essay—there will not be time. Corrections can be made by crossing out words and writing either above or after what is crossed out.

8. **Edit Your Final Copy.** Take at least five minutes to proofread your work. Look for lapses in sentences and sentences that do not make sense. Correct misspelled words, and rewrite awkward sentences. Many instructors will allow you to use a dictionary during an essay exam. Finally, in the upper left corner, write your name, class title and meeting time, instructor's name, and the date.

Study the sample essay exams that follow. Keep in mind that they were written under the pressure of a time limit and that the writers were **not** allowed to refer to text or notes. As you read the sample essay exam, notice these characteristics:

1. Abbreviated introductory paragraph: immediately begins answering question—the first paragraph is the thesis
2. Good paragraph structure: strong topic sentences, plenty of primary and secondary support—each body paragraph at least four or five sentences long
3. Logical order of ideas: most important point is stated in first body paragraph
4. Conclusion summarizes the paper in a single sentence placed at the end of the last body paragraph
5. Essay carefully proofread

ESSAY QUESTION

Topic: Analyze the causes that prompt the characters to act as they do in the short story "The Autopsy."

An analysis of "The Autopsy" reveals that all four living characters in the story are in many ways products of their environment.

The clearest example of this is the old fishmonger. The author describes him in great physical detail, making it clear that his work and hard life have made great demands upon him. His body, his face, and his hands all show the effects of the hard life he has lived. Perhaps even more tragically, the old man's emotions have been conditioned by the environment. It becomes apparent to the reader early in the story that the man is considered by the other characters to be lower class, hardly worth noticing. For instance, when the narrator arrives at the hospital for the business meeting and finds the fish merchant there, his feelings are made perfectly obvious. The narrator, even after recognizing the old man, does not bother to acknowledge him. It is not surprising that with the indifference shown him, the fishman accepts the role of an inferior person in society, expecting the cruel treatment from others that they almost automatically extend to him.

If the fishman represents the inferior role in a racially prejudiced society, the pathologist is surely the antithesis. Obviously accustomed to controlling his environment, the doctor notices no irregularities in his treatment of others. An example of his lack of feeling is given in the beginning of the story. As the doctor enters the hospital, he not only ignores the fishman, but he does not even verbally greet his visitor. It is apparent the doctor was raised in an environment which taught him to consider all members of other races as inferiors. In addition, he obviously believes that the power of his position makes him superior to some or most members of his own race. During the scene in the autopsy room when the old man is viewing his wife's body, the doctor is oblivious to any human quality or suffering. Two things could contribute to his lack of feeling; the first is his profession. Working at a job where he does not deal with living patients could have removed basic feelings of compassion towards others. The second, a more likely factor, could be his environment. A person in his position in a racist society could come to feel he is above common people, especially some old, black fishmonger who accepts the role of an inferior.

Another, more obvious example of the effects of environment can be seen in the lab assistant. The author uses a very graphic incident to illustrate the callousness of the lab assistant. Using the dead woman's thigh as a pin cushion while the husband watches him sew up the woman's mutilated body clearly illustrates the assistant's inability to feel compassion for the grieving man in front of him. This incident clearly suggests that the assistant has been influenced by the unfeeling doctor. While working on the old man's wife, the assistant displays the same feelings of social superiority as the doctor. An assumption that position and race separate humanity is obvious in both the doctor and the assistant.

Finally, the most ambiguous character is the narrator. He is also shown to be a product of a racially segregated society by his actions during the first meeting with the fishman. Unlike the doctor, the narrator does notice the old man; indeed, he acknowledges some human qualities in him. But while he is quick to notice his appearance, this businessman does not feel compelled to greet or console the old black man. Although the reader becomes aware of an uneasiness in the narrator, there is little action from him to indicate true compassion during the post-mortem scene. The reader is almost led to believe the narrator's sense of unease comes from embarrassment and not compassion. In the narrator, as well as the other characters, the reader is aware of a sense of position. Although the narrator may be uncomfortable due to some inner pangs of compassion, it is obvious the fishman, the doctor, and the lab assistant see nothing wrong with the roles they play, suggesting their actions are the result of environmental conditioning.

K. C. Boylan

Sample In-Class Essay #2

The students taking this exam were given the following instructions and were to respond to an essay that first appeared in *Newsweek* magazine. The article, written by Ginny Carrol, reported on a interview with Captain Carol Barkalow of the U.S. Army. The title of the article, "Women Have What It Takes," sums up the point of the article. According to Captain Barkalow, women should have every right to ask for combat duty if they want to fight on the front lines. She pointed out in the interview that women have fought in wars in the past, that the death of a woman warrior should be considered no more tragic than the death of a man warrior, and that the interpersonal relationships between men and women soldiers on the battlefield would be no different than the traditional relationship between men on the battlefield.

In "Women Have What It Takes," Captain Barkalow makes a case for military women being allowed to fight in combat. In response to her argument, students were asked to write a paper in which they agreed or disagreed with her position. The following essay was submitted by one student who took the exam.

Women Have What It Takes

During the past few decades, there has been a growing controversy over the issue of allowing women to serve in the military. Carol Barkalow, a West Point graduate and commander of an air defense platoon and a truck company, spoke to <u>Newsweek</u> writer Ginny Carroll concerning the subject shortly after the invasion of Kuwait and resulting Gulf War. In her interview, Ms. Barkalow took the position that women were fully capable of serving in the military and were equal to men in their overall suitability. While such a position may well raise some conservative eyebrows, a review of similar roles women have played in American history will demonstrate the veracity of Ms. Barkalow's belief.

During the American Revolution and the Civil War, a number of women were involved both overtly and covertly in the war efforts. In both wars, soldiers involved in active combat were later discovered to be women disguised as men. In many cases, the women involved were so convincing in their roles that the men they fought alongside and camped with refused to believe they were in fact women. In at least one instance, the United States government paid a pension to the husband of a "soldier" following her death. In addition to this type of direct combat involvement, other women acted as spies and couriers. For instance, during the Civil War, abolitionist Harriet Tubman and Sojourner Truth, both black women, tirelessly worked as spies to promote the success of the Union army and risked certain death if they were caught.

The history of women in the military continued into the present century with the advent of World War II. With fighting taking place in so many arenas, women were not at liberty to take a passive role, even had they been so inclined. While women were unable to serve in active combat, military positions were found for them in organizations such as the WACS and WAVES. In fact, one such woman was employed as General Eisenhower's driver, and other women filled a number of similar positions. Back in the United States, many women played an active role in the war effort by seeking employment and training in naval yards and factories, and the war-time stereotype of Rosie the Riveter was born. Although their jobs were primarily in the private sector rather than in direct, combat-related activities, the job duties of women in war work were hard and physically demanding. Because they were successful and dedicated in carrying out their efforts, women were able to prove to their male counterparts that they could undertake such responsibilities when called on to do so.

Within the last few decades, women have been accepted into military and paramilitary roles traditionally within the purview of men and have found success in those positions. As Carol Barkalow pointed out in her <u>Newsweek</u> interview, West Point began admitting female candidates in 1980. By 1990, men in the military had begun to recognize women as their peers because women had shown themselves to be worthy of their regard. Similarly, and at around the same time, civilian police departments began to hire and train female officers as a result of the Affirmative Action requirements mandating the hiring of minorities. While veteran male police officers were skeptical at first, women officers have since proven their competency on the job, on patrol, and not just behind a desk in a station house. Today the highest law enforcement position in the United States, that of Attorney General, is held by Janet Reno, and in Sacramento, California, the position of District Attorney is held by Jan Scully.

Although the idea of women in combat is still somewhat controversial, it is an idea whose time has come. It is axiomatic that diehard conservative males will continue to oppose the idea of women in the forefront of active combat, but as Carol Barkalow so eloquently pointed out, strong, valid arguments exist to refute each and every point of opposition. During the 200-plus years the United States has been in existence, women have made slow but steady gains in obtaining the recognition of their abilities and equality they deserve, and the battle has frequently been a difficult one. The experience of battling against those people they value and hold closest to them for so many years has made women inherently suitable to battle those who threaten the peace and liberty of us all. In fact, given the opportunity, women just may do a better job!

Kim Powers

EXERCISE 8.3

Assume you are writing an in-class exam for a health education class, and your instructor has told you to prepare to write on physical fitness. Try to anticipate the essay examination questions that you might be asked. List three potential questions:

1. _____

_____

_____

2. _____

_____

_____

3. _____

_____

_____

Note: The following examination (Exercise 8.4) must be completed during a single class period.

EXERCISE 8.4

At the very beginning of the class period in which you plan to write your practice examination, ask your instructor for your question and go to work immediately.

Write in ink; use 8 1/2 x 11-inch paper; write only on one side of the page; and skip every other line. Proofread your work.

Your practice examination will be evaluated and returned to you, or it will be evaluated with you in a conference. The following checklist will be used. Study it so you will know the basis upon which you will be graded.

EVALUATION CHECKLIST

1. Knowledge of subject (Coverage?)
2. Thesis (Short introductory paragraph?)
3. Essay structure (Best idea first?)
4. Topic sentences (At beginning of each body paragraph?)
5. Primary and secondary support sentences (Details?)
6. Sentence construction
7. Proofreading

Probable Grade _____

LESSON THREE: *Open-Book Exams*

Occasionally, an instructor will allow you to refer to your texts and notes during an in-class essay examination. Open-book exams, however, are not easy to write; they present special problems. The main problem is time pressure. Since you will be required to write at least 500 words during a typical essay exam—often in a fifty-minute class period—you cannot take much time to plan your answers. To function effectively during an open-book exam, you must formulate your thesis and an outline rapidly, then begin to write your paragraphs, using, whenever possible, information you need from your books and notes. Because of time limitations, however, you have to know exactly what information you want to use and where to find it. Therefore, studying before an open-book exam is just as important as studying before a closed-book exam.

The best organizational strategy for you to use is the one outlined in the previous lesson. Dispense with the introductory paragraph—concentrate on writing a good thesis. Use your best point first, and write just one concluding sentence instead of a full concluding paragraph.

Quoted materials must be enclosed in quotation marks and documented, and any material closely summarized or paraphrased should be documented, too. Use parenthetical documentation.

Study the following essay, written as one part of an open-book examination in an American literature course.

Question: Discuss the use of nature as a symbolic motif in William Faulkner's *The Bear*.

> Nature symbolism in <u>The Bear</u> by Faulkner is dominated by the bear and Sam Fathers as symbols of the spirit of the wilderness.
> "Old Ben is the wilderness, the mystery of man's nature and origins beneath the forms of civilization; and man's proper relationship with the wilderness teaches him liberty, courage, pride, and humility" (Hoffman and Vickery 325). Sam Fathers, the son of a Negro slave and a Chickasaw chief, symbolizes human ability to achieve the proper relationship to nature through contact with the wilderness. Both Sam Fathers and the bear bring Ike to an awareness of the wilderness, which he realizes is slowly

vanishing. " 'So it wont be until the last day. When even [the bear] dont want it to last any longer' " (Faulkner, 205). Because of his initiation into the mystique of the wilderness, Ike takes it upon himself to preserve the spirit of the wilderness after the killing of the bear and the death of Sam Fathers by refusing to contribute to its physical destruction. By repudiating his inheritance of the land, Ike hopes "to hold the earth mutual and intact in the communal anonymity of brotherhood" (Faulkner 247), a lesson he has learned from the wilderness. Ultimately, Faulkner juxtaposes the wilderness, a desired element in human well-being, with civilization, a corrupt evil that is a result of people not having a proper relationship to nature. The wilderness emerges as human salvation from civilization, but it is dying as that same civilization threatens to destroy it.

EXERCISE 8.5

If you feel that you need to practice writing an open-book exam (or if your instructor feels you need to practice), have your instructor assign you a topic, and negotiate an agreement about time limits, sources you may use, and documentation required.

Have your practice exam evaluated.

LESSON FOUR: *Take-Home Exams*

Instructors frequently assign take-home exams. Students are usually relieved upon hearing they will be able to write their exams outside of class because they want to be free of the tremendous time pressure of the in-class exam and because they need more time to study. Often, however, their relief is short-lived, for take-home exams can be very demanding. It is not unusual for multiple-part exams to be assigned, each part requiring a response of 500 words or more; furthermore, students are usually given less than a week to complete a take-home exam. These requirements are a great hardship on students who have heavy study loads or who work.

When your instructor assigns a take-home exam, be certain you understand exactly what is required and what is allowed. Several students in class will always find time to write thorough, well-researched answers, and your answers must compete with theirs. You must face this probability; it is a fact of student life, unfair as it may seem. Your best strategy in take-home exams—unless your instructor is adamant that you should not do any more than asked for—is to go above and beyond what is required. Some instructors will mark papers down if students go over the allowable length. Other instructors will mark papers down if students include references to library sources that were not requested. Your best plan is to take the time and effort to construct your answers carefully. Each take-home essay you write must be carefully constructed and perfectly edited.

Study the following essay. Students taking this exam were to analyze a specific short story, "The Guest."

The students assigned this take-home essay were given the following instructions and limitations.

Take-Home Essay Assignment

Write an essay in which you analyze the author's message or the author's technique in "The Guest" by Albert Camus. Your paper must—

1. be no more than 1,200 words in length
2. analyze some aspect of the short story
3. have clear essay structure
4. refer clearly to the author and short story
5. be carefully edited
6. include many examples to support your analysis.

The following essay was submitted by one student who took the exam.

Barbara Morden

English 1-A MW 1:30

Mr. Mehaffy

31 October 1992

                            The True Guest

     Each of the three characters in Albert Camus's short story "The
Guest" is a subtle and individual illustration of the title: they are
all really guests, though none of them fully understands the impli-
cations of this reality. Because of the French colonization of Algeria,
Daru and Balducci are guests ruling in a foreign land, while the Arab,
the only character who is native to the setting of the story, is
ironically a guest in Daru's schoolhouse even though it is a public
building in the Arab's own country. This irony effectively demonstrates
the more obvious interpretation of Camus's fascinating story, but the
"guest" the title refers to is not a character in person at all.
Integrity or honor, which all too often is only a "guest" in the lives
of people, is the real subject of Camus's thought-provoking narrative.
Balducci, Daru, and the Arab represent the different levels of personal
integrity that people possess and act upon during the course of their
lives.

     The character of Balducci is the easiest to understand and explain
in terms of personal integrity. Balducci is a soldier and a simple man
who follows orders and does what he is told without question. Camus
effectively portrays a universal type of honor through the somewhat
rigid characterization of Balducci. He is mature and symbolizes the old
school of thought. The attitudes he represents are clearly defined by
the manner in which he treats his prisoner, his unwavering commitment to
obeying orders, and his reaction to Daru's unwillingness to perform the

duties now expected of him. Balducci is also used to illustrate the differences in attitudes between generations. Younger generations are traditionally more questioning, flexible, and idealistic than their predecessors. A mature soldier is an excellent example of the older generation's unquestioning obedience and strict adherence to rules and regulations. Through Balducci, integrity is represented as how well a man executes his duty; and, therefore, how well a man executes his duty defines what he is. "Those are the orders" (Camus 3) is Balducci's justification for bringing the Arab to Daru. Though this character's integrity is short-sighted and finite, it is pure in concept because it is so simplistic. When the schoolmaster tries to tell the old soldier that he won't turn the Arab over to the authorities, Balducci replies, "If you want to drop us, go ahead; I'll not denounce you. I have an order to deliver the prisoner and I'm doing so" (Camus 5). It may be somewhat misguided, but it is an example of an elementary honor which the author illustrates through this character.

The simplistic nature of Balducci's duty-bound integrity is exposed as the story unfolds. This type of integrity appears to be not only limited in application and scope but even irresponsible when adhered to strictly. There are definite and sometimes disastrous consequences for following "the orders." Camus makes a strong statement about individual responsibility through the use of this character. Although Balducci is a minor character in the story, he is the catalyst that sets the conflict in motion, and the duty-bound integrity he represents is certainly ambiguous and potentially dangerous.

Another level of integrity is well-illustrated by the character of Daru. Daru symbolizes the embodiment of education and an enlightened, high-minded integrity and conscience. This character is drawn with more depth and subtlety than that of Balducci and is used to demonstrate that the black and white lines of honor are sometimes grayed by resolve and circumstance. Most readers find Daru's actions in the story exemplary and even heroic, but his actions are not really all that clear-cut. The author paints the picture of a man who loves Algeria more than France, but this same man is part of Algeria's oppression and is employed by its oppressors. Though Daru is the sustainer of life through the distribution of grain to the Arabs and teaches the Arab children, he is also like a ruler in his own little kingdom where the hostage pupils learn not about their own country but about French history, customs, and language. Quite simply, Daru is a fence-sitter; he represents the ambiguity which often exists in personal integrity. He cannot decide whether to set the Arab free or to take him to prison, so he takes him to the high plateau where one road leads to the prison at Tinguit and the other to the nomads and freedom. At that point, the Arab wants to know what he should do. Daru tells him bluntly, "No, be quiet. Now I'm leaving you" (Camus 9). The Arab knows the schoolmaster will be in trouble with the French authorities if the prisoner disappears, and he feels such an obligation to the man who has befriended him that he walks down the road to prison, knowing that he will almost certainly be put to death. This incident clearly contrasts Daru's integrity with that of the Arab. Daru demonstrates conditional integrity.

The last and highest level of integrity explored in this short story is illustrated by the character of the Arab. Camus uses this character to symbolize a perfectly consistent integrity, an integrity which is honest on both a personal and societal level. Throughout the story the Arab never takes any action which isn't completely consistent with the integrity he represents. Readers may expect the most integrity from Daru; after all, he is highly educated, and therefore moral. However, the common man, the Arab, is far more representative of the ideals that society reveres and esteems. Camus skillfully draws this comparison between the characters of Daru and the Arab. The schoolmaster is intelligent, learned, worldly, and high-minded, but he is also hesitant to become involved, unwilling to make responsible choices until he absolutely has to make them, and he is undoubtedly somewhat prejudiced as illustrated by some of the observations and personal thoughts he entertains concerning his Arab "guest." For example, he observes the Arab's "animal mouth" (Camus 6). On the other hand, Camus has created a symbol which can be missed because it is not obvious. The Arab personifies the attributes of humility, honesty, and humanity under the more general umbrella of integrity. He is the first to feel a bond in the story, for he says to Daru, "Come with us" (Camus 7). He shows no hesitancy to make choices which are consistent with his own personal honor, although he has many opportunities to do otherwise. Integrity is never just a "guest" in the ethics of the Arab.

The kind of courage and integrity which leads people to stand up for their beliefs even in the face of death is the kind of integrity which transcends all others. At the end of Camus' story, the Arab displays this exact kind of courage and honor. He chooses to do what he believes is morally correct despite the fact that his choice will lead him to almost certain death. His integrity never fails him. True integrity is never only a "guest" in the lives of people, but, unfortunately, the inferior progenies of real integrity are far more predominant in society and much easier to find.

LESSON FIVE: *Proficiency Exams*

Schools commonly require students to write **proficiency exams** to demonstrate their writing ability prior to awarding some major degree or certificate. Most colleges and universities, for example, require students to pass a proficiency exam before they receive their bachelor's degree. Some schools refer to such exams as the WPE, the Writing Proficiency Examination. In most states, those students who go on to earn their teaching credential must pass another writing proficiency test; in one state this is called the CBEST. Colleges and universities in other states require students to take the PPST or some similar exam. And there are many other writing proficiency exams students may be required to pass, depending on their majors.

SCORING GUIDE

4   The **4** essay reflects an exceptional performance of the writing task.
- thesis is clearly stated, may be compelling or thoughtful
- organization is exceptionally clear, transitions effective
- uses appropriate details and analyzes their significance
- fluent, demonstrating a clear command of language and varied sentence structure
- virtually free of errors in sentence structure, grammar, and mechanics

3   The **3** essay reflects adequate performance of the writing task.
- a central idea focuses the essay
- adequate organization and development
- may have a few problems in sentence structure, diction, and mechanics
- demonstrates adequate command of language and some sentence variety

2   The **2** essay approaches adequate performance of the writing task.
- may have an unfocused or simplistic central idea
- may be poorly organized, or may lack detail and specificity
- frequent problems in diction, grammar, mechanics, and sentence structure, which impede meaning

1   The **1** essay is clearly inadequate.
- may lack a central idea
- may lack coherence or adequate development although it may address the topic
- multiple errors in sentence structure, grammar, and mechanics impede understanding

---

Writing these proficiency exams is in some ways easier than writing short-time in-class exams. When writing proficiency exams, you will typically have two hours or more to complete the writing. When writing such essays, you should write fully developed introductory and concluding paragraphs as well as fully developed body paragraphs. Plan to write an essay that is 500-750 words long, and make sure you edit your work carefully before you submit it.

Proficiency exams are normally graded holistically by a committee made up of experienced English teachers. Your exam will be read by at least two readers, both of whom must agree that your essay is either passing or failing. In some schools all exams that receive a failing score are read by a third reader to give the student the benefit of the doubt. The term "graded holistically" refers to the fact that the instructors reading the exams are not allowed to make any marks on your exam; they simply read the exam to gain an overall impression and then compare its qualities to a scoring guide they have in front of them. The following scoring guide is typical.

Student essays given 4 or 3 scores by instructors are passing papers; those given 2 or 1 scores are failing papers. However, some schools use a six-point scale where 6, 5, and 4 papers pass and 3, 2, and 1 papers fail. While reading proficiency exams, readers occasionally refer to this scoring guide, which they typically keep immediately at hand, until they have it committed to memory. You should examine it carefully so you will know what your readers will expect when they read your exams.

Most proficiency exams will list two topics and ask you to choose one of them. When you receive your exam topics sheet, look quickly at both topics and choose one that looks interesting. After you have chosen one, stay with it: do not change topics, even if you later find that you don't like the one you have chosen. Changing topics after you have started will almost certainly lead to failure because you won't have sufficient time left to develop the second topic.

The topic you are given to write on when you take a proficiency exam will be general rather than specific. That is, you can confidently expect that you will be asked to write about something that everyone should know enough about to write a 500-750 word essay. Consider the typical proficiency exam topic below:

> Many parents are concerned about the negative effect of television on their children. Write an essay in which you explain what some of the physical, social, and psychological effects are that cause parents to worry. Include specific examples to support your ideas.

When writing on a topic such as this one, look carefully at the assignment and you will often see exactly what is desired in the way of a response. Here, the body paragraphs should include at least three, one describing each of the following effects: physical, social, and psychological. You could write more than this but not less.

The following is a typical holistic exam topic that has been given often in proficiency examinations.

EXAM TOPIC:

> Aging is an inevitable process about which people hold differing views. Some people are bothered by the physical process of growing older: the changes in appearance, activities, and health. Others, however, believe the mental changes—more knowledge, maturity, ability to understand life—far outweigh the physical inconveniences of growing older. Obviously, there are both positive and negative aspects involved in the process of growing old.

THE TOPIC TO WRITE ON:

> Discuss some of the positive and negative aspects of growing older, and explain why you feel aging is ultimately either a positive or a negative experience.

The first step in writing on this, as with any written assignment, is to analyze the question. The topic clearly states that you are to discuss both the "positive and negative aspects" of growing older. The topic also asks you to "explain why you feel aging is ultimately either a positive or a negative experience." You could easily discuss the positive and negative aspects in the introduction and then explain the point of the paper in the thesis. The body of the paper would then give as many examples as possible to support the major idea. The student who wrote the following exam used that approach.

What Do You Mean, Old?

Nobody asks for it, nobody wants it, everyone tries to avoid it, everybody fights it, but, so far, everyone eventually grows old unless he or she dies prematurely. Although growing old is a natural state of affairs, most people would just as soon avoid having to experience the physical problems that come along with old age. Even those who champion the advantages of aging don't look at newborns with their petal-soft skin, sparkling eyes, and flexible joints and wish them dry, wrinkly skin, droopy, dim eyes, and stiff, painful joints. But given the fact that virtually all humans would rather grow old than die before having a chance to enjoy life, most look forward to old age with a mixture of apprehension and anticipation. After all, growing old is not only a time when the body deteriorates; it is also a time when people have time to enjoy free time, family, and friends. Because growing old is a challenging and worthwhile adventure that calls into action all the mental, emotional, and physical resources that people have available, there are realities and myths which need to be addressed.

No one can deny that recognizable attitudinal and mental changes occur as people grow older. Many reach a generative state when past fifty. This is a time when many individuals search to put meaning into their lives and their work. Oftentimes these people might change jobs or even careers. They look for fulfillment by leaving something good for posterity. As they grow past that, in the later years, there can be a sense of peace and accomplishment because of a life well spent. In these years people in general use the faculties, experiences, and wisdom they have gathered over the years to guide the next generation. Although it takes them longer to learn new skills, it is a mistaken notion that old people must be forgetful and can't learn new things. A recent article in Scientific American discussed how many people continue to learn throughout life and published a picture of a ninety-nine-year-old who had just graduated with a Bachelor of Arts! And many of us can remember hearing that Colonel Sanders started a new business adventure, Kentucky Fried Chicken, after he retired.

While growing older, people can continue to be emotionally balanced. Good emotional habits need to be acquired while young and continued throughout life. By learning good stress-coping techniques and being open to change—change does not mean death—people can carry on normal, happy, fulfilling lives regardless of their age. George Burns is a good example of this. His wife and show business partner died many years ago, yet he not only survived, but with good coping skills, he went on to make many more money-making movies and made countless appearances on television shows and in theaters. He is nearing 100 years old. Many centenarians, when asked what their longevity secrets are, repeatedly remark, "I didn't worry," "I left it up to the Lord," "I drank a glass of wine every day," and the like. George Burns might suggest that his daily cigar is responsible for his longevity. The similarity between all those who have lived exceptionally long lives is that they had the ability to live their lives "one day at a time." Being emotionally balanced can give older people an edge in dealing with younger ones as they teach them, thus helping to leave a good legacy.

The physical process of growing old is viewed by many as the hardest with which to cope. Obviously, it is true that there are many physiological changes which also affect the emotions and the mind. There is no dichotomy here. Throughout our lives we lose about twenty-five percent of our neurons, and there are other changes in the remaining neurons. This affects the communication between brain and body. Also, muscles tend to shrink in size. Hormones decline. These are very real physiological changes. However, some myths must be expelled from people's minds. One medical doctor, in his book <u>Growing Old is Not for Sissies</u>, described his lifestyle and showed pictures of himself—his muscles are far from flat and flabby! Much of the physical deterioration commonly accepted as a normal part of aging is simply from lack of use. It has been consistently proven that exercise does help stiff joints. The synovial fluid needs to be moved so it does not crystallize and make the joints stiff. Ninety-year olds have been put on gentle exercise programs, and their muscles have increased in size. In a study conducted in the United States, several older citizens were able to give up their walkers after a steady program of exercise. Disabilities due to coronary heart disease have been reversed by using a good exercise program. And how much better is prevention? Good regular exercise, a prudent, low-fat, mostly vegetarian diet, good stress coping skills, and quiet "time outs" keep people feeling young and healthy into old age. In the same issue of <u>Scientific American</u> mentioned above, there were pictures of centenarians swimming and engaging in various lively activities.

People should remember that mental changes can be channeled into positive experiences, that the emotions can be tamed and used to benefit posterity, and that physical changes can be monitored to a great extent. It seems that life is just a matter of living each day, each minute, looking forward to the next day with clear cognitive skills, wholesome emotions, and a healthy, toned body. Can it happen? Absolutely! Is it happening to people? Yes. The questions to ask are, "If you didn't know how old you were, how old would you be?" and "If you had seventy more years to live, how would you plan to spend them?" A woman in France just turned one hundred twenty years old. This is, according to scientists, as long as humans can live under the conditions people are familiar with at this time. People would do well to plan their lives according to the one hundred twenty-year time line. They would have quite an incentive to keep good mental, emotional, and physical habits so as to guarantee themselves a happy, healthy, and long life.

Lillian Manship

Chapter Eight Test

To prepare for the Chapter Eight Test, you will need to review Chapters Three through Seven of *Survival*. Your final essay exam will require you to demonstrate a thorough knowledge of the writing strategies presented in these chapters. (You will not, however, be tested on your knowledge of documentation.) When you have completed all of the work in Chapter Eight and you have reviewed Chapters Three through Seven, ask your instructor for the Chapter Eight Test. Your instructor may give you one of the following:

1. A closed-book exam (500-750 words)
2. An open-book exam (500-750 words)
3. A take-home exam (500-750 words)

If the examination is to be written in class, it must be completed during a single class period. If your first attempt is not acceptable, you will be allowed to revise your examination or to write another one on a different topic. (You may be asked to rewrite or revise your take-home exams, too.) Your instructor will make this decision.

CHAPTER EIGHT ESSAY EXAM

Name _____   Date _____

Class _____   Instructor _____

Meeting Time _____   Day _____   Circle One: Original Paper

                                                                    Revision

IMPORTANT: REVISED PAPER MUST BE ACCOMPANIED BY THE ORIGINAL!!

Type of Essay

Check one of the following:

_____   1. Short essay answer

_____   2. Longer in-class essay

_____   3. Open-book exam

_____   4. Take-home exam

_____   5. Proficiency exam

Topic _____

EVALUATION CHECKLIST

1. Knowledge of subject

2. Thesis

3. Essay structure

4. Topic sentences

5. Primary and secondary support sentences

6. Sentence construction

7. Proofreading

Grade for Original Paper _____

Revision _____

APPENDICES

APPENDIX A: *Documentation*

APPENDIX A: *Documentation*

INTRODUCTION

Appendix A has only one purpose: to help you write your Works Cited section. An example or two of an entry for almost every type of source is listed in the following section. You only need to be sure you find and follow exactly the example of the source you have referred to in the body of your paper. Be exact: every comma, period, and colon must be used accurately.

PART ONE: BOOK ENTRIES

A BOOK WITH ONE AUTHOR

Herbert, Frank. Heretics of Dune. New York: Putnam's, 1984.

      [Author is listed last name first.]

Hill, Ruth Beebe. Hanta Yo. New York: Warner, 1979.

      [Name of publishing company is shortened—Warner Books becomes simply Warner.]

King, Stephen. Pet Semetary. New York: New American, 1983.

      [Cite city of publication and date of publication.]

TWO OR MORE BOOKS BY THE SAME AUTHOR

Wouk, Herman. War and Remembrance. New York: Pocket, 1971.

---. Winds of War. Boston: Little, 1978.

      [Give author's name in first entry only; in subsequent entries show three hyphens followed by a period to repeat the author's name. Note that publisher's name—Little, Brown and Company—has been shortened to Little.]

A BOOK WITH MORE THAN ONE AUTHOR

Collier, Peter, and David Horowitz. The Kennedys: An American Drama. New York: Summit, 1984.

      [First author is listed last name first; second author is listed first name first.]

Gibaldi, Joseph, and Waiter S. Achtert. MLA Handbook for Writers of Research Papers. 2nd ed. New York: MLA, 1984.

      [Second edition becomes 2nd ed. Modern Language Association of America shortened to MLA.]

Rose, Turner, et al., eds. U.S. News & World Report Stylebook for Writers and Editors. Washington: U.S. News, 1981.

      [If a book has more than three authors or editors, list the first person's name and use "et al."—meaning "and others"—in place of the authors' names. Use "eds." to indicate editors or "trans." to indicate translators.]

AN ANONYMOUS BOOK

Information Please Almanac: Atlas and Yearbook 1983. 37th ed. New York: Information Please, 1982.

      [If a work has no author, begin the entry with the title; ignore the articles "a," "an," and "the" when arranging items alphabetically.]

Urdang Dictionary of Current Medical Terms. New York: Urdang, 1981.

A TRANSLATION OF A BOOK

Ende, Michael. The Neverending Story. Trans. Ralph Manheim. Illus. Roswitha Quadflieg. New York: Doubleday, 1983.

> [After the author and title are listed, the translator is listed following the abbreviation "Trans." Here the name of the illustrator is given after the abbreviation "Illus."]

Kawabata, Yasunari. The Sound of the Mountain. Trans. Edward G. Seidensticker. New York: Berkeley, 1971.

Maude, Aylmer, trans. Anna Karenina. By Leo Tolstoy. Ed. George Gibian. New York: Norton, 1970.

> [List the translator's name first if you are documenting the comments of the translator. The author of the literary work being discussed is preceded by "By." The editor is listed after the author.]

A FOREWORD, AN INTRODUCTION, OR A PREFACE

Gannett, Lewis. Introduction. The Sea Wolf. By Jack London. New York: Bantam, 1972. v-xvii.

> [When you are citing what is written in an introduction, first give the name of the author of that section, followed by the word "Introduction" with the first letter capitalized but without underlining or quotation marks. The author of the work under discussion follows the word "By" after the title. The page numbers of the entire introduction, usually in lower case Roman numerals, are listed at the end of the entry. Note the use of periods throughout.]

Matlaw, Ralph E., trans. Preface. Fathers and Sons. By Ivan Turgenev. New York: Norton, 1966. vii-ix.

> [If the translator included a preface to explain the work, as is often the case, begin the entry with the translator's name if you wish to make reference to those comments.]

Naisbitt, John. Introduction. Megatrends: Ten New Directions Transforming Our Lives. By Naisbitt. New York: Warner, 1982. 1-9.

> [When citing something in an introduction that was written by the author of the work itself, the author's last name only is given after the word "By". Again, the total span of pages covered by the introduction being cited is listed at the end of the entry.]

A WORK IN AN ANTHOLOGY

Espinosa, Luzmaria. "La Cultura Chicana." Sacramento Edition. Ed. Ben L. Hiatt and Bill Howarth. Sacramento: Sacramento Poetry Exchange, 1982. 39.

> [A poem in the anthology is cited by author and title; the page number is listed.]

 Wells, H. G. "The Country of the Blind." Science Fiction: The Future. Ed. Dick Allen. New York: Harcourt, 1971. 66-68.

> [Begin by giving the author's name and then list the title of the work you are citing, placing quotation marks around the title. The name of the editor is placed after the title of the anthology; underline the anthology title. The total number of pages covered by the article is listed at the end of the entry.]

Worth, Helen. "Get Cooking!" The Complete Guide to Writing Nonfiction. Ed. Glen Evans. Cincinnati: Writer's Digest, 1983. 477-85.

> [Helen Worth is the author of the article, and "Get Cooking!" is the title of the article; Glen Evans is the editor of the anthology. The article appears on pages 477-485.]

A BOOK IN A SET OF VOLUMES

Crane, Stephen. "The Bride Comes to Yellow Sky." <u>The Norton Anthology of American Literature</u>. Ed. Ronald Gottesman et al. 2 vols. New York: Norton, 1979. 2: 926-35.

>[When referring to a work in a multi-volume anthology, begin the entry with the author's name and proceed as with any anthology, but insert the total number of volumes in the set after the editor's name. At the end of the entry, place the number of the volume the work is in, followed by a colon and the total page span of the work.]

Synge, J. M. <u>The Playboy of the Western World</u>. <u>J. M. Synge: Collected Works</u>. Ed. Ann Saddlemeyer. 4 vols. London: Oxford UP, 1968. 4: 51-175.

>[If the work being discussed is a play in a collection, it must be underlined and followed by a period if the play was originally published as a book. The title of the volume, the editor, and the number of volumes follow. The publishers name, Oxford University Press, Inc., has been shortened to Oxford UP.]

Wallbank, T. Waiter, and Alastair M. Taylor, eds. <u>Civilization Past and Present</u>. 4th ed. 2 vols. Chicago: Scott, 1961.

>[Place the number of the edition between the title and the volumes; the publisher's name, Scott, Foresman, and Company, has been shortened to Scott.]

Robinson, Charles Alexander, Jr., ed. <u>An Anthology of Greek Drama</u>. Classical Literature in Rinehart Editions 1. New York: Holt, 1964.

>[When you are citing a work in a series, you must include the name of the series. The name of the series will be given on the title page or the page facing the title page. Do not underline the series title or place quotation marks around it.]

ORGANIZATIONAL AUTHOR

The Carnegie Foundation for the Advancement of Teaching. <u>Three Thousand Futures: The Next Twenty Years in Higher Education: Final Report of the Carnegie Council on Policy Studies in Higher Education</u>. San Francisco: Jossey-Bass, 1980.

>[A book may have an organizational or corporate author. In this example, Jossey-Bass is the publisher, but in some cases the organization may be both the author and the publisher.]

A REPUBLISHED BOOK

Auel, Jean M. <u>The Valley of Horses</u>. 1982. New York: Bantam, 1983.

>[When citing a paperback printing of a book that was originally a hardbound, place the date of the first publication before the information about the book cited.]

Michener, James A. <u>Centennial</u>. 1974. Greenwich, CT: Fawcett, 1975.

>[If your reader may not recognize the location of the city of the publishing house, include the ZIP code abbreviation of the state.]

Toomer, Jean. <u>Cane</u>. 1923. New York: Liveright, 1975.

>[The original date of publication is often many years prior to the date of the edition you use.]

PUBLISHER'S IMPRINT

Thackeray, William Makepeace. <u>Vanity Fair: A Novel Without a Hero</u>. New York: Signet-New American, 1962.

>[A publisher's imprint is the special name used to identify a certain series or division of

the publishing company. Place the publisher's imprint before the name of the publisher—separate the two with a hyphen. In this example the imprint, "A Signet Classic," is shortened to "Signet"; the publishing company name, "The New American Library," is shortened to "New American." Although this old novel (first published in 1837) is republished, no original publication date is needed.]

A PLAY OR POEM

Baldwin, James. <u>Blues for Mister Charlie</u>. New York: Deli, 1964.

    [A play presented in a book is treated just as any other book.]

Field, Edward. "She." <u>Variety Photoplays</u>. New York: Grove, 1967. 15-16.

    [Title of poem is placed in quotation marks. Pages covered by poem cited are given.]

Jones, LeRoi. "The Death of Malcolm X." <u>New Plays From the Black Theatre</u>. Ed. Ed Bullins. New York: Bantam, 1969. 1-20.

    [This play title is placed in quotation marks because it was not published first as an individual book. Page numbers of entire play are listed at end.]

A REFERENCE BOOK

Bettelheim, Bruno. "Autism." <u>Encyclopedia Americana</u>. 1983 ed.

    [Encyclopedia entries need no page numbers since such books are alphabetically arranged. If the entry lists an author, list the author's name first; otherwise, alphabetize according to article title.]

Fink, Donald G., and Donald Christiansen, eds. <u>Electronic Engineer's Handbook</u>. 2nd ed. New York: McGraw, 1982.

    [Reference book with full publishing information, including the editors.]

<u>Moody's Analytical Overview of 25 Leading U.S. Cities</u>. New York: Moody's Investor Service, 1977.

    [In the case of reference works not commonly used by students and instructors, cite the full publication information.]

Neuman, Gerhard. "Ocean Currents." <u>Encyclopaedia Britannica</u>: Macropaedia. 1981 ed.

    [Specify "Macropaedia" or "Micropaedia." For articles in Macropaedia the author's initials are given consult the "Propaedia: Outline of Knowledge" for the author's full name.]

"Draconian." <u>American Heritage Dictionary</u>. 1982 ed.

    [List dictionary entries by subject heading. No page or publisher is needed.]

A PAMPHLET

<u>Air Pollution Primer</u>. New York: National Tuberculosis and Respiratory Disease Association, 1969.

    [A pamphlet entry is written as a book entry.]

Mulligan, William. <u>Dyslexia: Specific Learning Disability and Deliquency</u>. N.p.: California Association for Neurologically Handicapped Children. N.d.

    [The sponsoring agency is considered to be the publisher. Use "N.p." if no place of publication is given; use "N.d." if no date of publication is given.]

AN UNPUBLISHED DISSERTATION, THESIS, OR PROJECT REPORT

Bettcher, Margaret A. "Teaching Reading in the Innercity: A Focus on Teacher Training." Thesis. California State U., Sacramento, 1971.

> [The title of an unpublished thesis or dissertation is not underlined; the title of a published one would be underlined.]

Pinney, Theodore Charles. "The Biology of the Farallon Rabbit." Diss. Stanford U, 1965.

> [University is abbreviated as "U" to shorten length of entry.]

GOVERNMENT REPORTS

Asimov, Isaac, and Theodosius Dobzhansky. <u>The Genetic Effects of Radiation</u>. Understanding the Atom Series 1. Oak Ridge, TN: USAEC Division of Technical Information Extension, 1967.

> [Example of government publication not published by Government Printing Office in Washington. Note that the authors' names are given and that United States Atomic Energy Commission has been abbreviated "USAEC." Note also that the pamphlet is from a series.]

Berns, Waiter. "Affirmative Action vs. The Declaration of Independence." <u>New Perspectives: U.S. Commission on Civil Rights</u>. Washington: GPO, Summer 1984: 21+.

> [Use common sense when you are not sure how to list a government publication. In this case, an article is cited in a quarterly periodical published by the U.S. Commission on Civil Rights but printed by the Government Printing Office.]

Greenwalt, Kent. <u>Legal Protections of Privacy: Final Report to the Office of Telecommunications Policy, Executive Office of the President</u>. Washington: GPO, 1975.

> [With author]

United States. Commission on Civil Rights. <u>The Federal Civil Rights Enforcement Budget: Fiscal Year 1983</u>. Washington: GPO, 1982.

> [If no author is given, consider the sponsoring agency to be the author. Note the period after United States. Most U.S. Government publications are published by the Government Printing Office (GPO) in Washington, D.C.]

PART TWO: MAGAZINE AND NEWSPAPER ENTRIES

AN ARTICLE FROM A MAGAZINE

Franklin, D. "Embryo Transfer: It's a Boy." <u>Science News</u> 11 Feb. 1984: 85.

> [No colon or period is placed between magazine name and date of publication.]

Moritz, Michael. "A Hard-Core Technoid." <u>Time</u> 16 Apr. 1984: 62-63.

> [Weekly or biweekly magazines require complete date with day of month first. Do not include volume and issue numbers. Abbreviate the name of the month if it is in excess of four letters.]

Nolen, William A., M.D. "New Ways to Treat Arthritis." <u>McCalls</u> June 1982: 31+.

> [If the magazine appears once a month or every two months, give month and year; omit volume and issue. The + shows that the article continues on various other pages.l

"Vatican Warning: Cardinal Joseph Ratzinger's Report." <u>Time</u> 26 Mar. 1984: 70.

> [If the author's name is not given on an article, alphabetically arrange the article by title.]

AN ARTICLE FROM A JOURNAL

Axelrod, Pearl, and Natalie Trager. "Directing a Day Care Center." <u>Innovator: the University of Michigan School of Education</u>. 4.10 (1973): 10-13.

> [When the article cited appears in a journal that begins with page one each issue, list the title followed by a period and the issue number (volume 4, issue ten above). The year appears in parentheses.]

Bodmer, George R. "The Apple Ate My Paper." <u>College English</u> 46 (1984): 610-11.

> [If the article cited appears in a journal that uses continuous pagination throughout the year, (that is, each issue begins with the next number after the last page of the previous issue) give the volume number and follow it with the year of publication in parentheses. End the citation with a colon and the pages covered by the article.]

AN ARTICLE OR EDITORIAL FROM A NEWSPAPER

Campbell, Don G. "Autistic Child's Quick Recovery." <u>Los Angeles Times</u> n.d.: n. pag.

> [When the newspaper article being cited has been found in the vertical file, it will occasionally have no date of publication or page number listed. The abbreviation "n.d." for no date and "n.pag." for no pagination explains to your reader that the information is missing.]

Kirp, David. "A Civics Lesson in the Suburbs." Editorial. <u>Sacramento Bee</u> 3 Dec. 1984: B10.

> [If you cite an editorial in a newspaper, include the word "Editorial" after the title of the editorial. If no author's name is included, arrange it alphabetically according to the title.]

Mercer, Kathy. Letter. <u>Sacramento Bee</u> 3 Dec. 1984: B11.

> [A letter to the editor is identified by the word "Letter" immediately after the writer's name. Do not underline the word or place quotation marks around it.]

Sheehan, Thomas. "The Vatican Errs on Liberation Theology." <u>New York Times</u> 15 Sept. 1984, sec. 5: 23.

> [Note that the name of the newspaper is <u>New York Times</u> not The New York Times. If the newspaper is paginated continuously as is the Saturday edition of the paper above, list the section before the colon.]

"Vatican Reported to Have Sought Rebukes for Two Other Latin Clerics." <u>New York Times</u> 11 Sept. 1984: A14.

> [In the instance where the author is not listed, alphabetically arrange the article according to the article title.]

A REVIEW OF A BOOK, PLAY, OR OTHER WORK OF ART

Dewey, Phelps. "This World." Rev. of <u>The Old Ones of New Mexico</u>, by Robert Coles. <u>San Francisco Chronicle</u> 17 February 1974: 9.

> [When citing a review in a newspaper, after you give the reviewer's name and review title, identify the book being reviewed and its author or authors.]

Hedgpeth, Joel W. "Shifting Sands." Rev. of <u>Living with the South Carolina Shore</u>, by William J. Neal, et al. <u>Oceans</u> Nov. 1984: 59-60.

> [When citing a review in a magazine, arrange the information the same as for a newspaper.]

PART THREE: MISCELLANEOUS

AN INTERVIEW

Steck, Harold. "Waterfront Interview: Master of a Lost Art." <u>Waterfront: California's Boating News Magazine</u> Dec. 1984: 70-71.

> [When citing an interview in a magazine or newspaper, list the name of the person interviewed first. After the name of the person interviewed, give the title of the interview, if it is given, and the publication in which it appears.]

Steen, Lynn. Interview. <u>New York Times</u> 5 Dec. 1984: B17.

> [If an interview has no title listed, identify it by using the word "Interview" in place of the title. Do not underline the word or place quotation marks around it.]

Taylor, Horace. Personal Interview. 6 May 1984.

> [A personally conducted interview only shows the name of the person interviewed, the type of interview (i.e., private or telephone interview) and the date of the interview.]

A LECTURE OR SPEECH

Blanton, Marian. Lecture. San Francisco City College. 17 May 1984.

> [A class lecture can be cited by giving the lecturer's name, the title of the lecture (if one was given), the location of the lecture and the date. When no title is given, identify the citation with the word "Lecture" or "Speech" as appropriate.]

Smith, William E. "Integrating Writing Curriculum with Computers." Weber State College Conference. 11 May 1984.

> [When the title of a speech or lecture is given, list it immediately after the speaker's name.]

COMPUTER SOFTWARE

Castro, Paul K. <u>Music Mania Version 2.0</u> Computer Software. Castro Software, 1984.

> [When citing a computer program, give the author first, if known, followed by the title. Identify the entry with the words "Computer Software" after the title; these words are not underlined or placed in quotation marks.]

<u>Dosplus IV</u>. Computer Software. Micro Systems Software, 1984.

> [If author is not known, begin the entry with the title of the program.]

COMPUTER, INFORMATION, OR MICROFICHE SERVICE

Laster, Ann A. <u>Setting Up and Implementing a Technical Writing Course in the Two-Year College: A Method</u>. ERIC, 1974: ED 099 876.

> [When citing an information service, give the identifying number at the end.]

Katz, Abram. "Greenhouse Effect Real, but a Long Way Off." <u>New Haven Register</u> 1 Jan. 1984. NewsBank ENV 2: B11.

> [Entry for a newspaper article found in a microfiche news service. Be sure to list the section and microfiche numbers, in this case "ENV 2: B11."]

Cosner, Thurston L., et al. "Theories and Instruments for Student Assessment." <u>Community College Review</u> 7.4 (1980): 1-12. ERIC EJ 230 715.

> [Entry for a summary of an article previously published in an educational journal. The summary was obtained from an information service, ERIC (Education Resources Information Center), during a computer database search. Note that the number needed to identify the ERIC document is given: "EJ 230 715."]

Wagner, Mary Leu. "The Adult Minority Women in the Community College." Paper presented at the Annual Conference of the Eastern Community College Social Science Assn. Baltimore, 10-12 Apr. 1980. ERIC ED 190 195.

> [In this case the information service is the publisher of a paper not previously published.]

ONLINE SOURCES

Drew, J. R. "So That's Why They Call It the Big Apple." Qyabta [Online]. Available FTP: export.acs.cmu.edu Directory: pub/quanta Files: quanta-oct.ps.Z (Oct. 1989).

Holmes, Kathy. "Adult Responsibility." Bibliographic Instruction Discussion Group [Online]. BIL@BINGVMB.CC.-BUFFALO.EDU (23 Nov. 1994).

Burka, Lauren P. "A Hypertext History of Multi-User Dimensions." MUD History [Online]. http ://www.ccs.neu.edu/home/lpb/mud-history.html (no date).

> [The basic rule is to give the author's last name, followed by a comma and the first name. After that, give the title of the work, in quotation marks, and the title of the complete work, underlined (italicized if you are using a computer), if there is a title. Thus far, documenting online sources is the same as documenting traditional print sources. From this point on, however, everything is dramatically changed as you can tell from the entries above. Every colon, slash, period, hyphen and space must be exact. When you are documenting electronic sources, you must provide your reader with enough information to call up the source and read the original document you have quoted.]

RADIO AND TELEVISION PROGRAMS

"Lena Horne: The Lady and Her Music." Great Performances. PBS. KQED, San Francisco. 9 Dec. 1984.

> [Radio and television entries begin with the program and series titles and include the network, the local station, the city where it was aired, and the date of the broadcast. Other information can be inserted as necessary to help readers identify the program.]

Hemingway, Ernest. The Sun Also Rises. NBC miniseries. KCRA, Sacramento. 9 and 10 Dec. 1984.

> [Here Hemingway is listed first because the work is primarily based on his novel. In the case of a miniseries, give the dates of all parts of the production.]

MOVIES AND VIDEOTAPES

2010. Dir. Peter Hyams. With Roy Schieder. MGM, 1984.

> [In citing a movie, list title, director, primary actor or actors, distribution, and year.]

West Side Story. Videocassette. Dir. Robert Wise. CBS Video, 1961.

> [When citing a videocassette, filmstrip or slide program, list the medium just after the title.]

RECORDINGS

Goodall, Jane. A Lecture by Dr. Jane Goodall: Chimpanzee Behavior and Its Relationship to the Study of Man. Everest 33179, n.d.

> [A cassette recording of a lecture. Include the name of the speaker, the title of the cassette, the name of the recording company, and, if available, the recording date.]

Lennon, John, and Paul McCartney. "Eleanor Rigby." Revolver. Capital SW 2576, n.d. [A song on a record album]

PERFORMANCES

<u>Rigoletto</u>. By Giuseppe Verdi. Dir. Jean-Pierre Ponnelle. With Ingvar Wixell. War Memorial Opera House, San Francisco. 2 Dec. 1984.

> [In citing performances, give information about production, author, director, performer, place, and date.]

PART FOUR: ABBREVIATIONS

ABBREVIATIONS

Use the following abbreviations when necessary in your documentation.

N.p.	No place of publication given—use before a colon.
n.p.	No publisher given—use after a colon.
n.d.	No date of publication given
[1973]	Approximate date of publication
N. pag. or n. pag.	No page numbers given—or page numbers missing
(sic) or [sic]	Quotation is accurate; error is in original publication.
trans.	Translator(s)
ed.	Editor(s)
rpt.	Reprinted by, reprint
illus.	Illustrated by, illustrator
e.g.	For example
i.e.	That is
c. or ca.	About (approximately)
+	And other pages
qtd. in	Quoted in (for indirect quotation)
Apr.	April (Do not abbreviate May, June, or July.)
NE	Nebraska (Use ZIP code abbreviations for states.)

APPENDIX B: A *Guide To Stylistic Revision*

APPENDIX B: *A Guide to Stylist Revision*

INTRODUCTION

Good writing is clear, terse, and forceful. No reader should misunderstand what you are saying. Furthermore, your sentences should not drone on and on in a haphazard succession of excessively worded and loosely connected thoughts. And, finally, your style should engage the reader because your sentences are interesting and lively. Think about what you want to say; then write and rewrite relentlessly until you have stated your ideas plainly but gracefully.

The connection between sound thinking and good writing cannot be overstressed. Responsible writers must heed George Orwell's warning in Politics and the English Language:

> It is clear that the decline of language must ultimately have political and economic causes. . . . But an effect can become a cause, reinforcing the original cause and producing the same effect in an intensified form, and so on indefinitely. A man may take a drink because he feels himself a failure, and then fail all the more completely because he drinks. It is rather the same thing that is happening to the English language. It becomes ugly and inaccurate because our thoughts are foolish, but the slovenliness of our language makes it easier to have foolish thoughts.

The style guide that follows offers some suggestions to help you avoid the stylistic abuses that pervade much of what you read today. By studying "A Guide to Stylistic Revision," you can improve your style and your grades.

Avoid Trite Introductory Phrases

Purge your writing of trite introductory phrases, such as "Since the beginning of time," "Since the days of the cavemen," "Throughout time," "Throughout history," and "In generations past." Typically these introductory phrases are overused and too general. They are rarely used as they should be: to introduce a passage summarizing authentic historical information. Instead, they are used to falsely create the impression that the writer knows what happened millions of years ago. For example, a writer might assert that, "Since the days of the cavemen there has been a generation gap between the young and the old." This statement is far too general. Has there been a generation gap in all societies? Is the writer implying that the supposed generation gap caused conflict between ancient tribal elders and the young? The writer has not really thought through the matter and does not know exactly what happened and, therefore, should have avoided such careless generalizing. One technique of revising trite introductory phrases is to substitute verified concrete examples. For example, the statement "Since the beginning of time man has suffered degenerative diseases" might be changed to "The Stone Age dwellers of Great Britain, the Romans, the early American colonists, and modern-day Americans have all suffered from the same degenerative diseases." Using the specific examples makes the introduction more authoritative and more apt to engage the reader's interest because the examples create images in the reader's mind.

Eliminate Platitudes

Also omit or rewrite sentences containing platitudes. Platitudes are trite, space-wasting statements of what every reader already knows. For example, a writer might state, "Millions of Americans drive automobiles," or "Television sets may be found in almost every American home," or "Advertisements are communicated through a variety of media: radio, television, magazines, and newspapers." What reader needs to be told any of this? These platitudes become even more offensive when combined with trite introductory expressions.

Example

TRITE INTRODUCTORY PHRASE	PLATITUDE
Since the beginning of time,	people have found it necessary to eat.

Be especially cautious when writing the opening statement of your paper. Try to begin with a meaningful, thought-provoking generalization, one that will intrigue the reader. The platitude "Millions of Americans drive automobiles," for example, might be changed to "The Environmental Protection Agency wants millions of Americans to stop driving their automobiles." Almost every reader should be affected by that statement. If you are not sure whether or not a statement is platitudinous, ask for advice.

Support Your Generalizations with Specifics

1. Explain your ideas.
   Rising college costs are causing problems. This year a fresh group of parents and students must grapple with grim economic realities as admission notices arrive. Savings accounts are smaller, more inflation is almost certain, and competition for loans and scholarships is increasing.
2. Use examples.
   Johnson notes, for instance, that one of every three students filing for admission now asks for financial aid, compared with one of every four last year. For example, fewer students major in liberal arts programs to "learn how to work with people." But more students enroll in accounting programs.
3. Use facts and figures.
   The report estimates tuition and fees will cost $1,388, room and board on campus $3,054, books and supplies $350, and miscellaneous personal expenses (not counting transportation) $1,455, a total cost of $6,247.
4. Use quotations.
   Warren stated, "A family must save almost two thousand dollars a year for nine years for each child planning to attend four years of college."
5. Use anecdotes.
   When I attended the University of Michigan, costs were much lower. Tuition, for example, was only $125 per semester. Yet we were always short of money and welcomed the summer vacations when we could replenish our depleted bank accounts.

Reword Clichés

Avoid the use of clichés. In French, cliché means stereotype; in English, cliché means a prefabricated phrase, one that is commonly known and commonly used. Admittedly, some clichés are colorful; the problem with the use of these prefabricated phrases is that they show lack of imagination. Clichés are phrases that are so common that when you are given the first part, you can usually fill in the last part yourself.

Examples

common as dirt	the spirit is willing, but the flesh is weak
warm as toast	the blind leading the blind
old as the hills	a parting of the ways
sell like hotcakes	diamond in the rough
sleep like a log	the full flush of victory
bolt from the blue	the patter of rain drops
politics makes strange bedfellows	a fly in the ointment
left high and dry	part and parcel
variety is the spice of life	the old song and dance
point the finger of suspicion	live to a ripe old age
sly as a fox	to grow by leaps and bounds
slippery as an eel	to withstand the test of time

stubborn as an ox
goose is cooked
covers a multitude of sins

to let bygones be bygones
to be unable to see the woods for the trees
eat crow
to upset the apple cart

Other phrases, such as *"in today's society"* and *"in today's world"* are less colorful but just as trite. Although these phrases should ordinarily be avoided, occasionally they may be used with some effectiveness, but when they are used, they should be put in quotation marks to indicate to the reader that the writer knows full well that they are clichés, for instance, *"When in Rome, do as the Romans do."*

Euphemisms

Euphemisms are expressions employed to make unattractive ideas more pleasing or disturbing thoughts less troublesome. There are some topics about which people are reluctant to talk candidly. Therefore, they believe that if they can clothe them in words or phrases that are less disturbing the unpleasantness will be avoided. For example, people are reluctant to discuss death, toilets, disease, old age, sex, and menial jobs. People do not die; they *"pass away," "pass on, "enter into rest," "go to Heaven," "become deceased," "kick the bucket," "cash in their chips," "give up the ghost,"* or *"go to the happy hunting ground."* Hopelessly injured animals are not killed; they are *"put to sleep."* Secretaries are given the title *"Administrative Assistant"* but still given secretary's pay. Many less obvious euphemisms are used regularly by educated Americans: *"residential restrictions"* instead of *"no minorities allowed," "disadvantaged"* or *"under-privileged"* rather than *"poor," "credibility gap"* instead of *"lie," "underachievers"* rather than *"lazy."* Euphemisms are inescapable, but have the courage to screen them from your writing as much as possible. Most euphemisms are motivated by kindness, but many are condescending, and some are ruthlessly intended to delude and mislead—the tools of dictators and propagandists. Euphemisms reduce clarity and should be banished from your writing because they mask truth and reality.

Jargon

Omit any jargon in your college papers. Jargon, or "shoptalk" language, is the unique vocabulary or language used by a particular trade or profession, for example, police, military, education, business, law, or government. Instead of writing about burning houses and buildings, firefighters write about "structure fires." Instead of using forceful action verbs, military writers add "-tion" to make long, dull nouns: *"pacify"* becomes *"pacification,"* and *"demobilize"* become *"demobilization," "defoliate"* becomes *"defoliation."* Government writers *"finalize"* and *"definitize."* Business and management people seem fond of adding *"-wise"* to nouns to make adjectives, such as *"newswise," "moneywise,"* and *"taxwise."* Educators refer to counselors and advisors as *"student personnel counselors,"* to tutors as *"peer mediators"* or *"peer facilitators"* and to teaching as *"facilitation of learning."* Participants in the Watergate hearings in 1974 used considerable jargon: the words *"operative, " "inoperative," "transmission," "confidentiality," "parameter," "a highly sensitive matter," "deniability,"* and *"expedientiability"* were frequently employed. Business and legal writers often use words and phrases such as *"heretofore"* and *"herewithin enclosed."* Avoid jargon, especially if you are writing a technical paper for the nontechnical reader. Jargon reduces the clarity and conciseness of your writing and may confuse a reader not familiar with your terminology.

Gobbledygook

Gobbledygook is pretentious writing, the wordy and unnatural style that results when student writers try, unsuccessfully, to impress instructors with a more "intellectual" vocabulary and prose style. Remove or revise any pretentious writing in your papers. Do not make the mistake of thinking that your best written English is not good enough for your instructors and that you must use longer words, wordy phrasing, and long, involved sentence constructions to impress them. Use your own language— your natural written style. Specifically, you should avoid two types of gobbledygook.

The first type of gobbledygook to be' avoided is excessively wordy phrasing: the use of several words and long phrases when all that is needed is a short phrase or a single word. The simplest way to eliminate this type of wordiness is to reduce wordy phrases to their smallest one- or two-word equivalents.

announced himself to be in favor of	— said he favored
met with the approval of Jones	— Jones's approval
at the theoretical level	— theoretically
a long period of time	— a long time
at that point in time	— at that time OR then
resembling in nature	— like
finally, to conclude	— finally
exhibits a tendency	— tends
in many instances	— often
paid a compliment	— complimented
reach a decision	— decide
make an attempt	— try OR attempt
local level	— locally
utilize	— use

The second type of gobbledygook, or pretentious writing, occurs when the writer unsuccessfully attempts to be more impressive by using a more complex vocabulary. What happens, however, is that the larger words are often used improperly or in such a way that they cloud rather than clarify meaning. When pompous vocabulary is combined with excessive wording, the results may be very embarrassing for the writer, ludicrous in fact.

Read the following excerpt taken from a student's paper that argues for a particular interpretation of a poem by Leonard Cohen:

> . . . In an explication of this poem the archetypal is used to illustrate the foremost degree of definition and understanding.
>
> To solidify the lucidity of the poem, it is a necessity to briefly recapitulate the account. In the beginning, the man asks the subject, whom he has met on the train, to meet with him later in an apparent endeavor to begin a liaison. In response, the subject accepts the invitational proposal. The affair results in being parasitic; meanwhile, the man seems to be wandering in search of mortal happiness. At the end of the poem, the man believes that the subject is preventing his independency of the search; therefore, he decides to leave the subject and catch a train. He apologizes for his departure in dubious concern.
>
> By using the archetypal approach, the reader can detect a sense that man is a preginator in the first stanza . . .

The student's instructor was flabbergasted when she read this paper. In class discussion the student had always been straightforward and to the point. In a conference, the student revealed that because he was afraid his own vocabulary and sentences would not impress the instructor, he tried to imitate the way professional literary critics wrote. Obviously, the attempt was a disaster, and although this excerpt is an extreme example of how garbled writing can become when writers do not use their own vocabulary and writing style, it does serve as a warning. State what you are saying concisely and simply. Have no qualms about removing pseudo-intellectual language from your paper.

Slang and Obscenity

Slang (including obscenity) is not appropriate in your writing. Do not become overzealous in your attempts to combat euphemisms. For example, do not write an obscenity instead of *"sexual intercourse."* The obscenity may not be euphemistic, and while it has rhetorical impact, the word disturbs or angers too many readers for you to risk using it (just as the word has carefully been avoided here).

Other obscenities used for emphasis usually fail to achieve their intended effect, also. "Americans must take action immediately" will sound better to most readers than *"Americans must do something damned quick."* *"Social Security laws are in a hell of a mess"* might be an appropriate sentence in a conversation, but in a written argument the sentence would be better worded *"Social Security laws desperately need revision."*

Slang, for all its energy and colorfulness, is just not appropriate for your writing. *"This dude makes it to the meeting"* should be changed to *"The delegate attended the meeting."* *"Chick"* should be changed to *"woman"* and *"busted"* to *"arrested."*

Use the Correct Word or Phrase

Students commonly misuse certain words and phrases. For example, *affect* and *effect* are frequently used improperly. *Affect* should never be used as a noun; it should be used as a verb:

> He wondered how the new plan would *affect* the others.
> The north wind *affected* his sinuses.

Effect, on the other hand, can be used as a noun:

> He wondered what *effect* the new plan would have on the others.

But *effect* can be a verb, too:

> She wanted to *effect* changes in the organization.

Another misused expression is "the reason is because."

> *The reason* most students have difficulty finishing freshman composition *is because* they do not do enough homework.

The sentence reads much better after "The reason . . . is because" has been dropped:

> Most students have difficulty finishing freshman composition *because* they do not do enough homework.

Your instructor will point out inappropriate wording in your writing and explain how to correct the errors.

Repetition

Repeating words and phrases can be an effective and sometimes dramatic way of achieving emphasis and clear transition.

Example

> Now what does "let students move at their own pace" mean? Too often it means letting them come to class only when they want to. Too often it means let them do no homework. Let them take two semesters to finish a course that they should finish in one. But "let students move at their own pace" should mean let them know they must produce. Let them know they must attend class regularly and do homework every night. Let them work hard and be proud of what they write. Let them accept and master the challenge of meeting self-imposed deadlines. Let all of those who are able finish their work early, but let a deserving few continue their work another semester. Let students realize from the very beginning that a self-paced course is rigorous, but let them understand too that it is rewarding, and make them want to work.

Repeated words are sometimes ineffective and bothersome to the reader. While proofreading, you may discover that you have overused a transitional word or phrase, perhaps *of course, however, or moreover.* Or you may have created a monotonous tone by using one too many times in an attempt to keep your writing in the third person. All writers have words and phrases that they overuse. Watch for this kind of repetition in your writing. Reword or rephrase whenever necessary. using a dictionary or thesaurus to find synonyms.

Impersonal Use of "One"

In converting first or second person writing to third person, resist the temptation to use the impersonal **one**. When "one" is overused, the writing becomes boring and wordy.

Impersonal—
> *One* never knows where forest fires will occur. Many times *one* finds the hottest spots are in difficult places, deep in a box canyon or similar area—difficult to fly into and even more difficult to fly out of—places where maneuverability and good rate of climb absolutely must be there when *one* pulls up after *one's* fire retardant drop. *One* can do just that with the S-2 aerial tanker.

Revised—
> Forest fires never seem to break out where they can be reached easily. Many times the hottest spots are deep in box canyons or similar areas—tough to fly into and even tougher to fly out of—places where maneuverability and good rate of climb absolutely must be there when the pilot pulls up after a fire retardant drop. The S-2 aerial tanker can do just that.

Use Active Verbs

When the subject of a sentence performs an action, as in the sentence "Bertie mashed the garlic," the verb is **active**. The writer is using the "active voice." When the subject of a sentence receives an action, as in the sentence "The garlic was mashed by Bertie," the verb is **passive**. Whenever possible, use active verbs to give sentences force and clarity. Avoid passive verbs when they make writing wordy, unclear, impersonal, evasive or dull.

Example

PASSIVE   *It has been decided* that you are not ready for graduate school at this time.

ACTIVE   The Dean of Admissions has *decided* that you are not ready for graduate school at this time.

In some situations passive verbs are more desirable than active verbs, as when the subject is perfectly obvious or when the subject is not known.

Example

PASSIVE   The huge old jade plant *was stolen* from the front porch during the night. Only a forlorn pile of broken leaves *was left* scattered in the street. It was as if a member of the family *had been abducted, forced into a car,* and *spirited* away to some unknown fate.

ACTIVE   Someone *stole* the old jade plant from the front porch during the night. Only a forlorn pile of broken leaves *lay* scattered in the street. It *seemed* that someone *had abducted* a member of the family and *spirited* him away to some unknown fate.

Using the active voice in the second version caused problems. Since the abductor is not known, the word *Someone* has been inserted, taking away emphasis from where it should be, on the jade plant, as in the first version. Furthermore, the next sentence is not as accurate in the second version as in the first, since, strictly speaking, leaves do not "lay" anywhere. And then in the last sentence, the intrusive someone has been employed again, and because there is no alternative, the awkward sounding "him" has been used. A "family member" could not be referred to as *it*, but a jade plant is customarily an *it*, not a *him* or a *her*.

Editing for "It Is" and "There Is"

To liven up your sentences, cut the *"it is's"* and *"there is's"* and their cousins, such as *"it was's,"* *"it will be's,"* *"there was's,"* *"there were's,"* and *"there seemed to be's."* Writers overuse these phrases, mistakenly believing that these adverb-linking verb constructions make their sentences flow more gracefully. But actually all these weak expressions do is slow down sentences, drearily stretching them with unnecessary words. Unless your objective is to put your reader to sleep, edit most of them from your writing.

Wordy—

[It is] unfortunate that people do not have the gift of looking into the future.

Edited—

Unfortunately, people do not have the gift of looking into the future.

Wordy—

To assure society a satisfactory future, [it is] imperative that a program of zero population growth be implemented immediately.

Edited—

In order to assure society a satisfactory future, a program of zero population growth must be implemented immediately.

Wordy—

At present the world population is approaching 4½ billion, and [it is] doubling every thirty to thirty-five years.

Edited—

At present the world population is approaching 4½ billion and doubling every thirty to thirty-five years.

Wordy—

[There are] numerous problems [that are] caused by overpopulation.

Edited—

Numerous problems are caused by overpopulation.

Cut Unnecessary Words

Do not rely on needless verbage to meet the required word limit for an assignment. Edit each paragraph for general wordiness. Ordinarily you can revise a wordy paragraph to say the same thing better, in half the words.

Wordy—

High school, college, and university students have the knowledge now more than they ever did in the past that a degree from an institution of higher learning can be the key leading down the trail to jobs that are better and lives that are richer. But the prospects of a degree, especially for members of the lower middle class and the working class of society, have a tendency to descend with costs which are rising. Already a son or daughter who wants a college education for four years can expect to pay four years of payments which can total up to a total of fifteen thousand dollars or possibly even more. (112 words)

Revised—

Students know a college degree can lead to better jobs and richer lives. But the prospects, especially for the lower, middle, and working classes, descend with rising costs. Already four years of college can cost fifteen thousand dollars or more. (40 words)

Study the following breakdown:

—High school, college, and university students (6 words)	—students (1 word)
—know more than they ever did in the past now that (11 words)	—know (1 word)
—a degree from an institution of higher learning (8 words)	—a college degree (3 words)
—can be the key leading down the trail (8 words)	—can lead (2 words)
—to jobs that are better and lives that are richer (10 words)	—to better jobs and richer lives (6 words)

Awkward Sentences

Sentences can be awkward for many reasons. Much of the advice in Chapter Two and in "The Guide to Stylistic Revision" is given to help you avoid awkward writing. For example, vague pronoun reference, tense shifts, passive verbs, faulty parallelism, and misplaced modifiers all cause "awkward" sentences. When these problems and other kinds specifically covered in *Survival* show up in your writing, your instructor will mark them so you can refer to the appropriate sections for suitable remedies. Suppose, for example, an instructor reads the following sentence:

In the early days of our grandparents: the supposition could be made that crime and corruption were not unknown since by way of tradition they have handed down their feelings.

The author would be directed to study the section on *Gobbledygook*. Sometimes, however, a sentence will be marked *Awkward* because this general label offers an easy way for the instructor to point out a bad sentence—one that does not read well, or one that does not "sound good." Awkward sentences should be rewritten. Reading the sentence aloud may make you "hear" the problem. If after reading a sentence marked *Awkward* you cannot see how to revise it, request assistance. Here are some awkward sentences and suggested revisions:

Awkward—

The meaning of "The Bear" by William Faulkner deals with the close alliance with nature when people learn the ritual of the hunt.

Revised—

"The Bear" by William Faulkner deals with people's close alliance with nature when they learn the ritual of the hunt.

Awkward—

The reason for legalizing off-track betting is on the grounds of lost tax money.

Revised—

Off-track betting should be legalized to prevent the loss of tax money.

Awkward—

This statement was about the only one which all of the Indians who fought in the Battle of Little Bighorn agreed.

Revised—

This statement was one of the few about which all of the Indians who fought in the Battle of Little Bighorn agreed.

Awkward—

Attempting the insulation of television viewers by taking for granted they are complete idiots is poor taste.

Revised—

Attempting to insulate television viewers by assuming they are complete idiots is in poor taste.

Awkward—

All along for their struggle to reach equality with the male officer, the women have run into much opposition.

Revised—

All during their struggle for equality with male officers, women have run into much opposition.

Parallel Construction

Parallel construction—or parallelism—is stylistic symmetry achieved by repeating grammatical constructions. The basic tactic in achieving parallelism is to use the same kinds of words, phrases, or clauses in pairs or series—for example, a noun paired with a noun, or three adjectives teamed in a row.

Example

1. Three Adjectives—Predicate Adjectives

   His tie is || red,
   || white, and
   || blue.

2. Three Verbs—Compound Predicate

   The cornered mountain lion || snarled,
   || snapped, and
   || lunged.

A breakdown in parallelism occurs when an item in a pair or series is not the kind of construction the reader expects. Sentences lacking parallelism lack balance and rhythm—they do not flow well, and they should be revised.

Example

For breakfast John has two scrambled eggs, a mound of fried potatoes full of bacon bits, three pieces of buttered toast, and drank coffee until he finished the whole pot. (not parallel)

In the above example, the reader is thrown off balance upon encountering "and drank coffee until he finished the whole pot." That part of the predicate should be revised to read, "and a potful of coffee." Here are some general suggestions about parallel construction:

Correlative Pairs

Be on the lookout for these **correlative conjunctions**—they work in pairs.

either — or
neither — nor
both — and
not — but
not only — but also
first — second . . .

Place each conjunction in the pair next to the sentence part being correlated.

Example

Not Parallel	*Parallel*
Either automation is one of the major enemies of the American worker *or* the means to provide future employment and prosperity.	Automation is *either* one of the major enemies of the American worker *or* the means to provide future employment and prosperity.

Team Modifiers

When separated modifiers are teamed, fewer words are needed and parallelism is improved. Use similar grammatical constructions, such as two adjectives, and place them together either before or after the word or word group being modified.

Example

Not Parallel	*Parallel*
The *gusty* north wind, *which was cold*, blew steadily for three days.	The *cold, gusty*, north wind blew for three days.

Phrases in a Series

Try to use similar grammatical constructions in a series of phrases—a succession of coordinate phrases.

Example

Not Parallel	*Parallel*
For many, college is a time filled *with constant mental strain, with feeling physically fatigued, and by periodic depression.*	For many, college is a time filled *with constant mental strain, physical fatigue,* and *periodic depression.*

Note that the preposition *with* in the example above has not been repeated in the parallel version.

with ‖ constant mental strain,
‖ physical fatigue, and
‖ periodic depression.

Unless special emphasis is desired, the introductory word—an adjective, a preposition, or a pronoun—need not be repeated in each phrase in a series of short phrases. But when one or more of the phrases in the series contains five or more words, repeat the first word at the beginning of each phrase.

Examples

to investigate, prosecute, and publicize (single words and short phrases)
to investigate, *to* prosecute, and *to* publicize (special emphasis)
to the store near his aunt's house and *to* the Mercury Cleaners on Broadway (more than five words)

Dependent Clauses in a Series

When writing a series of dependent clauses, keep them parallel. The first clause in the series ordinarily can be used as a model for the rest.

Example

Not Parallel	*Parallel*
Jimmy believes that the lost continent of Atlantis is below the Bermuda Triangle, and an underwater civilization flourishes there.	Jimmy believes that the lost continent of Atlantis is below the Bermuda Triangle and that an underwater civilization flourishes there.

As can be seen in the example above, the signal word "that" is repeated in the second dependent clause to make the two clauses parallel. Also note that it is the missing signal word that makes the example "not parallel."

In a series of long dependent clauses beginning with the same signal word, repeat the signal word in each dependent clause. (A long dependent clause is one that contains five or more words.)

Example

A state treasury surplus of 4 billion dollars can be expected by the end of next year || *if* the economy continues to improve, *if* proposed income tax reform laws are implemented, and *if* the state budget for next year can be cut eight percent.

If the dependent clauses are short (fewer than *five* words), there is usually no need to repeat the signal word.

Examples

Although Frank lost his ring
and Jamie became seasick, || everyone else had a good time sailing on San Francisco Bay.

Those students *who* studied daily
and completed every exercise || finished the course before those who tried to take shortcuts.

Position Modifiers Accurately

A modifier is a word, phrase, or clause that describes, limits, qualifies, or distinguishes another word. Modifiers must be positioned accurately to make the meaning of a sentence clear. Avoid the squinting modifier, one that can modify either the sentence part before it or after it.

Squinting modifier—
   She asked the salesman *tactfully* to express his opinion.
Revised—
   She *tactfully* asked the salesman to express his opinion.

Or—
   She asked the salesman to express his opinion *tactfully*.

Also avoid placing modifiers in the wrong parts of the sentences. Misplaced modifiers can be confusing and occasionally embarrassing.

Misplaced modifier—

The president and vice-president of the company were forced to show the memo to the board of directors *that implicated them in the plot.*

Revised—

The president and vice-president of the company were forced to show the memo *that implicated them in the plot* to the board of directors.

Misplaced modifier—

After they finish taking the pretest, the instructor wants to have a conference with the students.

Revised—

The instructor wants to have a conference with the students *after they finish taking the pretest.*

Be especially careful not to write *dangling introductory phrases and clauses* that do not modify the subjects of the main clauses immediately following them. The subject of a main clause must be the "doer" of the action in the introductory word, phrase, or clause.

Dangling introductory phrase—

Hopefully, all students will complete the course early.

Revised—

All students *hope* to complete the course work early.

Or—

The instructor *hopes* all students will complete the course work early.

Dangling introductory phrase—

Naive and innocent, the intrigues of politics amazed him.

Revised—

Naive and innocent, he was amazed by the intrigues of politics.

Dangling introductory phrase—

A good buy, many people purchased the tool kit.

Revised—

Because the tool kit was a good buy, many people purchased it.

Dangling introductory clauses—

While riding on the freeway, the truck ran over the bicyclist.
After learning the art of throwing pots, a modest living was made.
Because it was too dull, the grass would not cut evenly.

Revised—

While riding on the freeway, the bicyclist was run over by a truck.
After learning the art of throwing pots, he was able to earn a modest living.
Because the mower was too dull, it would not cut the grass evenly.

Capitalization Rules

Capitalize the following:

1. Persons, races, nationalities, languages
   Examples

George	But not—
William B. Smith, Jr.	blacks
Asian	white
African-American	
Indian	
American	
Italian	
Chinese	

2. Specific places
   Examples

Boston	Detroit River
North Carolina	Lake Tahoe
Mexico	Pacific Ocean
Appalachian Mountains	West (section of the country)

3. Specific organizations
   Examples

   The Sierra Club
   The State Air Resources Board
   The National Aeronautics and Space Administration
   NASA
   The House of Representatives
   Senate

   But not—

   government
   state government
   the state
   the federal government
   the legislation

4. Historical events, documents, and periods
   Examples

   the French Revolution
   World War Two
   Declaration of Independence
   Magna Carta
   the Dark Ages

5. Days, months, holidays
   Examples

Monday	But not seasons—
April	spring
Christmas	summer
Memorial Day	fall
	winter

6. Titles of courses

   Examples

       The West as an Idea in American Literature
       English
       Spanish
       Math 101
       Anthropology 2
   But do not capitalize—
       mathematics
       anthropology
       sociology
       chemistry

7. Titles of books magazines, journals, newspapers, movies, plays, poems, songs, record albums, articles, chapters, speeches, papers, and other publications.

   Capitalize the first word and all other words in the title except—
       articles (a, an, the)
       prepositions (in, on, over . . .)
       conjunctions (and, but, or . . .)

   Examples

Catcher in the Rye (book)	"My Last Duchess" (poem)
Encyclopaedia Britannica (book)	"America the Beautiful" (song)
Time (magazine)	*Nashville Skyline* (record album)
English Journal (journal)	"Automakers Urge Mandatory Belts" (article)
New York Times (newspaper)	"The White Race and Its Heroes" (chapter)
The Godfather (movie)	"Inaugural Address" (speech)
Hamlet (play)	"Nature Symbolism in 'The Bear' " (paper)

8. Official titles

   Examples

       Dr. Robert Lee, Jr.
       Professor Johnson
       Treasurer James E. Burns
       President John F. Kennedy
       Mr. Pong
       Mary B. Jorgenson, Doctor of Pharmacology
       John Marshall, Chief Justice, United States Supreme Court

   But not—

       Mary B. Jorgenson, pharmacist
       James Johnson, a chemistry teacher

9. Religious names, terms, titles

   Examples

God	Hinduisim
Christ	the Bible
Allah	the Koran
Buddha	Jews
Saint John	Muslims
Holy Communion	Hindus
Christianity	

10. In addresses

Examples

> 20178 Park Street
> Ford Motor Company
> English Department
> Claims Department, Pacific Mutual Life Insurance Co.
> Mountain View, California

11. Names of buildings, ships, airplanes, automobiles, brand names

Examples

Empire State Building (building)	But not—
Titanic (ship)	shepherd in German shepherd
Boeing 747 (airplane)	oak
Mercedes (automobile)	roses
Tide (brand name)	

12. Outlines

Examples

> I. Background of Project Mercury
>   A. Impact of Sputnik
>   B. Creation of NASA
>   C. Objectives of the Project

Abbreviations and Symbols

In general, avoid abbreviations in the text of a paper. Spell out the names of months (e.g., "February"), units of time (e.g., "hours," "century"), units of measurement (e.g., "miles per gallon," "centigrade," "kilometers"), geographical names (e.g., "New York," "United States"), and items often abbreviated in conversation and journalism (e.g., "television").

Some terms, however, are almost always abbreviated in a paper (e.g., "Mrs.," "a.m.," "PhD," "BC"). Current style favors omitting periods and spaces in abbreviations consisting entirely of capital letters and in some almost entirely capitalized (e.g., "AD," "USSR," "PhD"). The intitials in names are followed by periods and spaces (e.g., "J. F. Kennedy," "Franklin D. Roosevelt"). Most abbreviations made up of single lowercase letters contain periods but not spaces (e.g., "a.m."), but some have neither periods or spaces (e.g., "rpm").

Although the general rule is to avoid abbreviations, use common sense. In some papers it may be easier for readers to read abbreviations, such as "US" or "FBI," rather than the spelled-out versions many times. What is important is that readers should not have to puzzle over the meaning of an abbreviation. Some writers will spell out the term once and accompany the full name with its common abbreviation placed in parentheses, for example, "National Aeronautics and Space Administration (NASA)" and then use the abbreviation in the rest of the paper or even alternate between the spelled-out and abbreviated forms. In some cases the abbreviation placed in parentheses is not necessary, for example, in a paper referring to the United States many times.

The above guidelines apply only to the text of a paper. Abbreviations should be used according to directions in parenthetical documentation, Notes, and Works Cited. For further information and examples, consult Appendix A and Lesson Five of Chapter Four (page 214).

Symbols may be used (e.g., "$1,200," "47.33%," "-11°F"); you may prefer not to when a paper contains only a few figures (e.g., "1,200 dollars," "47.33 percent," "– degrees Farenheit" or "eleven degrees below zero"). [Also see "Numbers," page 382.] Symbols likely to be unfamiliar to your readers should not be used.

[Sic] or (Sic)

Errors within quotations may be designated by the word *sic* in square brackets or parentheses, i.e., [sic]. Any error found in quoted material will be considered yours unless you designate it. Never correct an error in a quotation, however. Instead use the [*sic*], placing it immediately after the error.

Numbers

Write as words numbers one through nine, but use numerals for 10 and above.

Examples

The witch granted her *three* wishes.
Greta saw *11* grotesque statues lining the driveway.

As an alternative to the above convention, you may spell out numbers that can be said in one or two words when you are writing a non-technical paper containing only a few numbers.

Examples

For more than *twenty* miles the road twisted and turned through the mountains.
The new school will cost at least *seven million* dollars.
More than *two-thirds* of the parts were defective.

No matter which of the above conventions you follow, dates, years, addresses, and times followed by a.m. or p.m., pages, dimensions, and decimal fractions should be stated as numerals.

Examples

His big break came on *July 12, 1973*.
The artifacts were probably used before *11,000 BC*.
Deliver this package to *21533 Hastings Avenue, Apartment 3C*.
At *10:33 a.m.* a sharp earthquake shook the building.
For your research notes use *4-by-6-inch* index cards.
Only *33.5%* of the recruits passed the examination.

Always use symbols or abbreviations when numerals are used.

Examples

The telephone company sent him a bill for *$263*.
Currently, *55%* of the college population is female.
Raise the connecting rod *12 cm*.

With very large numbers—millions, billions, trillions—numerals and words may be mixed.

Examples

Electronics sales may surpass *$400 billion* by 1990.
That image of Saturn was obtained when Pioneer 11 was *2.5 million* kilometers from the planet.

Never begin a sentence with a numeral. Either write the number in words or reorganize the sentence so that the number appears later.

Examples

Fifteen thousand dollars was more than he could afford for tuition.
He could not afford to pay *$15, 000* for tuition.

For the sake of appearance, numerals should be used consistently in a paper.

Examples

Don't write *3%* in one place and then *five percent* in another.

Don't write *$36.25* in one place and then *fifteen dollars* in another.

Don't write *18th* century in one place and then *twentieth century* in another.

Do not change the numbers in a passage you are quoting. Quote the passage exactly as it appears, no matter how you have been stating numbers in the rest of your paper.

APPENDIX C: *Suggested Subjects*

The following list presents 350 subjects used by many students in papers they have written. You should be aware that not every subject will be considered acceptable to your teacher. Furthermore, every instructor will offer other subjects for consideration. Select two or three from the following list and discuss the merits of each before you begin writing. Keep in mind, too, that almost every subject listed is a general subject and will need to be narrowed.

Abortion
Academy Awards
Accidents
Actors/Actresses
Acupuncture
Adoption
Advertising
Affirmative Action
African-Americans
Agent Orange
Agnosticism
Agriculture
Air Pollution
Airline Safety
Alcohol as Fuel
Alcoholism
Alternative Energy
Americans with
    Disabilities Act
Androgony
Animal Experimentation
Animal Rights
Arab-Israeli Conflict
Architecture
Art
Artificial Hearts
Artificial Intelligence
Artists
Asian-Americans
Astrology
Astronomy
Atheism
Athletes
Autism
Auto Emissions Control
Automation
Automobile Safety
Automobiles
Balanced Budget
Baseball

Battered Women
Beauty Contests
Behavior Modification
Best-sellers
Bicycles
Bilingual Education
Biodiversity
Birth Control
Black Humor
Black Nationalism
Books
Bosnia
Bovine Growth Hormone
Boxing
Boycotts
Budget Deficit
Busing
Camping
Cancer
Capital Punishment
Careers
Caregiving
Carpal Tunnel Syndrome
Censorship
Central America
Character Education
Charities
Child Abuse
Child Custody
Child Rearing
Childbirth Methods
Children's Rights
Church and State Separation
Civil Disobedience
Civil Rights
Civil War
Class Action Suits
Clichés
Cloning
Collapse of the USSR

Collective Bargaining
College Education
Comedy
Communes
Computer Crime
Computer Hackers
Computers
Computers in Schools
Congress
Conscientious Objectors
Conservation
Conservatives
Cooking
Corporate Welfare
Cosmetic Surgery
Cost of Living
Crafts
Crib Death (SIDS)
Crime
Cuba
Cults
Cultural Diversity
Cyberspace
D.C. Statehood
Dancing
Dating
Day Care
Designer Genes
Down-Sizing
Drug Testing
Drugs—Legal and Illegal
Eating Disorders
Ecology
Elections
Endangered Species
Environmental Groups
Ethics
Euro-Americans
Families
Family Reunions

Famines
Feminism
Fetal Alcohol Syndrome
Floods
Folk Medicine
Folklore
Food
Food Banks
Fourth Amendment
GATT
Gambling
Garbage
Gays in the Military
Genealogy
Generation X
Genetic Engineering
Global Economy
Global Warming
Graduation Requirements
Gulf War Syndrome
Handicaps
Helmet Laws
Hispanic Americans
Holistic Healing
Hostages
Housing
Human Rights
Hunger
Hunting and Fishing Rights
Illiteracy
Immigration
In-vitro Fertilization
Income Taxes
Indigenous Peoples
Inflation
Information
Institutions
Interest Rates
Internet
Internet Censorship
Internships
Inventions
Jingoism
Junk Foods
Jury Trials
Justice System
Juvenile Delinquency
Ku Klux Klan
Land Use Planning
Latin America

Law Practice
Laws
Learning Disabilities
Liberal Arts Education
Liberals
Lifestyles
Literacy
Lottery
Luxury Taxes
Lyrics
Marriage
Martyrs
Mass Transit
Materialism
Matriarchy
Medical Costs
Medical Practice
Mental Illness
Mental Retardation
Metric System
Mexican-Americans
Military Base Closings
Military Draft
Military Life
Military Spending
Militias
Minimum/Subminimum Wage
Minorities
Mixed Marriages
Money
Moods
Moon
Motorcycles
Movie Rating System
Movies
Music
Music Videos
Musicians
Mythology
NAFTA
NEA Grants
National Debt
National Park System
Native Americans
Natural Disasters
Neighbors
New South
Nobel Prize
Noise Pollution
Northern Ireland

Nuclear Non-Proliferation
   Treaty
Nuclear Power
Nuclear Waste
Nuclear Weapons
Nudism
OSHA
Occult
Oceans
Off-Road Vehicles
Oil Drilling
Oil Spills
Old Growth Logging
Orphanages
Overpopulation
Ozone Layer
Parents
Parole
Patriarchy
Performance Art
Pesticides
Philanthropy
Photography
Plea Bargaining
Police
Political Campaigns
Political Prisoners
Politicians
Pornography
Prayer in School
Prehistoric Entities
Presidents
Prisons
Private Schools
Professional Sports
Proficiency Tests
Provincialism
Psychiatry
Public Television and Radio
Quality of Life
RU-486
Racism
Rainforest
Rape
Rapid Transit
Real Estate
Recessions
Recycling
Refugees
Registration for Classes

Rehabilitation Programs
Relatives
Religion
Rent Control
Reservation Casinos
Robotics
Rock Music
Rodeos
SATS
Savings and Loan Scandal
School Lunch Program
Schools
Science
Science Fiction
Second Amendment
Secondhand Smoke
Sex Education
Sexism
Sexual Harrassment
Shelters
Sibling Rivalry
Singles Bars
Smoking
Smoking Bans
Social Class
Social Security
Socialism
Software
Solar Energy
South Africa
Space Colonization
Space Programs
Space Weapons
Speed Limits
Spirituality
Sports
Stadiums
Standard of Living
Standardized Tests
Stereotypes
Steroids
Sting Operations

Stock Market
Stress
Strikes
Strip Mining
Student Government
Subliminal Messages
Suburbia
Subversive Organizations
Success
Superfund Clean-up Sites
Superstition
Supreme Court
Surgical Implants
Surrogate Mothers
Tariffs
Taxes
Technology
Teenage Marriage
Teenage Pregnancy
Telecommunications
Television
Term Limits
Theater
Theologians
Third World Debt
Third World Politics
Three Strikes Law
Throwback Genes
Tolerance
Tourette's Syndrome
Toxic Wastes
Trade Deficits
Trade Embargoes
Traffic Congestion
Transportation
Trauma Care
Truancy
Trucking
Tuition
U.S. Postal Service
UFOs
Unemployment

Unexplained Phenomena
Unification of Germany
Unions
United Nations
Urban Decay
Urban Planning
Urban Renewal
Values
Veterans
Videos
Vietnam War
Violence
Virtual Reality
Volunteer Work
Voter Redistricting
Wages
War
War Crimes
Water Quality
Water Resources
Welfare
Wetlands
Wilderness Preservation
Wind Power
Witchcraft
Wolves in Yellowstone
Women in Military Academies
Women in the Military
Wood Energy
Workers' Compensation
Working Parents
World Bank
World War I
World War II
Writers
Writing
Yoga
Youth
Zen
Zero Population Growth
Zoning Laws
Zoos

Index